O'MALLEY OF NOTRE DAME

O'Malley of Notre Dame

BY JOHN W. MEANEY

A NOTRE DAME SESQUICENTENNIAL BOOK

University of Notre Dame Press
Notre Dame   London

Library of Congress Cataloging-in-Publication Data

Meaney, John William, 1918–
    O'Malley of Notre Dame / John W. Meaney.
        p.   cm.
    Includes bibliographical references (p.) and
index.
    ISBN 0-268-01505-8
    1. O'Malley, Frank, 1909–1974.   2. English
teachers—United States—Biography.   3. University
of Notre Dame—Faculty—Biography.   4. English
philology—Study and teaching—Indiana—Notre
Dame—History—20th century.   I. Title.
PE64.04M4   1991
820.9′00092—dc20
    [B]   90-50968
                                                          CIP

"redeem the time"

Contents

Acknowledgments

to
Rev. Louis J. Putz, CSC, for help and encouragement always.

to
Tom Stritch for suggesting the appropriate motto for this book: "redeem the time," a phrase, as he says, "always in Frank's mouth;" and for his incisive comments.

to
Rufus Rauch for his patient and most helpful criticism of the text and for many interesting reminiscences.

to
Phil Gleason for sending me the working paper about O'Malley by Arnold Sparr.

to
my daughter, Carol, for making the photo of O'Malley's grave.

to
my wife, Ruth, for ms. corrections and suggestions.

to
the Notre Dame Archives for pictures and photocopies of documents.

to
David A. Hazel, Principal of Clinton High School, for information about O'Malley's school years.

to
O'Malley's sister, Mrs. Alice Spellissy of Framingham, Mass., for help with the early years.

to
all of O'Malley's colleagues and former students who responded so generously to my calls on their memories and notes. Bill Slavick and Garry Bolger even shared with me collections of reminiscences which they had gathered for their own publications.

1
Beginnings

There were only two people on campus who were genuinely interested in souls; one was Father Craddick, prefect of religion, who wondered whether your soul were soiled or clean; and the other was Frank O'Malley who wondered whether your soul was alive or dead.[1]

We thought he was just another student when he first came in. It was early September 1936 and our first session of the required freshman course in English composition and rhetoric was meeting in the southwest corner room, ground floor, of the new College of Commerce building. Our class cards told us that our instructor was to be a Mr. Francis J. O'Malley, but none of us had ever heard of him. Some students in the front row stood up and began talking to each other near the open door. Just after the bell rang a very well-dressed young fellow with light reddish hair came in and slowly closed the door, waiting for the loitering students to move out of his way. When he slowly walked with clicking heels to the desk platform and stepped up behind the desk we decided that this must be not another student but Mr. O'Malley. He looked younger than some of the students among us and was not as tall as many, but it would have taken a very fastidious student to come in dressed as he was in tab collar and an expensive tan suit.

He seemed not only very young but shy as well. He stood for a few seconds smiling faintly and looking out the windows to his left, blinking his deep blue eyes a few times under his tan eyelashes. Then he said in a clear tenor voice:

"I will take up your cards if you will pass them to your left."

As he collected the cards at the ends of the rows he muttered thanks to the students who handed him the irregular bundles. He returned to his standing position behind the little desk with the cards in a pile before him. His head was like an inverted cone tilted forward, sloping down from the neatly combed red hair to

1

a tiny chin and neck. Light from the windows glinted across his gold-rimmed glasses as his long white fingers rearranged some of the cards that were upside down in the pile.

"Mr. Edmund P. McMahon; Mr. R. A. Rothacker ... " He checked faces and the pronunciations of names, looking up to see where in the room the hand was raised. When this process was finished he tapped the cards into a neat deck, then took a rubber band from his pocket and put it around them.

He began his remarks by saying that he wanted to get to know each of us personally and where we were starting from in our study of English. Still he was avoiding any direct look at the class, his gaze almost a squint as he kept his face turned toward the bright sunshine and green lawn outside.

He told us that he wanted us to develop as soon as possible a sensitivity to the power and beauty of concrete language, the expressions of things seen, heard, tasted, smelled, and touched or felt in what he called the kinesthetic sense. To suggest the type of writing that he had in mind he opened a book that he had brought with him and began to read us a passage:

> There was something about living on the sea that kept time from getting into a man. Being alone so much and not talking—that was a part of the story. Leaving things on the land and expecting to come back to them just as you left them—that was a part, too. It was like having a playroom and leaving your toys there, going out and growing up, and then coming back and being able to play with toy horses just the same as ever. Anyway, months and years on the ocean did not count up. Not the way they did on land. Oh, Uncle Thomas had wrinkles all right. Especially at the corners of his eyes. His face was always crinkled up there, and it made him look as though he was smiling even if he wasn't. Hard knocks had made his broad back like an oak plank and his hands like sheet anchors. When he took hold of things, things came along. He could knock a grown man down as if he was a ninepin. He was cured with salt like a prize ham.[2]

He read rapidly in a kind of monotone without any accent more regional than American radio.

Next he picked up chalk and stepped to the blackboard to write out our assignment for next time:

(a) Compose an essay of 500 words approximately elaborating this subject: Personal Pleasures, honest in statement and pleasant in tone.

(b) Plan and organize the paper before you write, and submit your plan or organization scheme with the completed paper.

(c) Write out also and submit a brief criticism of your own completed paper. Be mindful of these questions: (1) Is there any padding, that is, any needless, excessive phrasing? Or is your expression stripped down to the swiftest, sharpest form you can presently manage? (2) Are you sure you have committed no grammatical errors of any kind? Indicate your doubts. (3) Is every sentence neatly formed and punctuated? (4) Have you paragraphed properly? Does each paragraph contribute to your subject, and what specific contribution does each paragraph make?

Add any other comments or mention any other doubts you have.[3]

By the time that we had written down the assignment the bell rang. O'Malley waited at the desk for a few minutes to answer questions. Then slowly he backed away and went clicking on his metal-capped heels out of the building and across the quadrangle, bare headed, smiling, and bowing from the waist in a courtly manner toward anyone that he knew. He was wearing wingtip cordovans.

When we saw him at the next class two days later he made another short written assignment and then, after taking up our papers, read to us the James Joyce short story called "The Dead." As he reached its beautiful ending his voice was ringing like a gong upon the words:

A few light taps upon the pane made him turn to the window. It had begun to snow again. He watched sleepily the flakes, silver and dark, falling obliquely against the lamplight. The time had come for him to set out on his journey westward. Yes, the newspapers were right, snow was general all over Ireland. It was falling on every part of the dark central plain, on the treeless hills, falling softly into the dark mutinous Shannon waves. It was falling, too, upon every part of the lonely churchyard on the hill where Michael Furey lay buried. It lay thickly drifted on the crooked crosses and headstones, on the spears of the little gate, on the barren thorns. His soul swooned slowly as he heard the snow falling faintly through the universe and faintly falling, like the descent of their last end, upon all the living and the dead.[4]

During the third class meeting he returned to us the papers assigned on the opening day, and they were mostly graded "Average." Nevertheless, we found the margins covered with his comments and suggestions in red ink. He had a forceful, flowing scrawl that plunged ever forward, without hesitation or correction, dropping here in a heavily spread downthrust and then swinging out there in a wide loop to the next word. In a way the rapidly flowing line of his writing, interspersed with loops and slashes, seemed a visual equivalent of the tense monotone in which he read to us. For a class of forty or forty-five all of this close personal attention to every paper had clearly taken a good bit of time.

Sometimes his marginal comments were just a single word: "verbose," "stodgy," "turgid," "trite," "indefinite," or "vague." In other places on the top or bottom margins his remarks would amount to a restatement of a point that he had tried to stress in class: "Nouns and verbs, because they represent things and actions and not the qualifications of things and actions represented by adverbs and adjectives, strengthen and fortify the expression."

Further assignments continued to nudge us toward the use of concrete language: a paragraph to be entitled "Boys are very rich in the treasures of sense," then one to be called, "We normally never see the world at all."

After a few days of this some of us began to understand what he was after, and our efforts began coming back with grades of "Exceptional!" or "Exceptional +" or even, occasionally, an "Exceptional + +." The marginal comments were extended to: "Thank you for the great care and the enormous effort evidenced in this paper. It is satisfying to observe real interest!" or "Some of your impressions are exquisitely good."

When that stage had been reached we discovered something else about his reward system. He began reading aloud to the class the papers that he particularly liked, without mentioning the names of the authors. We all looked about us and promptly discovered by smug smiles here or there who the authors were. So a kind of fame began to be added to the generous and even extravagant praise of his marginal comments.

There was also time nearly every class to hear his reading of a passage from some professional writer, for example, from D. H. Lawrence:

> And so we steam out. And almost at once the ship begins to take a long, slow, dizzy dip. . . . Up comes the deck in that fainting swoon backwards—then down it fades in that indescribable slither forwards. It is all quite gentle—quite, quite gentle. . . . To tell the truth there is something in the long, slow lift of the ship, and her long, slow slide forwards which makes my heart beat with joy. It is the motion of freedom.[5]

Sometimes the man with the rust-colored hair would ask us to take a sheet of paper and write a critique of the reading. That meant that the next class period would see him returning two written assignments, each covered with his red ink comments and pleadings. The entire semester became a prolonged paper transaction, papers flowing in and papers flowing back. He used every form of repetition to hammer into our consciousness the need for sensitivity to primary sense impressions. On top of it all he was demanding freshness and originality in our sensory observations. And in spite of his unending persistence he managed to include some variety and even an occasional bit of puckish humor in the assignments that he wrote on the blackboard, turning his red scrawl to white:

> Write a segment of your autobiography: (1) Do not tell the whole story of your life thus far. (2) Take some incident, one time, some period, some person, some place, perhaps a moment of intense emotion. Camping trips, hikes and games are proscribed. (3) The paper should be reasonably long (possibly 500 words) and should have at least 5 paragraphs. (4) You needn't be too glowering. Take your subject lightly, easily, even blithely. . . .

One day in October our very urbane little teacher came into class carrying his usual eleven-inch stack of our folded papers with the rubber band around the middle and a current issue of *Scribner's Magazine*. After he had handed back our papers and had written out on the board our assignment for next time he opened the magazine and read to us a short story called "The Swede" by a writer named Harry Sylvester. We learned later that

Sylvester had been a student at Notre Dame and a classmate of O'Malley's. Knute Rockne was never mentioned in the story, but he was clearly the coach called "The Swede." To us new students just absorbing from every side the mystique of Rockne's greatness the great shock of that story was the perception that the author, one of his football players, did not really regard Rockne as a great man, seeing his faults as well as the power of his emotional leadership. The story ended with the words, "all of us cried that first day of his long death, the heart having a longer memory than the mind."[6] O'Malley paused when he had finished the reading, his pale eyebrows rose a little, and he said again more slowly and a little louder: "The heart having a longer memory than the mind." Then there was another long pause during which he just stood there blowing a silent breath from his mouth, something like a sigh. He dismissed us soon after that, and several brash fellows went up and asked him what he thought about Rockne. But he only scoffed and smiled at them. He would not say.

In November we discovered still another dimension of his reward system. The university published a quarterly literary magazine called *Scrip* (named for the wallet carried by medieval pilgrims), and it was distributed quarterly to all of the students in the residence halls. Mr. O'Malley was its faculty adviser, and his classes were the prime source of its literary material. Those freshmen of his who had learned the knack of concrete writing were surprised to find some of their class papers published. To the anonymous fame of classroom citation he was thus able to add a kind of campus fame as well.

But still the sensory drill assignments went on. He asked us to "list all the possible things, places, acts, persons, moods, feelings, anything in your experience suggested by each of the following: (a) Geography, (b) August, (c) Snowfall." We were asked "to search for things in your experience which the myopic, the insensitive ignore." Then, "from current periodicals of the popular, 'mobocratic' type like *Collier's, Satevepost* and others, gather at least 25 examples of trite phrasing. Cut them out and paste them to ordinary theme or typing paper. Note source and date." With an assignment to describe a person well known to us he filled the board with his instructions: "In describing people, this is your primary problem: you must individualize, 'peculiarize' the person you select. To achieve this individualizing, this differentiating, you must emphasize details, details of clothes, face, posture, manner, talk, walk, particularly those things which belong uniquely to your subject, those details which make him undeniably and unavoidably himself. Arrange your details in suitable and effective sentences and paragraphs. And there should be at least 3 or 4 paragraphs of at least 5 or 6 sentences each. Employ the diction which will give your portrait its best effect. Observe and reflect carefully before writing. Avoid unnecessary introductory and concluding paragraphs. Make sure that your whole sketch is unified. You might try to see and to present your person interiorly as well as exteriorly; that is, suggest his qualities of mind and heart as well as his appearance, his physical presence. Don't generalize. Actually fix your eye on the person. Recreate him so that I can through you see and hear and recognize him definitely, unfalteringly. Be mindful that a person, not a type is desired. And remember that your purpose throughout is to present your subject, not yourself. Check yourself on each of the foregoing urgencies."

Sometimes he asked for a single paragraph description of well-known people around the campus: "(1) Harry, the chief soda jerk of the University. You will find him in the cafeteria at these hours: Monday 11 to 5 and 7 to 9:45, Tuesday 8:30 to 12:30 and 5 to 9:45. (2) The Lady of the Laundry Delivery, (3) The Tallest Campus Policeman, Mr. Zerbe. Suggestions: (1) Don't offer information merely about these people. Offer me no statistics about height, weight, breadth. Try to pictorialize, to image them at a given moment. And don't include more than you can actually observe at a given moment from a given position. (2) Don't attribute motives or impulses or qualities to these people beyond the things you observe. (3) Don't waste a single sentence. Use no vague or general words. (4) Try to get a primary effect or a dominant impression of each. (5) Notice and register all characteristic manual gestures, facial motions, peculiarities of voice — and so on."

Later he asked us to do a single-adjective description of (a) Mr. Layden, the football coach; (b) Mr. Boland, the assistant coach; and (c) Mr. McCarthy, Dean of the College of Commerce. "Each has a particular dominant identifying physical quality that can, if you try hard enough, be reduced to a single adjective."

Having defined content words as nouns, verbs, descriptive adjectives, and descriptive adverbs, he assigned us to "Characterize each in a single sentence containing all necessary structural words but no more than seven content words, all of which should be image-bearing, ten of those ravenous wretches who sit at your table in the university dining halls." After he wrote that on the board he waited for us to copy it into our notebooks and was fingering the cord of a window shade, smiling faintly as he heard the snickers around the room.

Sometimes his instructions were almost specific enough to do the writing for us: "Compose a three-sentence description, emphasizing vivid nouns and verbs, of your foreign language professor. In re Essentials: Use only image-bearing nouns and verbs. Avoid all anaemic verbs, especially the copulative verb *to be* in all its forms. And, likewise, be wary of all forms of *to have*. Perilous and ruinous, too, are verbs like *appear, seem, look, remain, become*. Have a horror of the phrase *gives the impression of*. In re Modifiers: Since you are, in this short piece, to concentrate on strong nouns and vivid verbs you should not have too many modifiers. You will be wise not to employ more than four adjectives or adverbs in the whole piece. And the few you use must be image-bearing. I do not want to see adjectives like *pleasant* or *patient* or *delightful....*"

He did not neglect place description, either. He asked for "a city in autumn or spring or winter, a city in rain, a city in daylight, a city square, a suburban park or village, a forest, a wilderness, a warehouse, a cathedral, a church, a house, a shop, a courtroom, a mill, a garden, a lake, a river, mountains, a coast, a ship, a canyon.... But you should be sure to understand that the secret of a good description of a place or locality, whether an entire city or town or simply some special section or part of it is the realization of the ways in which it is distinguished from all other places.... Title the paper carefully. Please!!! Your titles generally are matter for shuddering, for tears, for sneers, for jeers."

Known campus places also crept into our assignments: the interior of the book store, the exterior of the post office, the exterior of Washington Hall, the Commerce Building lobby, the main building porch, the Engineering Hall foyer, a Cavanaugh or St. Edward's Hall corridor, or the Brownson Hall locker room.

Even when the snows came he did not wear a hat. He would arrive a little breathless from his fast walk across the campus, his hair flecked with snowflakes, and he would remove his tan gabardine overcoat and put it on the chair which he never used for sitting. The suits might rotate from blue to gray to tan to brown, but always there was the white shirt with the tab collar and the conservative tie.

It seemed to us that we were getting close to the heart of the matter one day when he began a consideration of poetry by writing on the board:

I. *Method:* Poetry suggests, symbolizes, creates, intensifies, does not state baldly or flatly as does pure prose. The method may be illogical. The poet may ignore sequences and logical conclusions.

II. *Arrangement:* Lines and Stanzas

III. *Rhythm:* Sometimes regular, organized, prosodic, metred, sometimes not, but always organic, living, the curiously vital, vivid flowing away of the poem, the movement communicated by the words of the poem which the reader must himself discern.

IV. *Rhyme:* Chime. Incidental but familiar in poetry. It accentuates the rhythm, frames the poem, but many poets will do without it.

V. *Sound Pattern:*
   a. *Alliteration:* Not merely the repetition of initial consonants, one should look within words.
   b. *Assonance:* The repetition of similar vowels in varying consonantal patterns.
   c. *Consonance:* Repetition of similar consonants in varying vowel patterns.
   d. *Repetition:* Reaffirmation of the same word or phrase.
   e. *Line changes:* Long line followed by a short, etc.

VI. *Imagery:*
   a. *Sensory Impressions:* Remember that the poet deals with realities, with the immediate or remembered things he himself can see, hear, smell, taste, touch. You can always be ready to classify the sense images in a poem.

b. *Figures:* Especially similies and metaphors.

c. *Symbols.*

VII. *Words:* Terms and epithets and collections of words having special value, potency, richness, fineness, words which stab grooved and channelized readers into wakefulness. Indeed in words especially does the poet reveal his *creative, making* power.

After he had finished writing all of that he went back to the "Imagery" paragraph and found room to write on a slant to the left of it: "(Of course, the poet often goes *through* reality, *beyond* reality.)"

The poem that he read to us as an example was Gerard Manley Hopkins's "Pied Beauty":

Glory be to God for dappled things—
   For skies of couple-colour as a brinded cow;
     For rose moles all in stipple upon trout that swim;
Fresh-firecoal chestnut-falls; finches' wings;
   Landscape plotted and pieced—fold, fallow, and plough;
     And all trades, their gear and tackle and trim.
All things counter, original, spare, strange;
   Whatever is fickle, freckled (who knows how?)
    With swift, slow; sweet, sour; adazzle, dim;
He fathers-forth whose beauty is past change:
     Praise him.[7]

He suspected that there was not a person in the class who had ever heard of Hopkins before. So he waited a few seconds and then read the entire poem again in a slightly lower tone, his voice riding the rhythm of the thing in sheer delight. Then he lifted his eyebrows at the end, slowly closed the thin black book, and walked out as if there were nothing more that could possibly be said.

To our surprise, he never followed this up with any assignment asking us to write a poem. Perhaps he had found that poetic prose was as much as we could handle. Anyway, he began the next semester by assigning another description of place, and his cautionary words suggest the level of our general advance by then: "This time there must be no romantic wandering—no nostalgic and sentimental blathering. Take some place, in whole or in part, by one view or another, some place which you do know, which you have or have had experience of and describe it realistically and imaginatively. Don't moralize; don't tell a silly story; don't cite statistics."

Eventually, almost reluctantly as if he were only doing it because people expected it of him, he gave us some assignments of logical essays: "Answer with careful reasons these questions: (a) Are the old maxims about the advantages of hard work now outgrown? (b) Should college courses prepare for the 'New Leisure'? (c) Is 'rugged individualism' wholly detrimental? (d) Should city dwellers go back to the land?"

Or, again, he asked us to, "Deal with one of the following questions: (1) Is national isolation conceivable in the world today? (2) Is sectional isolation in this country conceivable? (3) Should child labor be prohibited everywhere? (4) What evidences of barbarism do you see in our present civilization? (5) Is newspaper reading really educative?"

Once he asked us to do an essay in agreement or disagreement with a statement by Robert Maynard Hutchins, the new president of the University of Chicago: "The hope of doing a better job of training young people in the practices of a profession by having the universities do it is quite illusory."

But the poetic prose was clearly creeping back when he asked us to write an "informal essay utilizing one of the following ideas: (1) expressive hands; (2) echoes and shadows; (3) woodsmoke; (4) voices and gestures; (5) watermusic; (6) fire-engines; (7) music moods; (8) motoring at night; (9) on finishing a book; (10) on the departure of visitors; (11) on unanswered letters; (12) on play going; (13) on burrowing among bed clothes." He apparently had a theory that freshmen could, at best, be asked to observe and experience with sensitivity their own sharp sensory perceptions of the world. Reasoning and intuition were for the later years. In the freshman year he wished to ask only what we were most capable of. And by our response to that challenge he selected us for future attention, much as the rigorous training of aviators might begin only after a physical exam.

Whenever any of us would meet him on the off days at the intersections of campus paths he would always stop for a brief chat, inquiring as to our health, our perplexities and satisfactions. But it was clear that his mind was usually far away on other things, and as we answered he hardly heard us; he had to ask, "What? What?" He would veer away, making barely audible comments, then circle back, looking at his cordovan shoes, smiling silently. Finally, after a decent interval of visiting, he would raise a hand in a wave and be off, walking as fast as before. He seemed to us a kind of messenger from another world, a world of ideas, certainly, but of rare enthusiasms, too, and of indignations at the follies around us. It was a world of sensitivity and dedication that we longed to enter, and we soon found that he was more than a messenger from it: he was also a missionary for it. But he was a missionary who persuaded without suasion, simply by being. We were like moths following his light.

As an instructor at Notre Dame it was part of his job to teach freshmen students, but it was apparently the part that he enjoyed most of all. It mattered little to him which college they were starting in. Our class was in the College of Commerce. Other years he might happen to be assigned one in the College of Arts and Letters. In either case he was confident that he would find there sensitive souls needing to be saved from the boring routine of the general curriculum, people who would become "friends of the work," as he called them. They would change their majors to English because of him, switching into the College of Arts and Letters in order to be able to do that.

As we got to the end of the second semester he spent several days very diligently and carefully doing something else that had apparently been given to him as a responsibility: outlining for us the bibliographic procedure for writing research papers complete with footnotes and references. It was not a chore in which he took the greatest personal interest, but he did handle it with great thoroughness.

On the last class day he handed out for our use during the summer a five-page reading list in modern fiction:

> Each year many students ask earnestly for reading sugges-
> tions. And, to satisfy such seekers, I am offering this notably
> variegated list of American, British, and Continental sto-
> rytellers. Yet these are not "guaranteed" readings: I have
> chosen merely to mark a number of the representative fic-
> tionists of the modern world. Of course, I am hopeful that
> the average person, selecting wisely, may discover some dis-
> tinct pleasures among these writers.

1. Baring, Maurice .... *Cat's Cradle,*
Coat without Seam, Robert Peckham.
2. Bates, H. E. .... *Day's End, The Fallow Land.*
3. Beerbohm, Max .... *Zuleika Dobson,*
Christmas Garland.
4. Belloc, Hilaire .... *The Man Who Made Gold,*
The Postmaster General. ... [8]

And so the enormous list continued through 133 authors. However, there was no mention of James Joyce, D. H. Lawrence, Dostoyevski, or Kafka. Perhaps he took into account our ages of eighteen or nineteen and decided that we were not yet ready to deal with these figures.

My own experiences of O'Malley's freshman composition class were typical of many. For example, Henry Adam writes:

> I was in Frank O'Malley's English composition class as a freshman for a year. O'Malley's intellectual impact on me and most of the class was significant. He dedicated himself to expanding our intellectual horizons and to nurturing our consciences. He challenged us to stretch our imaginations with essay assignments such as, *The Taste of an Apple.* He carefully read our papers and sprinkled them with cryptic notations—a considerable amount of labor. Honest effort and improvement produced generous grades.
>
> O'Malley taught us much about Christian perspective and the essence of an ethical life. I remember the time that someone in the class invoked, "Honesty is the best policy." O'Malley awakened us with, "Honesty is a POLICY?"
>
> In the classroom O'Malley—reserved and somewhat sardonic—kept the atmosphere lively and fun. When he returned papers he had graded he often would comment—"Ah, Mr. Brennan, you wrote with the angels," or "Mr. Berres, another paper like that and you will be eternally damned!"
>
> The noise of a power mower just outside our ground floor class room infuriated O'Malley. He would close the windows and pace about the room declaring, "Someday I shall deal with that fellow!"[9]

Phil North recalls a day in the fall when the disturbance was the Notre Dame marching band going back and forth on the quadrangle outside playing the "Victory March." O'Malley would have to stop his lecture and wait for them to pass on. Finally, as he heard them approaching again, he burst out with, "God! You'd think they would know it by now."[10]

We were, in general, products of Catholic high schools all across the country, and we had been sent to Notre Dame to receive what our parents trusted would be a Catholic higher education. The University of Notre Dame trusted the same and had prepared for us a carefully restricted environment of on-campus residence halls. Freshmen lived in freshman halls, and all halls were closed and locked every night at ten. Those who arrived later than that had to contact a night watchman for admission and had to sign in. The next day they had to explain to the hall rector, a priest living on the first floor, the reasons for their late arrival. Lights in the halls were also turned off at ten, and about eleven the rector on the first floor and prefects on the upper floors made their rounds down the lighted corridors, opening every door for a bed check to be sure that all were present or accounted for.

There was a chapel in every hall and several Masses every morning. Students were encouraged to attend Mass in the morning and to receive Communion before going out to the dining hall for breakfast. There was a daily *Religious Bulletin* slipped under our doors with the mail delivery, constantly propagandizing for more morning Communions. In order to be eligible to receive Communion we must not only be in a state of Grace but we must also have abstained from all food and drink, even water, from the previous midnight.

That we were docile enough to submit to all of these strictures and requirements came from the fact that we and our families were Tridentine Catholics, conditioned for more than three-hundred-seventy years by the Council of Trent and the garrison mentality that it formed in the Church. O'Malley had been conditioned by the same influences, and yet he had somehow broken free into his bright and intense other world. He was only ten years older than most of us, but we could see nothing in his background to account for his difference from us.

He was born August 19, 1909, in Clinton, Massachusetts, a small New England milling town some forty miles west of Boston and a little north of Worcester. His father was Michael Francis O'Malley who had been born in County Mayo, Ireland, in 1878 and had immigrated to the United States in 1885. He had taken a job as a weaver in a Clinton cotton mill, a far cry from the seafaring traditions of the O'Malleys in County Mayo where there was a saying that "There never was a good man of the O'Malleys but he was a seaman." In 1905 he married Ellen Tierney who had been born in County Galway in 1884 and had come over in 1897. Their first child was our Francis Joseph, and he was to be joined by four sisters in later years.

Clinton was a predominantly Catholic town because of the many Irish who lived and worked there in cotton, woolen, and carpet mills. There were nearly a hundred of the O'Malleys alone. The family of Michael Francis O'Malley lived in the parish of Our Lady of the Rosary, and young Frank attended the parochial grade school. There was no Catholic high school in the town, so he went on to Clinton High School. There Frank O'Malley played inter-class football and basketball, took a minor role in the senior class play, and was one of the editors of the 1926 yearbook which remarked that his "nonchalance in the senior play won for him many feminine admirers."[11] In general, the yearbook noted that, "From a bashful freshman to a senior dignified or otherwise—mostly otherwise, has Francis emerged. His original wit has afforded numerous laughter during an otherwise monotonous class." He was also to be remembered, it said, as one to whom one could go for help in any subject.

After graduation from high school Frank needed to earn some money for college, so he worked for two years as a clerk at the Evans Drug Store on High Street in Clinton. Finally, in 1928, he enrolled as a freshman at Notre Dame, living at 2134 Carroll Hall. In those days the east and west wings of the Main Building were low-priced student dormitories named Carroll and Brownson Halls. So 2134 would be the designation not for a room but for a sheet-enclosed space containing a bed and little else. The 1929 *Dome* described Carroll Hall as: "Rows of desks, rows of sheets, like tents, rows of wash-bowls and lockers—the nightly prank, the scampering feet, the suppressed laugh—upstairs to sleep, downstairs to study—a happy group who keep the old traditions of their honored hall—these the things which make a year in Carroll an everlasting memory."[12]

The president of the university at that time was Father Charles L. O'Donnell, C.S.C., a poet much admired by Frank O'Malley for poems such as:

WONDER

I have never been able to school my eyes
Against young April's blue surprise,
Though year by year I tell my heart
This spring our pulses shall not start
Nor beauty take us unaware,
Beauty that is the blue of air,
Blue crocus and a bluebird's wing,
Water, blue shadows, everything
The sky can lay a finger on,
Blue twilight and the white blue dawn.
But every year in spite of this
Stern blunting of the edge of bliss,
When April first with blue-veined feet,
In any wood, down any street
Comes as I know that she must come,
My foolish heart beats like a drum,
My eyes, for all the tutoring years,
Are faithless in their truant tears.[13]

Such may be the source of a later Professor O'Malley's assignment to his freshman class of a paper on the subject, "Blue."

Among other officials and faculty of the university that year were Father J. Hugh O'Donnell as Prefect of Discipline, Father John F. O'Hara as Prefect of Religion, Father Charles C. Miltner, Dean of Arts and Letters, Father Julius A. Nieuwland, Professor of Organic Chemistry, and Mr. Knute Rockne, football coach.

A football player named Frank Leahy was a member of the Student Activities Council.

The University Theatre produced *Julius Caesar*.

Football fever was reaching its all-time high and entered even into the student pranks: the pompous Prefect of Discipline, Father O'Donnell, who had once been a football player, found continual embarrassment in a chant of hidden students which began with a loud yell of "Who lost the Yale game?" followed by the chorus: "J. Hugh O'Donnell." Much later Bill McGowan (class of '41) was to write: "When Father Hugh O'Donnell was president I worked a bit in his office and got to know him fairly well. He appeared pompous and formal and somewhat ill at ease in private conversation, but he was really a kind and generous man. I was talking to Frank O'Malley about him one day in the cafeteria, and Frank agreed generally with my observations. 'However,' he said, 'I do wish Hugh would stop talking like a monument.'"[14]

In the 1929–30 academic year Notre Dame's football team was undefeated and untied, winning a national championship with Frank Carideo at quarterback, Jack Cannon at guard, Frank Leahy at tackle, and Jumping Joe Savoldi in the backfield.

When Frank O'Malley, then resident in Walsh Hall, graduated in 1932 as valedictorian he had come to know in his classes or around the campus: Father Peter E. Hebert, Professor of Ancient Languages; Mr. Devere T. Plunkett, Instructor in Classics; Mr. Paul C. Bartholomew, Instructor in Politics; Mr. T. Bowyer Campbell, Assistant Professor of History; Mr. William H. Downey, Assistant Professor of Economics; Mr. Charles Phillips and Mr. Paul Fenlon, Associate Professors of English; Mr. Norbert Engels, Mr. John T. Frederick, Mr. James A. Withey, Mr. Richard Sullivan, Mr. Thomas P. Madden, Mr. Rufus Rauch, and Father Leo L. Ward, Assistant Professors of English; Mr. John P. Turley, Instructor in Latin; Father Leo R. Ward, Assistant Professor of Philosophy; and Mr. Paul R. Byrne, Librarian. Many of the above were among the "bachelor dons" whose ranks at Notre Dame O'Malley was soon to join.[15]

Among his classmates were: Charles McCarragher, Dom Napolitano, Louis J. Putz, Jerome J. Wilson, and Joe Petritz.

The University Theatre had presented *A Merchant of Venice* and three one-act Irish plays, in one of which the part of Paddy Farrell, a messenger, was portrayed by Thomas Stritch.

Frank O'Malley's picture as Associate Editor of *Scrip* showed him still without glasses, and it was reported that he "did fine work for *Scrip* this year, as he does for every activity that attracts him. His work, both in criticism and fiction, shows a touch that is typically his, a touch that appeals to any one who enjoys good writing."[16]

O'Malley was also active in the Scribbler's Club which held "meetings every Tuesday night in Howard 'Rec'. Completely oblivious to the incongruity of the surroundings with the aims and purposes of the group, they meet to carry on the old tradition of writing. Firmly believing that 'the only way to learn to write is to write,' the Scribblers write ... and write. Poems, short stories, essays and plays are read before the club by their authors and criticisms are open to all members. Criticism is never wanting: constructive and destructive, disparaging and encouraging it tumbles from all quarters to fall upon the happy or hapless author.... The most prized tradition of the Scribblers is the position of honorary president. The fact that this position is held by Mr. Charles Phillips makes it more than a mere tradition. Mr. Phillips, author, lecturer and professor, has not only inspired members to their best literary efforts but has counseled them wisely in many of their works. He is a friend to every Scribbler."[17]

Another Tuesday evening club was the Patricians which had been organized three years earlier for "the promotion and sustenance of a genuine interest in the classical arts and literatures at Notre Dame.... Such variegated subjects as the literary moods, influences, and literary technique of the Ancient Greek and Latin writers, Hellenistic Art and Culture, English Literature and the Classics, Comparative Studies in Ancient and Modern Architecture, Classical Music, and Current Literature on the Classics were discussed by the members this year.... The club does not restrict itself solely to the consideration of the great books and great authors of Greece and Rome, but also gives not a little attention to the great classics of other nations: Shakespeare, Dante, Corneille, Goethe, Cervantes, as well as Plato, Virgil, Homer, and Saint Augustine constitute a group of literary Titans to whom the Patricians look with interest and admiration.... This year Frank O'Malley was President and by his amazing zeal and energy did much to stimulate the activities of the society. In every way he conducted himself in office in a manner august and Roman. He read papers very frequently on subjects such as 'The Hellenism of Walter Savage Landor', 'Dante, the Great Medieval Mind', 'The Historical Accuracy of Livy', and 'The Significance of Aristotle's *Poetics*'."[18]

The landmark events of the 1931–32 academic year were:

Oct. 1: first football pep meeting of the year prepared as a tribute to Knute Rockne who had died the previous March 31.

Nov. 2: Father Nieuwland went to a meeting of the American Chemical Society in Akron, Ohio, and announced his discovery of synthetic rubber.

Nov. 4: A Rockne Memorial Drive was opened with a nationwide radio program featuring Will Rogers, Mayor Walker of New

York, Mayor Cermack of Chicago, Rev. Matthew Walsh, Grant-
land Rice, Chick Meehan, and the Four Horsemen.

May 1: Father Charles O'Donnell, the university president,
stressed Notre Dame's historical and religious traditions and
urged perpetuation of them in a stirring address at the opening
of May devotions.

O'Malley's mother came out from Massachusetts for his graduation. The campus people who met her were mostly impressed
by her intense religious devotion. At every ceremony she sat quietly
praying her rosary. Frank probably returned home with her for
the summer of 1932. He loved his vacations at home even if, as
in some of the later years, he would be returning to teach during
the summer session at Notre Dame. Even a few weeks in Massachusetts were worth the long train trip.

Promptly after his graduation *maxima cum laude* Francis J.
O'Malley sat down and wrote a letter of application directly to
the university president, Father Charles O'Donnell, expressing his
interest in continuing his studies toward a master's degree by
working in the field of history on the university's archival collection of the letters of Archbishop John Baptist Lamy of Santa Fe,
New Mexico, and requesting an appointment to the faculty of the
university.

He gave Father Leo R. Ward as a reference. So Father O'Donnell forwarded the letter to Father Ward and asked for his advice.
Father Ward's recommendation was so positive and enthusiastic
that Father O'Donnell made the appointment forthwith. The result
was that O'Malley was listed during the 1932–33 academic year
as an instructor in the History Department while he completed a
master's thesis entitled "A Literary Addendum: Willa Cather's
Archbishop Latour in Reality—John Baptist Lamy—a Presentation of his Letters, Life, and Associates during the Missionary
Years in the Diocese of Santa Fe." Clearly, his original stimulus
for this work came from his reading of Willa Cather's *Death
Comes for the Archbishop*.

Since Cather had written that book without access to the archival letters, O'Malley wrote to let her know of his work, and at
her request he sent her a copy of the thesis and photostats of two
of the letters. She was rather unhappy about his including her
name and that of her character, Archbishop Latour, in his title,

but she finally withdrew her objection as long as the thesis was to be available only in the library and was not published. All the rest of his life O'Malley would enjoy telling his friends about that exchange of letters, mimicking Willa Cather saying, "My Dear Young Man."

The concluding words about Archbishop Lamy in his thesis anticipated the style of some of O'Malley's later poems:

> The dim short vision of the eye did not darken his venturing heart, or limit to its narrow outlook the wide-embarking horizon of his soul. And the times were ready for the prophet who filled up the valleys of ignorance and levelled the hills of laziness and straightened the crooked paths his people walked.
>
> Archbishop Lamy had the grand vision. Trustful and with steady sight he looked westward, where uplifted radiantly, motionless and far on the burning cloud, he saw all his heroic and difficult days, the satisfying vision of a time to be. In splendid portent, the beams of faith and truth and hope lighted the doorway of this pioneer.[19]

Such were some of the works, the environment, the teachers, and the associates who helped to form Frank O'Malley in his early years at Notre Dame. One of his associates who has written about that formation is Tom Stritch, a kind of early partner of O'Malley's as brilliant young men about campus. They always had some hilarious joke going between them, as in the time they were communicating by telegram out of the campus Western Union office in Badin Hall, insisting that the formal telegram delivery take place even if it be only between Badin and Morrissey Halls. As Stritch remembers, "Frank and I were great friends, but we were college-boy friends. Frank loved to laugh, and laugh we did, at nothing and everything, as young people do."[20]

Stritch says that O'Malley greatly admired English Professor James A. Withey and "gave him much credit for helping the technique of his teaching."[21] And certainly Stritch's description of Withey's technique sounds a good bit like O'Malley's: "in the red ink with which he so copiously criticized student writing, he understated everything. His labors were incredible: he required a piece of writing for every class meeting, and all his classes met three times a week. Nearly every one of those was returned to the student, graded and criticized, and his comments were penetrating and effective."[22] However, O'Malley's comments were not so strictly limited to understatement. On the contrary, overstatement was often a good part of his fun.

Stritch writes that O'Malley was "the most brilliant teacher of the humanities Notre Dame has ever known. . . . He was by far the best classroom lecturer I ever heard—he genuinely enlarged the minds and hearts of innumerable students who became his fervent disciples. His work was primarily religious; he scamped what was rational and logical, and lived and preached intuition, feeling and prophecy. It was good for his message that his pulpit was in the Department of English, not theology, which gave him greater range and variety. . . . He was a bold prophet. Where he got the sense of his mission I don't know; he had it when we were both undergraduates, in 1932."[23]

A young man with such a bold sense of mission already formed before he had ever taught a course at the university must surely have inherited the personality spark that one saw in his deep blue eyes. And yet, theirs was not merely the "hard, gemlike flame" of a Walter Pater[24] that burned in esthetic delight. O'Malley's flame burned also for philosophy, theology, and religion, although his freshman recruits of 1936 had as yet little anticipation of what his future direction of leadership and development would be.

2
The Wave of Religion

A great wave of heightened religious consciousness began to rise and sweep across Notre Dame shortly after O'Malley's arrival there in 1928. There had been earlier waves, perhaps the first of them being the very founding of the institution in 1842 by Father Edward Sorin and his little band of religious brothers. Father Sorin had later developed great respect for the work of Orestes A. Brownson, the gadfly New England convert to Catholicism and supporter—along with Emerson and Thoreau—of the Brook Farm Experiment. Brownson became a famous journalist and critic in the nineteenth century, a fierce defender of Catholicism against the Eastern Protestant Establishment. Sorin tried several times to bring him to the Notre Dame campus for speeches, but he never succeeded. Brownson died in Detroit in 1876 and was buried there. Ten years later Sorin succeeded in having Brownson's body disinterred and reburied on the Notre Dame campus in the crypt chapel of Sacred Heart Church. Many generations of students have walked up the center aisle and crossed the white marble floor plaque with the Latin inscription to Brownson without knowing the name or the reason for his burial there. During the year of his residence as a student in Carroll Hall next door, Frank O'Malley must have walked across that plaque many times, but he was not one who failed to become acquainted with Brownson's work. When he later developed his course in Modern Catholic Writers, Brownson was included.

But the religious wave of which Brownson was a part had long since swept past the Notre Dame campus and into history. During O'Malley's early years at Notre Dame a new wave, a new excitement in Catholic thought, was beginning to reach the place, and it probably originated in what was called the Oxford Movement in England and with some parallel upwellings of Catholic scholarship in France and Germany. It was this wave, which eventually culminated in Vatican Council II, that O'Malley rode through most of his life.

From England the first great name was John Henry Cardinal Newman. As a young student and teacher of divinity subjects Newman had joined in the early 1830s with his Oxford colleagues to assert "Over against the aridities of empiricist philosophy and Utilitarian ethics . . . a renewed awareness of transcendent mystery and a renewed sense of human life as guided by a transcendent power to a transcendent goal."[1] Newman and the others were Anglican clerics, but they found their studies taking them closer and closer to the position of the Roman Catholic Church. Finally Newman and William George Ward converted to Roman Catholicism in 1845. As Christopher Dawson wrote in 1950: "the coming of the converts had a revolutionary effect on the structure of the English Catholic community. For it brought in the upper middle class element which was to be the ruling class in the new Victorian England: not only the leaders of religious thought in the universities but members of families which had long held an important place in Parliament and public life. . . ."[2]

Even the spirits of Catholic students as far away as the University of Notre Dame eventually received a lift from these conversions. By the time of Frank O'Malley's undergraduate years the name of Newman evoked a special pride. It may have been in the courses of Rufus Rauch or of Father Leo R. Ward that O'Malley first heard of Newman, became an admirer of Newman's arguments from the Fathers of the Church, and also found esthetic delight in such a sentence as this from the essay *On the Scope and Nature of University Education:*

> Quarry the granite rock with razors, or moor the vessel with a thread of silk; then may you hope with such keen and delicate instruments as human knowledge and human reason to contend against these giants, the passion and the pride of man.[3]

But O'Malley may well have rated as Newman's greatest day the one in 1866, when he received into the Roman Catholic Church the young Gerard Manley Hopkins of Oxford. It was the poetry of Hopkins that was to make the most profound impact on the religious and aesthetic sensibility of Frank O'Malley for the rest of his life. He was later to write that "Newman's spirit had a quiet grandeur, like the quiet ocean rolling rhythmically or like great fields moving in winds that are even. Contrastingly, the spirit of Hopkins is sometimes like the upsurging of the ocean in cliffs of tumult or like the terrible sharp pain of scythes and knives, cutting into the very grain, the vein of the soul."[4]

During O'Malley's undergraduate days in the late 1920s and early 1930s at Notre Dame, there began to appear many indications of the Catholic intellectual renaissance that was originating in Europe and spreading to America. The Benedictine Abbey of Solesmes in France, long known for its skill in Gregorian chant, made recordings that became very popular in religious goods stores in the United States. Also, the Abbey of Maria Laach in Germany was marketing religious medallions, chalices, and vestments of excellent design. A distinguished quarterly publication called *Liturgical Arts* was founded in New York by Otto Spaeth and edited by Maurice Lavanoux. St. John's Benedictine Abbey in Collegeville, Minnesota, began to be known for the excellence of its liturgical studies. A granddaughter of Newman's fellow convert from the Oxford Movement, William George Ward, married an Australian speaker in the Catholic Evidence Guild, and the two of them, Frank Sheed and Maisie Ward, founded in London and New York the Catholic publishing house of Sheed and Ward. Its carefully chosen and well-designed publications began to appear in the campus bookstore with not only an intellectual but even a tactile and olfactory impact. They very paper that they used, in common with other British publishers, had a distinctive smell and feel. The choir of Moreau Seminary under the direction of Father Carl Hager, C.S.C., achieved great skills in Gregorian chant and began to be greatly appreciated at High Mass on Sundays in Sacred Heart Church.[5]

During the presidency of Father Charles L. O'Donnell, C.S.C., there began a policy of inviting to the campus for talks and courses a distinguished list of English and continental converts to Catholicism, beginning with Gilbert Keith Chesterton in 1930. Chesterton had described his feelings about his conversion as being like those of "an English yachtsman who slightly miscalculated his course and discovered England under the impression that it was a new island in the South Seas. . . . I am the man who with the utmost daring discovered what had been discovered before. I was a pagan at the age of twelve, and a complete agnostic at the age of sixteen.

I never read a line of Christian apologetics. I read as little as I can of these now."[6] Both faculty and students welcomed him enthusiastically. They jammed his lectures in Washington Hall. Rufus Rauch has reported:

> When Chesterton came to Notre Dame in the fall of 1930, I called on him several times at his house on Pokagon Street— after the first call, always by invitation.
>
> In the course of the conversation, not easy for a young instructor of twenty-six—though he was always charming and most considerate—as a kind of ploy I asked him what he thought of the poetry of T. S. Eliot. In 1930 there were relatively very few readers who had become aware of *Prufrock,* of *The Waste Land,* and then of the newly published sequence of *Ash Wednesday,* Eliot's first great religious poem. Chesterton, in his high pitched voice in an accent which seemed to me a hybrid of cockney and Oxford English, said, "Oh, yes. He has just published a long poem," and Chesterton quoted the opening passage:
>
> > "Because I do not hope to turn again
> > Because I do not hope
> > Because I do not hope to turn
> > Desiring this man's gift and that man's scope. . . . "
>
> "Quite dizzy-making. I suppose that's one way to conversion. What do you think?" What did I think? . . . I had learned a lesson. The first part of the *Ash Wednesday* sequence had been published in the April 1930 issue of *The Criterion,* Eliot's prestigious quarterly. Chesterton to my surprise had read it, remembered it, could quote it, and in his way was approving of it.[7]

The student editor of *Scrip* wrote:

> I shall always be tremendously pleased to think that I first met Gilbert Keith Chesterton in a book-shop. As the man who introduced me to him said, "You never know who's around the corner." I could just as well have met him in front of a drugstore or a hardware store but, think, afterwards I might have been unable to dissociate him from soda-fountains and light bulbs, or silverware and pyrex plates. . . .
> At the time of that first meeting he was standing in the aisle

of this particular book-shop, "browsing," he said, "over the books." Finally he caught sight of a volume, *A Short History of Women,* I think, and picked it up. An amazed chuckle came from him and then a laugh. He has a unique way of beginning a chuckle at his feet, and then, body quivering as the chuckle travels upwards, of ultimately bringing it to a fullfledged hearty laugh. What he thought can best be described by what he said after he had read a page or two. "A short history of women! Fancy that. I never thought anyone would ever attempt to write a short history of women!" As he turned from book to book I watched him. He wore a hat that I shall never associate with anyone else except a French *abbé.* About his shoulders was thrown a fog cape some mysterious person might throw about his shoulders—perhaps Sherlock Holmes. In his hand he carried a cane, "my *ciupaga*" he called it. "I brought it back with me from Poland." But he is not a French *abbé,* nor is he mysterious. He is about the most affable and likeable person I have ever met."[8]

Younger faculty members—Fenlon, Manion, Rauch, Connolly, O'Grady, Engels, and Ronay—gave a party for him in the Sorin Hall rooms of Professor Charles Phillips and used "devious and nefarious ways to find a sufficient supply of good ale and real beer for their guest" in spite of the prohibition laws. "On another occasion, Chesterton was taken, by his own request, on a tour of speakeasies in South Bend. . . ."[9]

Chesterton enjoyed and was grateful for his reception at Notre Dame, and he memorialized the visit with a poem that began thus:

> I have seen, where a strange country
> Opened its secret plains about me,
> One great Golden Dome stand lonely with its golden
>   image, one
> Seen afar, in strange fulfillment,
> Through the sunlit Indian summer
> That Apocalyptic portent that has clothed
> her with the Sun.[10]

In 1932 there were several lectures on campus by Etienne Gilson, the distinguished historian of philosophy from the Medieval Institute at the University of Toronto. Then, in 1933 and 1934 there were visits by William Butler Yeats and the Irish poet, Seamus MacManus. But the most important visitor by far in 1934 was the neoscholastic philosopher, Jacques Maritain. Rufus Rauch was one of the very few faculty members who had ever heard of Maritain. He had published an article in *Thought* in September 1931, entitled "The Esthetic of Maritain." (It may have been the first article about him in a U. S. publication).

O'Malley had probably known of Maritain's work from Rauch's course in his undergraduate days, and he had admired greatly the Maritain book translated under the title *The Philosophy of Art* (later reissued by Scribners as *Art and Scholasticism*). It gave the most coherent and satisfactory theory of art to be found anywhere: beginning with the perceptions of the senses, as in Aristotle, ideas were assumed into the working reason of the artist, formed, shaped into things of beauty and then recommunicated through the sensory media to the perceptions of an audience. Things received a "blessing" by their entry into the mind of the artist, for they lived there in a state better than that of their raw existence in nature. Hence, the distortions of modern artists were no distortions at all but the surviving traces of the artistic molding within the mind.

And yet, the main interest in Maritain derived from his personal odyssey. He and his wife, Raïssa, had been brilliant students in the classes of Henri Bergson at the Sorbonne, but the void of religion in their lives had induced them to form a suicide pact to be carried out if by the end of the year 1906 they had not found a prospect of salvation. Then they met the fiery French writer Léon Bloy and were converted by him to Catholicism. After careful study of the works of St. Thomas Aquinas, Maritain found his lifelong vocation which he summed up in the words: "Woe to me if I shall not have Thomisticized!" His lectures reinterpreted the medieval Latin of St. Thomas into the circumstances and applications of modern times with an incisive delicacy and sensitivity, and with it all, there was a positive aura of sainthood about the man. The rumor was that he spent most of his preparation hours in religious contemplation rather than reading.

Maritain returned for further lectures in 1936. He was a slightly stooped man with a handsome face set off by a small but elegant moustache and goatee. Over his chest there always hung the ends of a homely gray shawl. His mental precision was reflected in a hand gesture used for emphasis: the forefinger and thumb forming a small circle and appearing at key words, for instance, in his philosophical distinctions between the individual and the person. After his lectures the students came up with copies of his books in their trembling hands to request autographs of the learned and holy man.

O'Malley later wrote:

> I remember when Desmond Fitzgerald, the former Cosgrave Minister of Defense and External Affairs and now Senator of Eire, was visiting and teaching at Notre Dame before the second world war, he mentioned one day his own and his wife's reaction to the coming to their place in Dublin of Jacques and Raïssa Maritain: "Why it was like having holiness itself in the house." The rightness of this remark became clearer when Maritain himself came to stay at Notre Dame for a week and to give at the university for the first time the lectures that later appeared under the title, *Scholasticism and Politics*. Hearing him, seeing him, meeting him in the casual places of the campus was a splendid spiritual experience for many of us. The kindness, the quickness, the gentleness of his mind and of his very physical self impressed—in a way they will never forget—the students and faculty who faithfully came to his lectures. Many of us felt that we did indeed encounter in Maritain a holiness of intellect and personality that we had hardly discerned in any other human being. These are not extravagant words. There are, happily, a great many people in our country who could tell of a response in kind. For Maritain's wisdom, though it is directed to the salvation of the world, is still not of the world. The true humanist himself, he understands, in his living work, the relationship between God and twentieth-century man, between nature and supernature, matter and spirit. He makes the might and efficacy of this relationship vivid and real to all our generations.[11]

By 1934 the new university president, Father O'Hara, made a trip to Europe specifically to recruit the speakers and teachers for Notre Dame who later became known as "Father O'Hara's Foreign Legion."[12] The first of them to arrive was a member of the Irish landed gentry, former editor of the *Dublin Review,* a convert named Shane Leslie, who came for the winter and spring of 1935.

Tom Stritch was a student in Leslie's course in Jonathan Swift and found him a "strange and oddball person. I read his life of Swift during the course and found it jerky, eccentric, highly personal and more: it was arcane and semimysterious, as if the author had some special understanding, some key to an inner temple where no one else might enter, but from which there emanated flashes of insight."[13] Rufus Rauch remembers:

> I was giving a course in Shakespeare that spring; I was asked to turn it over to Shane, to give him something to do. He came up with the grotesque proposal to Father Leonard Carrico, the Director of Studies, that we put on a production of *Hamlet* and stage it in the stadium. Among other startling effects, we could have the Ghost emerge from the firey fumes of Purgatory, and in the grand finale have the football team march in as the Danish Army!
>
> Shane showed up at St. Mary's to give a lecture in plaid kilts, cross-gartered stockings, and tam on his head, the full regalia of his Irish clan.
>
> He (and other visiting professors) were not always happy with the guest quarters assigned to them in Alumni Hall: a beautifully panelled sitting room-bed room with bath, but rather sparsely furnished: a small oak table as a desk, a metal cot as a bed. Shane's plea to the rector for a more comfortable bed went unheeded, so on his last day at Notre Dame he got himself a can of deep red paint and in huge letters scrawled his inscription on one of the walls: 'Hic jacet Seanus Leslianus', the paint dripping down like blood.[14]

Leslie was followed by the publisher, Frank Sheed, in March 1935, who may also have been there earlier. Rauch says of Sheed that "he gave some powerful and exciting lectures to Notre Dame audiences. (We became friends early on. Beryl and I spent the summer of 1936 in Europe; we saw the Sheeds several times in London.) ... It was my impression that Frank Sheed was Father O'Hara's consultant and advisor in bringing most of those European writers and intellectuals to the campus. ... "[15] Father Martin d'Arcy, S.J., educated at Oxford, also came over in 1935. Then, in the fall of 1935, came Desmond Fitzgerald, a former Sinn Fein rebel from Ireland, poet, playwright and editor, politician and minister who became a great friend of Frank O'Malley.

The two of them often went on drinking rounds of the downtown hotels, and they exchanged letters for many years afterwards. Rauch recalls that "Desmond Fitzgerald was a most delightful man, conversationalist, raconteur. He had fought as a very young man in the famous Easter Rising of 1916, survived, was imprisoned. I remember Father O'Hara calling the English Faculty together to announce Desmond's forthcoming tenure at Notre Dame for a year or two. He described Desmond as a scholar who dared to quote St. Thomas Aquinas in the Irish Dail! Some members of the faculty were a bit skeptical. During the spring semester, Desmond took over my course in the Metaphysical Poets. Though the students enjoyed his stories and his readings, his forte was really not literary criticism or classroom teaching."[16]

Arnold Lunn, an English convert and critic, came for some lectures in October 1935. He was also an irrepressible enthusiast for Alpine mountain climbing (he walked with a limp that resulted from a climbing accident). Rauch reports that Father O'Hara was interested in developing a graduate program in Apologetics. It was for that purpose that he brought Lunn to the Faculty. Lunn's great distinction, besides his reputation as a mountain climber, captain of the British Olympic Ski Champions, etc., was precisely as a conversationalist and apologist for the Catholic religion. He took on such opponents as Sir James Jeans, Haldane, Coulton, each of them in a long series of exchanged letters, later published in book form in each case."[17]

Lunn was followed by Robert Speaight, the English actor and writer, in 1936. It was during Speaight's visit that Edward VIII's abdication speech was scheduled to come over the radio, so he invited in a group of students to his elegant quarters in the northwest corner of Dillon Hall's first floor to hear it, expressing satisfaction afterwards that the king had done the decent thing.

St. Mary's College joined with Notre Dame in 1937 to offer courses by Charles DuBos, the famous French man of letters who had written eleven volumes of literary criticism, mostly on English and American writers, and had translated the American novelist Edith Wharton into French. Rufus Rauch remembers that the *New York Times* ran a shipboard photo of his arrival and that he was accompanied by a secretary as well as by a wife and daughter.[18] Tom Stritch writes that: "DuBos was a courtly and elegant gentleman. He rented a house on Angela Boulevard just south of

Notre Dame's golf course, and there kept a Sunday afternoon salon. I judge his work to be like that of his American contemporary Paul Elmer More: humanistic, sincere, learned, tasteful. A deeply felt religious sense made DuBos rather more than More."[19]

The final import of 1937 was a man who came to stay and who gave to the entire lecture program the critical mass that it needed to dispense with Father O'Hara's recruiting trips: Waldemar Gurian. He seemed to know everyone in the European intellectual world. He had been born in 1902 in St. Petersburg to a Russian-Jewish father and a German mother. His mother became a Catholic convert in 1911 and took young Waldemar to live in Berlin. After some years in a Dutch Dominican school, he returned to Berlin to do his doctoral studies under Max Scheler. Then he became a writer for Romano Guardini's *Schildgenossen* in Cologne. With Hitler's rise to power Gurian had taken his family into a near destitute exile in Switzerland whence, through the good offices of Desmond Fitzgerald and others, he received his invitation to Notre Dame. He arrived with "his own swift and incisive brilliance, a mighty erudition, wide knowledge of world politics and political theory, remarkable insight into the nature of totalitarianism, the main theme of his work, a genuine feeling for literature, especially his native Russian authors, broad experience in intellectual labors both large and small and, above all, a clear model, based on his German experience, of what a Catholic intellectual journal might and could be."[20]

Gurian knew that his German friend, the political scientist Ferdinand A. Hermens, was then teaching at the Catholic University in Washington, D.C., so he persuaded Notre Dame's political science department to recruit him. Then with Hermens, Father Leo R. Ward, and Frank O'Malley, Gurian began planning for the establishment of a first-class political science journal at Notre Dame. They decided that it should be launched following an impressive symposium in that field, which they held in 1938, with talks by Jacques Maritain, C. J. Friedrich of Harvard, Goetz A. Briefs of Georgetown University, Mortimer Adler of the University of Chicago, and others.

In January 1939 the first volume of the quarterly *Review of Politics* appeared under the editorship of Waldemar Gurian with F. A. Hermens and Francis J. O'Malley as managing editors. That entire volume was made up of talks from the great symposium. It was clear from that content that the "politics" intended by the title were truly Aristotelian, embracing the concerns of man in society, a perspective perhaps best articulated by O'Malley some ten years later when he wrote that "*Review of Politics,* without complacency and with the temper of humility, would make the image of man, man's awareness of his existence, clearer to himself. For ten years it has worked towards this clarity, since it realizes that if man really reaches the point where he can see himself, his history and his institutions in right proportion, he may then be able to save his soul from the sword and his life from the power of dogs."[21]

Gurian and O'Malley worked so well together on the *Review* that they developed a deep respect and affection for each other. Gurian was a tall and very fat man who wore somber European suits and sometimes a black and flat-brimmed felt hat with a low crown after the manner of Sephardic Jews or of Amish men. He carried a heavy leather briefcase always bulging so much with papers that its top would not snap into place but had to be held together by the two buckled belts. O'Malley scampered bare-headed at Gurian's side as the two made their way like a Laurel and Hardy act across the campus toward the cafeteria in South Dining Hall. Sixteen years later in the memorial that O'Malley wrote for Gurian in the *Review* he said that "Waldemar Gurian was a presence—physically, intellectually and spiritually. . . . his impact upon the life of the university has been the greatest and the most enduring"[22] of those invited there by Father O'Hara. O'Malley recognized that Gurian did not stir warmth, but he felt that "the majority of the faculty held him in enormous respect."

Indeed the respect was almost compelled from the earliest days of Gurian's appearance there. He had arrived in 1937 while Arnold Lunn was making a return visit, giving his usual light-hearted and gossipy talks in Washington Hall, even throwing in one on mountain climbing. Gurian went to one of Lunn's talks and sat in the front row, occasionally frowning and grimacing, shaking his head from side to side. Eventually Lunn tossed off some remark— probably an underestimation of the Hitlerian danger—that was more than Gurian could take. The big man stood up and moved ponderously to his right, then with his high-topped shoes squeak-squawking all the way, he went up the aisle and out of the building.

Lunn continued with his good-natured chatter as if nothing had happened. But Gurian did not go home. He went around to the foot of the stairs that led down from the west stage exit and waited. When Lunn eventually came out, Gurian yelled up at him and denounced him. Students streaming from the building clustered around, finding the side show more interesting than the main event. They would cheer first one and then the other in the long and loud argument. The next day the *Scholastic* came out with one of its best headlines of all time: "Man Mountain Meets Mountain Man."

About the same time that Gurian arrived there was also a visit by still another English convert from Oxford, Christopher Hollis, who later in his memoirs summarized his glowering colleague very well:

> He was a man of immense reading who had a knowledge of the literature both of contemporary and past European politics immeasurably greater either than my own or than of anyone else at Notre Dame. If he had a fault it was that he estimated opinion too exclusively from what he had read in print. . . . he often confidently lectured me on the state of English opinion, and his judgment here, where I could check him, was often curiously at fault through gross exaggeration of the importance of some obscure person, an article by whom he had read in some newspaper.
>
> Gurian was a true Continental savant. Life to him consisted of reading and writing and of nothing else. He was indifferent to what he ate, where he lived, how he was clothed. I do not imagine that he ever in his life took any exercise. . . .
>
> He was as unyielding as a man can be in conversation. I never knew him to shift his ground an inch because of anything that anybody else said to him. . . . Frankly, I was quite frightened of his unceasing attacks. I have been to the door of the cafeteria, and, seeing him within, have not dared to enter, and have gone to get my meal elsewhere. . . . Gurian delighted in gloom.[23]

Nevertheless, Gurian made many contributions to Notre Dame's intellectual and spiritual life, not the least of them in his continuing recruitment of outstanding faculty members from Europe. For instance, he was responsible for the invitation which brought over to the philosophy department Yves Simon, the distinguished student and follower of Maritain, in 1939. At Notre Dame the situation was much the same as that James Hitchcock described of U. S. Catholic institutions generally: "theology was often not taught at all or was taught badly, while major effort was concentrated on the teaching of philosophy."[24] In the words of Tom Stritch, the Notre Dame students of the 1930s "were universally agreed that the required courses in religion were a waste of time and that the staff of the department was . . . a motley collection of misfits. . . ."[25]

The same Father O'Hara who had brought the university to such concentration in philosophy had also been somewhat responsible for the sad state of its religion department. While he was Prefect of Religion he had begun the *Religious Bulletin,* that mimeographed propaganda sheet so interested in the quantities of religious experience on the campus. Frank O'Malley as a young faculty member and floor prefect in his residence hall might be detailed by the rector to check every weekday morning the numbers and names of students attending Mass. And yet, O'Malley himself seldom attended such Masses. He would generally attend Mass once a week, on Sunday, at Sacred Heart Church. He would always bring with him a Saint Andrew's missal nearly three inches thick, and he would stand in the rear of the church. This made it easy for him to slip out and have a cigarette until the sermon was over—the sermon generally being a pietistic and almost totally unintellectual effort by some member of the religion department. Thus it was that O'Malley's spiritual growth came almost without piety. This sometimes caught students by surprise. A budding young intellectual might confide in O'Malley that he had lost his faith, expecting understanding and compassion, only to have O'Malley scoff him away as an impossible creature. O'Malley might be in revolt against Notre Dame's religion department, all of its works and pomps, but he was alive with spiritual faith, and he loved the Church. He matured at a period in Notre Dame's history when the waves of European converts brought a sense of the excitement to be found in rediscovering the Church and of coming to know it better than many of the churchmen of that day.

There were other symposiums that also advanced the intellectual climate at Notre Dame: a mathematics symposium in 1938 brought participants from Harvard, Yale, and Princeton; a physics symposium in the same year brought the astronomer Canon Georges LeMaître from Belgium, Arthur Compton from the University of Chicago, Carl Anderson from Cal Tech, and Harlow Shapley from Harvard. There were also faculty additions of great distinction in science: Arthur Haas, Karl Menger, Eugene Guth. But the big event for the humanities was the politics symposium of 1938. A follow-up symposium on religion and modern society took place in early 1940, offering talks by Anton C. Pegis and Robert Pollock of Fordham, Bernard J. Muller-Thym of St. Louis University, Walter M. Horton of Oberlin, Leo R. Ward and Frank O'Malley of Notre Dame. O'Malley's lecture was entitled "Modern Literature and the Religious Attitude toward Life." It was a tour de force performance, well received in spite of the fact that no question period was provided after it. Nevertheless, the total impact of the symposium seemed considerably less than that of the great effort which had launched the *Review of Politics* just over a year before.

Apart from the stimulating visits of lecturers and new faculty, the other great source of the spiritual resurgence was books and periodicals. Christopher Dawson probably never spoke on the campus (although he gave lectures at St. Mary's College nearby at the invitation of Sister M. Madeleva, C.S.C., in a program chaired by Dr. Bruno Schlesinger), but O'Malley knew his written works very well and often quoted them in his classes:

> A new kind of life has inserted itself into the cosmic process at a particular point in time under definite historical circumstances and has become the principle of a new order of spiritual progress.
>
> The creative process which has reached its end in man starts off again from man in a second ascent, the possibilities of which are as yet unrealized, and which are to be grasped not by Reason, which lives on the systematization of the past, but by Faith, which is the promise of the future.[26]
>
> Catholicism has always insisted that man's nature is twofold. He is neither flesh nor spirit, but a compound of both. It is his function to be a bridge between two worlds, the world of sense and the world of spirit, each real, each good, but each essentially different. . . .

This is not a Manichaean opposition between the essential
evil of nature and the absolute good of spirit. . . .

In the Sacraments, in the life of faith, in every act of
spiritual will and aspiration of spiritual desire, the work of
divine restoration goes ceaselessly forward. In that work is
the whole hope of humanity.[27]

One of O'Malley's favorite places for giving his readings, apart
from his classes, was the institution called "The Grail" located
on a farm near Loveland, Ohio. It had been founded by an aris-
tocratic Dutch lady and was dedicated to helping American girls
explore the implications of the Catholic life. The staff included a
former secretary of Mortimer Adler from the University of Chicago, and the group also operated another farm called "Childerly"
near Chicago where O'Malley also gave occasional readings.

As an undergraduate, O'Malley had in many classes been seated
next to Louis J. Putz through the accident of the alphabetical
seating arrangements. Putz was a young seminarian from Germany who brought to Notre Dame first-hand knowledge of the
Catholic Action developments in Europe. The Young Christian
Workers (JOC) movement had been founded in Belgium by Canon
Cardijn in 1925, had spread to France in 1926, then expanded into
a Christian Agricultural Youth (JAC), Young Christian Students
(JEC), and an Independent Christian Youth (JIC).[28] Shortly after
his ordination as a C.S.C. priest in 1936, Father Putz began
forming Catholic Action cells among the Notre Dame students.
This development helped to contribute to the generally rising tide
of excitement about things spiritual and liturgical on the campus,
but O'Malley showed little or no interest in it.

About this same time James O'Gara and John Cogley were
founding the Catholic Worker Movement in Chicago with many
advisory visits from Dorothy Day and Peter Maurin of the New
York Catholic Worker Movement. Father Putz and Professor Jerome Kerwin of the University of Chicago, a sort of unofficial lay
Catholic chaplain of Calvert House, the Catholic Student Center
there, also helped.[29]

Another development at the University of Chicago in which
O'Malley had great interest was the Committee on Social Thought
headed by John U. Nef. Since his own decision not to pursue
graduate study beyond the master's degree level, O'Malley had

been strongly advising his students against graduate study, but he seems to have been brought willy-nilly to respect for this program, at least. Perhaps it was because Gurian had introduced him personally to Maritain, and he found that Maritain was a warm friend of Nef's, always staying at Nef's house when he was in Chicago. At any rate, O'Malley began telling his students that if they must do graduate study this was the place to go. Rauch says that O'Malley eventually changed his stance on graduate study and "encouraged interested and qualified students to apply for Danforth Fellowships, intended for prospective college teachers and requiring a strong religious commitment on their part, and Woodrow Wilson Fellowships at Princeton, which were more open-ended. Frank wrote strong letters of support for such applicants; competition became keen among colleges and universities across the country; in the vast majority of cases applications from Notre Dame graduates were successful. Danforth applications required personal interviews with a selection committee. Frank for a number of years was a member of the selection committee for the Midwest region which held the meetings and interviews at Northwestern University. And for a good many years Notre Dame ranked very high among all colleges and universities in the number of Danforths and Woodrow Wilsons awarded."[30]

A little coterie of former O'Malley students had become graduate students with the Committee on Social Thought: Bob Heywood, Frank O'Laughlin, Erwin J. Mooney, Jr., and myself, with Heywood also serving as Secretary for the Committee. This group was often visited by O'Malley on weekends, and it sought through Calvert House, St. Benet's Bookstore, and the Thomas More Association to continue the exploration of spiritual developments from Notre Dame days. A young Benedictine named Father Gerard O'Brien came through occasionally and would say Mass facing the little congregation. Heywood began to take priests at Masses literally: when they said "Ite, missa est" (Go, the Mass is ended) he would get up and leave. This eliminated some of the encrustations of centuries—the Opening of the Gospel of St. John and the final prayers at the foot of the altar. None of us realized it at the time, but what we had been caught up in both here and at Notre Dame was the great wave of spiritual development that was carrying Catholicism toward Vatican Council II, still nearly twenty years into the future. Frank O'Malley was our companion in riding that wave. It suited his temperament as a prophet.

Phil Gleason writes of "the great Catholic intellectual and cultural revival of the interwar period. This was primarily a European phenomenon and was closely linked to the revival of Neoscholastic philosophy and theology. . . . Against this background it is understandable that apostolically inspired American Catholics began to speak of a Catholic renaissance, of creating a Catholic civilization, of building a Catholic culture integrated around faith and radiating outward into all the realms of life and thought."[31] At Notre Dame, Frank O'Malley was saying that Catholics would "construct man, construct society, construct creation."[32]

3
The Major Course

Development

In 1936 at the age of twenty-seven, Frank O'Malley was thinking about the possibility of further graduate study in the field of English. He had completed his master's degree work about three years earlier. However, Notre Dame's Graduate School did not offer a doctoral program in English. Just then an article appeared in *Commonweal* by the distinguished Catholic layman, Hugh S. Taylor, who was a Professor of Chemistry at Princeton:

> There is a very short and simple answer to the question why men should go to Princeton and it is: to promote the Catholic life. Paradoxical as such a reply may seem at first sight to be, it gains force from consideration, and especially from understanding of what the Catholic life consists. Monsignor Fulton J. Sheen in his final chapter of "The Mystical Body of Christ," recently published under the imprimatur of the See of Westminster, writes: "Catholic Action is immanent in the sense that it demands spiritual perfection in the laity. . . . Catholic Action is transitive inasmuch as it applies the fruits of the Spirit to those inside and outside the Mystical Body of Christ."
>
> It is this final "outside" which pertains to the problem in hand and of this Monsignor Sheen says: "Catholic Action means, if we follow through the logic of the Holy Father, that different groups and classes will be Catholicized by and through the Catholics *in those groups* [italics of Monsignor Sheen]—that is, that the stage will be cleansed by and through Catholicism on the stage, that the medical profession will be made moral by and through Catholic doctors, that law will be made honest by and through Catholic lawyers, that the working classes will be saved from Communism for the

Communion of Saints by and through Catholic workers themselves."

They should go to Princeton and other secular colleges and universities who, with full determination to promote Catholic living *ad intra,* seeking, as far as they are able, the spiritual perfection of their own lives, are determined also to promote Catholic living *ad extra,* to play their part in Christianizing students of history, politics, economics, language and literature, science and engineering by and through themselves as "Catholics in those groups," in Christianizing the professors of chemistry and physics and biology and geology by the spiritual influence and academic distinction of the Catholic professors in those fields of effort. There is no other reason why Catholics should go to Princeton and this reason is sufficient and compelling.[1]

O'Malley was impressed. He thought about it a long time, and then he very carefully drafted a letter to Professor Taylor. He never owned a typewriter, of course, and did not know how to type. But he took the letter to some departmental secretary, probably in the English department, and had it typed. A copy is still on file in the O'Malley Papers of the Notre Dame Archives.

April 26, 1936

Dear Dr. Taylor:

Please accept my thanks for the enormous satisfaction I had in reading your important Commonweal article on Catholic scholars and Princeton opportunities. God knows that our Catholic universities, except in distressingly, pathetically rare instances, are not justifying themselves at all on the graduate level and, unless they wish to represent themselves as full of ugliness and intransigence, I think that they must honestly accept the implications of your analysis. Certainly, Catholic young men should avail themselves more frequently of the splendid chances offered by our finest secular universities; then, competent with the substance and integrity and order of thoroughgoing and principled study, they can return to teach in their own colleges and to attempt really and reputably the harmonization of faith and scholarship, of religion and life. There is no licit reason why Catholic philomaths, professing, in Maritain's apposite terms, "to preserve in the present the actuality of the eternal", should not master the stuff and system of the most adequate "profane" learning, before they set themselves up as experts in the business of spiritualizing knowledge.

To me, one of the greatest tragedies—perhaps I should say horrors—is the complacency with which some of our Catholic educators—both of hierarchical and of modestly clerical degree—view the problems of training and developing the intellect. They talk hollowly and windily and sanctimoniously of character as their primary object in education and, in consequence, mark themselves as more or less anti-intellectual, as dull heads working into dead ends academically. It is sad that so often, so very often, their utterances are as meaningless as the wind shifting in dry grass, their achievements merely "shape without form, shade without colour, paralyzed force, gesture without motion." You may feel that I am excessively excited, but I do wish heartily, deeply that more of our Catholic schoolmen would submit their minds to this insistence of Dr. Robert Maynard Hutchins, whom I quote with approximate exactitude: "The moral virtures are formed by a life-long process, to which a university education contributes, but which it cannot be its primary purpose to supply. A university education must chiefly be directed to inculcating the intellectual virtues and these are the product of rigorous intellectual effort." Catholic presidents and administrators may mutter much about the magnificence of John Henry Newman, but it takes the voice of the president of the University of Chicago to articulate the true educational ideology of the English cardinal.

I do not judge wrongly when I aver that the attitude of Catholic educators, the attitude of "salvation in the bag," is devitalizing their academics, seriously spoiling their intellectual productivity and influence. You may be sure, Dr. Taylor, that your opinions have found much sympathy among those lay teachers in Catholic colleges who grow bitterly tired of witnessing daily and unceasingly a pietistic contempt for realities. It would, I suppose, be a good thing if such professors would publicly express their disgust; but, indubitably, public disgust would lead to private decapitation. Besides, the Catholic university professor, immersed in mute misery, as too often he is, would perhaps, in his day of freedom, be unreasonably violent and clamorous. He would scarcely limit himself to your emollient and praiseworthy urgencies.

                              Most sincerely yours,
                              Francis O'Malley[2]

O'Malley's letter reached Dr. Taylor after a considerable controversy had taken place over Taylor's original article, a controversy in which Notre Dame's *Religious Bulletin* had joined. So Taylor's reply shows a good bit of gratitude for O'Malley's letter:

                                        May 18, 1936
My dear Professor O'Malley:

I want to thank you most sincerely for your very wonderful letter concerning my article in the Commonweal and the reactions that it produced among Catholic lay-professors in Catholic institutions. I am not insensible of the difficulties under which you labor and it is for that reason that I felt it necessary to write the original article. I at least can be articulate in matters of this kind where others, who might do better, are of necessity silent. I welcome your letter the more because I feel that in the religious bulletin of Notre Dame University an unfair advantage was taken of the article that I had written. I think any one who will carefully read the third paragraph of my article must finally admit that I never made a plea that all Catholic students should go to secular universities. I set a very high standard for those who should go to Princeton and other secular colleges. My own feeling is that the heroes of the religious bulletin—I think they are named McGutsky and Stooge—quite properly belong in the Catholic colleges. My specifications for the secular colleges is a very high standard of Catholicism as well as a high standard of academic ability. I do not think that the feeble-minded girl, quoted in the religious bulletin, who took poison because evolution was supposed to be true, is any fit and proper person for a secular college. Indeed, I question whether such a person should be a candidate for any college. My own feeling is that perhaps a state institution for the feeble-minded or perhaps a Catholic insitution for such would best have served her purposes.

I knew, however, that my article would arouse a storm of protest but I recognize that some of this protest is not entirely disinterested. Vested interests are sometimes at stake. I am thoroughly convinced, however, that the Catholic Church in America must sooner or later depart from her position of segregation, which in some cases seems to be over-played. The Catholic Church has a mission to all nations and that includes the educational elect of the country. If segregation is complete I do not see how we can go on to preach to such people and these include students as well as professors. My own solution is that the bishops should deliberately send the best of their undergraduates, who are best from the spiritual and intellectual standpoint, into the secular colleges. I recognize that that will seriously diminish the quality of those who now find their way into Catholic institutions, but they will be sacrifices made on the altar of missionary effort. It is my belief that the best of the clergy should also be sent to these intellectual centers and that the same serious efforts should be made along these lines in this country as have been made for a generation or so now in England. I wish there were a comparative analysis of the conversions to the Faith in England and in America over a period of the last decade or so. I know there has been an enormous influence among the intellectuals in England relative to that which has occurred here; the smallness of this latter simply appalls me. I am convinced that if a serious effort along these lines were made in this country, the Catholic educational situation would benefit by it within a generation. Because, as you express it in your letter, they could go back to the Catholic colleges "competent with the substance and integrity and order of thorough-going and principled study. . . . to attempt really and reputably the harmonization of Faith and scholarship, of religion and life."

The opposing criticism that has occurred in reference to my article has been of a quality that might have been expected. What has surprised me have been the private expressions of appreciation from archbishops, bishops, priests and educated Catholic laity, which have enabled me to resist the temptation to bring the argument down to the level which the opponents have tried to set, and have left me with a sense of thankfulness at having essayed the effort, because of the good wishes that have come to me from those whose good wishes I sincerely appreciate, your own among the number.

Very sincerely yours,

Hugh S. Taylor[3]

Apparently the correspondence between O'Malley and Taylor went on for a long time, but the rest of it has not been saved. It led to one of the most crucial decisions of O'Malley's life. He was offered—probably through the good offices of Hugh Taylor— a teaching fellowship that would have enabled him to begin doctoral studies at Princeton University. But in the meantime something else had been going on at Notre Dame.

Father Leo L. Ward, chairman of the English department, had completely reorganized the English majors program, largely at the urging and with the collaboration of his two brightest young professors, Rufus Rauch and Frank O'Malley. In fact, the entire program was built around Rauch and O'Malley. English majors were to take six-credit-hour courses called the Philosophy of English Literature I and II in their junior and senior years with Rauch teaching the junior section and O'Malley the senior one. Just as this reorganization was about to go into effect O'Malley's fellowship offer from Princeton came through. He agonized over the decision that he must make. He realized that the big reorganization which he had so largely influenced would surely fall through if he were to leave at that time. So his loyalty overcame his ambition, and he decided to stay at Notre Dame. As he later summarized the episode in a resume, "I was appointed University Scholar by the faculty of Princeton University in 1938 but resigned in the same year to continue necessary work at Notre Dame."[4] The necessary work was the Philosophy of English Literature course, Part II (English 99) which built upon and presupposed the Part I (English 97) taught by Rufus Rauch. As the syllabus of the courses explained:

> These two courses make up a whole unit of intensive study extending over the junior and senior years for all students following English as major subject. In Part I . . . in the junior year, the subject matter is made up of an ordered sequence of selected works taken from the English literature of the Middle Ages and of the Renaissance. In Part II . . . in the

senior year, the subject matter is selected from the literature of the last two centuries, including a few major works of American literature.

The historical background of the literature is examined, in its various aspects—social, political, philosophical, religious—for the purpose of broadening and deepening the student's capacity to read the literature with understanding and pleasure. The literature is not to be turned into so many historical documents; primarily the historical elements admitted to consideration are intended to widen and inform the student's approach to literature, and to give his mind freer and more sympathetic access to the literature of periods removed from our own by accidents of time and historical change. Literature is to be preserved as an art, and is not to become merely or primarily a supplement to the study of history or of other sciences. . . .

The study of literature should be placed under a special debt to philosophy, and, at a Catholic university, to philosophy as we find it in our own tradition under the aegis and sovereign influence of religion. Philosophy, especially in our own tradition, provides a whole, ordered view of man's nature, and therefore helps to give balance and objectivity to the mind of the student. It opens and directs the mind to what is universal and immutable in nature, and therefore prepares the mind for what is truly beautiful and imperishable in literature. Philosophy and literature are in no real way antithetical, but truly complementary. . . . [5]

Within this sequence the Philosophy of English Literature I (Rauch's course) began with an introduction on the idea of a liberal education. Here the readings included Newman's *Idea of a University* and Robert Maynard Hutchins's *Higher Learning in America,* plus two papers from a symposium on the university in a changing world: the introduction by W. A. Kotschnig, and "The Conception of a Catholic University" by Dietrich von Hildebrand.

Next, Rauch focused on the philosophy of art with a section on the nature of man (with Christopher Dawson's *Enquiries into Religion and Culture* and E. I. Watkin's *The Bow in the Clouds*); then a section on the nature of art (with Maritain's *Art and Scholasticism,* Eric Gill's *Art in a Changing Civilization,* and Bede

Jarrett's *Social Theories of the Middle Ages*); and finally a section on the study of literature (with Newman's *Idea of a University* again, Louis Cazamian's *Criticism in the Making,* and T. S. Eliot's *Selected Essays*).

In considering the literature of the English Middle Ages, Rauch began with a section of lectures on the medieval backgrounds, touching Dante's *Divine Comedy,* the *Selected Writings* of Thomas Aquinas (edited by Rev. Martin d'Arcy in Everyman's Library), Jacques Maritain's *Angelic Doctor,* Chesterton's *St. Francis of Assisi,* and Etienne Gilson's *Medieval Universalism.* The two major literary works then studied were William Langland's *Vision of Piers Plowman* as translated by Wells in the Sheed and Ward edition (with collateral readings from Christopher Dawson's *Medieval Religion* and R. H. Tawney's *Religion and the Rise of Capitalism*) and Geoffrey Chaucer's *Canterbury Tales* (with readings from G. L. Kittredge, *Chaucer and his Poetry* and Middleton Murray, *Heaven and Earth*).

Rauch's lectures on the English Renaissance gave attention to four areas: (1) St. Thomas More (with related writings by William Roper, R. W. Chambers, G. K. Chesterton, and Hilaire Belloc). (2) Poetry in the works of Spenser, Shakespeare, Drayton, Donne, Herbert, Vaughan, Marvell, Crashaw, and Herrick (with critical comments by Helen C. White and T. S. Eliot). (3) Drama in Marlowe, Dekker, Jonson, Shakespeare, and Webster; and, finally (4) Prose works of Sidney, Jonson, Bacon, Browne, and Walton.

In this course, taught in the top room of the Law School's southwest corner tower, a space that had an almost medieval feel to it, the English majors of 1940 had their junior year's fundamentals. Then one day in late spring of 1939 Mr. Rauch distributed to the class a mimeographed letter from Frank O'Malley:

June, 1939

Since the reading requirements for English 99, *The Philosophy of English Literature II,* must obviously be extensive, I am suggesting that you anticipate next year's labors by reading during the summer as much as possible of the following material, assigned for

Part V, The Philosophy of Realism and Naturalism

A. Required: Fielding, *Tom Jones* (ML).

Recommended: Smollett, *Roderick Random* (E) or *Peregrine Pickle* (E) or *Humphry Clinker* (WC).

B. Required: Jane Austen, *Pride and Prejudice* or *Sense and Sensibility* or *Persuasion* (all in NC).

C. Required:

    1. Dickens, *Pickwick Papers* (NC) or *Bleak House* (NC).

    2. Thackeray, *Henry Esmond* (NC) or *Vanity Fair* (NC).

    3. Meredith, *The Ordeal of Richard Feverel* (ML) or *Diana of the Crossways* (ML) or *The Egoist.*

    4. Either Anthony Trollope, *Barchester Towers* (NC) or George Eliot, *Middlemarch,* or *The Mill on the Floss* (NC), or *Adam Bede* (E).

Recommended:

    1. Charlotte Bronte, *Jane Eyre* (NC).

    2. Emily Bronte, *Wuthering Heights* (NC).

D. Required: Dostoyevski, *The Brothers Karamazov* (ML).

Recommended: Turgenev, *Fathers and Sons* (ML).

E. Required: One novel representative of French Naturalism.

F. Required: Thomas Hardy, *Jude the Obscure* (ML).

Recommended:

    1. George Gissing, *New Grub Street* (ML).

    2. George Moore, *A Mummer's Wife* or *Esther Waters* (E).

G. Required:

    1. Mark Twain,

        a. *Innocents Abroad* or *Life on the Mississippi* (HMC) or *A Connecticut Yankee* (HMC).

        b. *The Man That Corrupted Hadleyburg* or *A Mysterious Stranger.*

    2. Henry James,

        a. *Portrait of a Lady* (ML) or

        b. *The Ambassadors* (HMC).

    3. Theodore Dreiser,

        a. *Sister Carrie* (ML) or

        b. *The Financier* (G & D) or

        c. *The Titan* (G & D).

Recommended:
1. Sinclair Lewis, *Main Street* (G & D).
2. Thomas Wolfe, *Look Homeward, Angel* (ML).
H. Required:
1. Bennett, *The Old Wives' Tale* (ML).
2. Galsworthy, *The Man of Property.*
3. Maugham, *Of Human Bondage* (ML).
4. Conrad, *Lord Jim* (ML) or *Victory* (ML).
5. Virginia Woolf, *Mrs. Dalloway* (ML).
6. Aldous Huxley, *Point Counter Point* (ML) or *Antic Hay* (ML) or *Brave New World* (G & D).
I. Required: Thomas Mann, *The Magic Mountain* (ML).

(Key: ML—Modern Library; WC—World's Classics; E—Everyman; NC—Nelson's Classics; G & D—Grosset & Dunlap; HMC—Harper's Modern Classics.)

While reading, you must try to avoid the pedantic approach. Your chief interest must be given not to academical trivia but to the assumptions and values upon which the authors have written. Remember, too, that when you say interpretation of literature is *philosophical,* you do not mean merely that you apply a mean, narrowing authoritarianism to literature and then judge it ruthlessly. Rather you must work as follows:

1. You must try to discern and understand *in the writings themselves* the intellectual and spiritual currents and forces which affect, disturb, underlie, and fortify the literature of the age.

2. You must attempt to determine the valid and invalid features of the thought-forces and art-theories operative in the literature, with reference to Christian and scholastic criteria.

3. You must be genuinely and vigorously philosophical in the most proper sense of the term: you must think deeply and keenly and creatively about your reading; and you must understand that it is neither constructive nor organic smugly to enforce formulae and syllogisms acquired by rote.

> I shall be wishing you the most
> pleasurable of all your summers.
> Frank O'Malley[6]

After our pleasurable summer of reading we returned to the campus in the fall to find that no further mention was ever made of our summer's list—no checkup on how much of the reading we had done. Apparently he felt that there was no point in checking: we had either done it or we had not. The result would be clear enough eventually. Instead, he distributed to us three new mimeographed pages the first day that we attended his class, which met in the first floor classroom along the west edge of the College of Commerce Building and toward the south end. The pages were a syllabus of the course:

English 99: THE PHILOSOPHY OF ENGLISH LITERATURE
Modern England and America

I. THE AGE OF REASON AND THE NEW CLASSICISM

The defection from the Christian order and the modern emphasis upon the order of nature; the influence of the new scientific philosophy and of the literary theories of the later English Renaissance

Plato: The Republic
Aristotle: Poetics
Horace: Ars Poetica
Milton: Paradise Lost
Dryden: Religio Laici, The Hind and the Panther,
   An Essay of Dramatic Poesy
Pope: Essay on Criticism, Essay on Man
Swift: Gulliver's Travels
Johnson: Preface to Shakespeare, Lives of the Poets
   (Milton, Dryden, Pope, Addison)
Austen: Pride and Prejudice

Recommended: Willey, Seventeenth Century Background; Burtt, Metaphysical Foundations of Modern Science; Dawson, Progress and Religion (I, VIII); Gilson, Unity of Philosophical Experience (Part II); Maritain, Three Reformers (Descartes); Gregory, T.S., The Unfinished Universe (Parts I and II); Dampier, History of Science (Chs. II, III, and IV); Randall, Making of the Modern Mind, (Books II and III).[7]

The syllabus went on through the major topics of "Romanticism" (with Rousseau, Blake, Wordsworth, Coleridge, Shelley, Keats, and Byron) and then "The Literature of the Later Nineteenth Century" (with Newman, Carlyle, Ruskin, Arnold, Mill,

Tennyson, Browning, Dickens, Thackeray, Eliot, Hardy, Conrad, Twain, James and Henry Adams). Finally, its "Conclusion" mentioned principally Hopkins, Claudel, and Chesterton. But we were to find that O'Malley, once into the course, treated his syllabus more as a theoretical and possible outline than as a plan of procedure. We scarcely heard him mention some of those authors again. He was not one to be bound down to some pedantic agenda, not even one of his own making. His procedure was as different from that of Rauch as were his mannerisms.

Rauch had always sat at the desk with a literary text open before him. He would discuss background readings with the class, but he always came back to specific passages in the literature.

O'Malley, by contrast, never sat in his classes. He always stood behind the desk and lectured about ideas. He apparently assumed that we had read the assigned literary works and the background readings. There were, occasionally, conferences scheduled with the individual students during which we were expected to ask questions. But he always came to class with a set of note pages on which he had written out his entire lecture, and he delivered this in a mounting crescendo of sensitivity, the finger tips of his hands barely touching the papers. Sometimes as his rhythmic delivery continued and his voice rang like a bell on the sounds of the words his eyes would narrow to slits and his eyebrows would rise. I sometimes imagined myself at those moments creeping silently forward to peep around the edge of the desk and confirm that his feet were not touching the floor at all! He seemed to be hovering there, steadied only by the light pressure of his finger tips.

Frank Duggan (Class of '48) recalls that

> Although he didn't speak in a whisper or slur his speech, his tone was usually low and conversational—at least toward the beginning of class; it would get louder as the class wore on and his earnestness mounted. There was also a slight sibilance in his speech, caused by his habit of not opening his mouth very wide when he talked. The result was that students had to listen carefully.
>
> To a visitor who might have dropped in while the class was in session, perhaps even to some of the students in it, it might have appeared that Frank was talking to himself

rather than to an audience. He didn't invite questions or conduct any kind of dialogue with his students; he simply lectured at a steady pace, in a soft voice, seldom looking up, as if what he said had to be said whether anyone heard it or not. There was frequently... a kind of earnestness in his manner: it was clear that what he said he thought important and that he intensely believed it. At times his vision of things was dark, but again and again he interjected some comment that affirmed his religious convictions, specifically his belief in Christ. He was, more often than not, a spell binder.[8]

There were some students who scoffed that he was not an original thinker. A professor of philosophy was said to have given it as his very guarded opinion that O'Malley was not rigorous in mind. And yet, no one scoffed at Toscanini for not being the composer of the works that he conducted. O'Malley did not teach literature; he conducted it. The writers were his themes, and he wove them subtly together for contrast, repeating in endless patterns, sliding at times into a diminuendo of scorn and then crashing out in soul-felt climaxes. He wove his spell around us, and we sat there day after day in the same respectful silence that an audience expects and enforces in a symphony hall. Interrupting questions were not welcomed, and a noisy, late-arriving student who broke the spell of the lecture might be greeted by an extended pause and then a scathingly sarcastic tongue lashing.

Probably none of us could have defined the essence of great teaching, but we felt that we knew it when we saw it. It had something to do with personality, with caring deeply, with high seriousness, with dedication, even asceticism, with living and drama, especially self-dramatization. The proof was in the words and the spell, their way of delivery.[9]

By about 1943 the English department faced up to the fact that its Philosophy of English Literature courses contained a great amount of material from Greek, French, German, and other non-English sources. So it changed the name to the Philosophy of Literature. About 1957–58 Rufus Rauch dropped the junior section of the course, and this eliminated the requirement that all English majors take O'Malley's senior section. Nevertheless, O'Malley continued with the course for the rest of his life, sometimes offering it on alternate years.

At some point, however, O'Malley put aside a good many of his "Philosophy of Literature" course lectures and substituted others. The Notre Dame Archives have his original folders marked "Old Series" in his own hand. An outline of later course directions is to be seen in the notes of Joseph G. Blake from 1967–68.

In spite of new literary figures added the emphasis is the same, and the sharp one-liners continue:

"Man's nature is to abide with matter and interpret it with spiritual values. . . . "

"Socrates died a victim of truth. There was for him a philosophical necessity for death. . . . "

"Jesus Christ is a force greater than knowledge and more terrible than truth. . . . "

"Pieper knows that the poet and the philosopher must be capable of wonder. . . . "

"For Solovyev, Christ stood in the center of human history. . . . "

"Buddhism denounces all reality as unworthy of existence. It expresses negative universalism. The Christian seeks an active realization of the final end—divine humanity. It is both our individual and communal activity. An organization is needed to promote this. This is the universal church, a living organism. . . . "

"The world which drove Swift insane prevails today more ferociously. Swift was gifted with an objective mind capable of recognizing evil in all its falsehoods. He hated the world because it was no place for a human being to live. . . . Swift cursed the world as a matter of course. Benjamin Franklin loved it."

"Germans are the most romantic of all the great peoples. Their romantic philosophers were a mixture of high truth and high nonsense. . . . "

"Rousseau had abnormal interests in the feelings. The *Confessions* are a consideration of the anatomy of feelings in an exaggerated form. He idolizes feeling in excessive detail. Extreme individualism is the mark of his work, the result of his egoistic sentimentalism. . . . He writes of the supreme duty of maternal care for children. Yet he himself ignored the care of his own children. He disposed of them—severing all paternal ties, forever. . . . He could cry at the thought of virtue, but he could allow a young maiden to bear the blame for his crime. . . . "

"de Maistre was an arch-conservative but the most original thinker of his age. . . . he concealed the spirit of a Hebrew prophet."

"True mystics are not abnormal. They are exceptional and of superior quality. They are super-normal. They are more advanced on the road to perfection. There is no essential difference between us and them. We should hold that a sublime character can be found amidst us. . . . Poetry expresses the natural desire for the mystical in the soul. . . . St. Paul explains that he has heard unspeakable things which man may not utter. . . . Bergson once said that he saw in mystics a superior kind of common sense. We do not attain the sublime by escaping reality. . . . There can be no poetry unless there is a firm grasp of reality. For verse is not a matter of feeling. . . . Real poetry requires sublimation of emotions and feelings. . . . The man who is fully conscious is called a seer— that is to say, we can make existence clairvoyant. . . . Blake said the things of the spirit are the only reality. . . . The soul needs to give thanks as much as the intellect needs to understand. And perhaps all is summed up in silence. . . . Some may call it adoration."

"We have been described as passengers on a raft carried along in a stream. We drift and are dimly aware of dangers. We need to know the origin of this threat. The wars we know may by chance . . . spring from religious not military and economic causes. A philosophy of despair is not without reason. A theology of God's absence is united with a philosophy of absurdity. We need a transcendental explanation of this unrest. . . . There are voices so free they startle us. The poets and the artists are these voices."

"The prophet has no biography. He stands or falls with his message. We can grasp the essentials of the prophetic gift if we look at the Jews. . . . They have left phrases burned into the heart of eternity."

"Rimbaud and Blake and Kafka detach from conventionality and are in line with the prophets. . . . The poet finds the hidden crack in mystery. The poet and the prophet find the illogical logic. Poetry and prophecy are from a consciousness that transcends experience."

"The art of poetry tries to save the warmth of life from oblivion. . . . There is a curious union of happiness and anguish—in this rests the secret of the poet."

"Poetry can never be complete until it recognizes the object of its gratitude and its rapture. . . . We are enslaved by determinism and rationalism. Yet poetry opens a window. This great cry of love and surprise rang in the ears and hearts of so many. . . . This cry of love and surprise makes us still lift our hands toward the light."[10]

Through all of his days the course still revolved about his basic message: "Cherish your Catholic heritage and redeem the time."

The Lectures

O'Malley's words come off the pages of our notes and reconstruct the intensity of their first delivery. Recall the setting: the wisp of a man, avoiding eye contact with his audience, gazing fixedly at his text, and reading with such a voice as if nothing else on earth that moment were of equal consequence.

Plato's philosophy is basically an ethical one: its final necessity is that of winning true virtue by true knowledge. This is foreign to the modern mind. The Greeks meant by philosophy a serious attempt to understand the world and man. Its prime aim was finding the right way of life and the conversion of men to this way.

Plato always asked, "What is the highest good? What is the ultimate end of life?" His answer was happiness. But happiness or pleasure has different kinds and levels, and it is the duty of the philosopher to determine which are the higher and which the lower pleasures, which are to be sought and which avoided. The pleasures of sensation are the lower ones, but they powerfully affect the natural mind, even though they are impure. The pleasures of the mind are pure. Thus, human consciousness has three elements: (1) appetite or the instinctive desire for sensation, (2) reason whose function is to rule the appetite, and (3) will which must compel the appetite to accept the guidance of reason. The charioteer (reason) controls a white horse (will) as well as a black horse (appetite).

Before our soul is born into this changeable world it experienced true being in another, unchangeable world, and now its education is largely a process of remembering that true being. The soul is in its best estate and most clearly remembers when it is a lover of beauty and a lover of wisdom.

Plato can be called a realist because he believed in the independent reality of ideas. He did not make being depend upon the

activity of the mind. For him the highest happiness or the highest
good of man was in nourishing the soul on the vision of the
unchanging, eternal world of ideas as contrasted with the tran-
sitory world of sense.

The rapture of the lover of beauty and of wisdom is a kind of
divine madness, and it is the best of the four kinds of divine
madness that men can know: (1) divination or prophecy, (2) purification, (3) poetry, and (4) love of beauty and knowledge.

The ancient Greeks considered that poetry, being inspired, was
a divine possession, a supernatural utterance of the gods, a kind
of frenzy which not even the poet could understand. When Plato
asked a poet what he meant by some of his poetry and found
that the fellow didn't even know what he was talking about, he
came to the conclusion that poets are concerned merely with imitating a world of shadows, not the real world of ideas. And it
was for this reason that he very reluctantly excluded poets from
his ideal republic. They would not exercise and strengthen the
higher nature of man but the lower. They would impair reason
and make for self-indulgence in the things of sense. Lyric poets
are just not in their right minds. Poetry, like painting, is concerned
with presenting a world of mere appearances. It is creative, but
it creates only imitations of things one step removed from reality.
And it creates without really knowing what is good or bad for
man; so it is unreliable in a well-ordered society. It may influence
men toward bad things.[11]

*It was about this time, apparently, in the fall of 1939, that
O'Malley began smoking cigarettes. After his lecture one morning
he stepped off the podium and walked over to the window on his
right. There he took out a package of cigarettes and lit one. When
he removed it from his mouth, he was holding it awkwardly from
below, between his thumb and forefinger, like a beginner.*

Aristotle holds his explanation of poetry within the human
order, without any question of divine inspiration. For him, poetry
derives from man's natural powers or instincts of imitation and
rhythm. Our love of imitation is founded on a love of recognition
which is, in turn, a form of knowledge. Our basic instinct for
harmony and rhythm accounts for man's use of metrical poetry
even earlier than his use of prose writing. Aristotle is far more

certain that poetry is imitation, however, than he is that it must be metrical. Because poetry is an art which imitates by language alone—unlike music and dancing—meter remains a secondary aspect of poetic creation. . . .

Aristotle's theory of imitation was an outgrowth of his metaphysics. He holds that we cannot separate ideas and things; because if we did, confined as we are to a knowledge of things, we could not prove that ideas exist. For him, ideas do exist but in things and not apart from them. A thing is a process of development, involving for its correct definition the elucidation of its idea and an indication of how its parts relate to each other and to the whole. Matter is the organic process viewed as potentiality. The idea or form or concept is the same process viewed as fulfillment. Everything is at the same time matter and form, matter with reference to what is above it in the scale and form with reference to what is below it. Nature presents an ascending series of forms, each lower form being the necessary condition of the realization of the higher, and each higher form the justification of the lower.

The culminating point of nature is man. And man's own process is a progress of spiritualization, a realization of the soul. Above man and nature is the end of the series in this ascending scale— that which is not relative at all but absolute. That absolute is pure form, the pure idea immaterialized. God is the life of pure thought, containing as content no foreign matter but only thought itself. He is the mover—though unmoved himself—of the universe, and this not by virtue of his own action but by being simply the end of the whole universe toward which all things move by an inner compulsion. Thus Aristotle's metaphysics is not of being but of becoming. It is a process of unfoldment, a development. But his philosophy of becoming ends finally in being.

Fine art, for Aristotle, is no longer twice removed from reality (as in Plato's imitation of an imitation). It becomes the expression of a higher truth, a universal which is not separate from the particular but inherent in it. A work of art becomes an image of reality itself penetrated by the idea and through which the idea shines more brilliantly than in the actual world. Thus it is the function of poetry not to mirror the surface of things but to bring out more clearly the ideas which things are striving to realize in nature. And so art imitates that creative force which we see in nature working rationally toward an end, succeeding in general but sometimes failing because of defects in material. Fine art would create for things more nearly perfect embodiments of those ideas not quite clear in things themselves. It is not a copy of things as they are but an imitation of things as they ought to be. And yet, while philosophy tries to state the universal in intellectual terms, art always represents particular things in sensuous terms. While art is always concerned with the concrete and sensuous it is also concerned with the universal. It expresses truths not as abstract ideas but as concrete manifestations. Aristotle recognized as much as Plato the emotional power of art and its consequent danger but he believed that its content of truth made it of great benefit to society. . . .

Artistotle's conception of organic unity is absolutely central to his theory of art: the whole of a work of art is not just a fortuitous collection of parts; it is an organic unity which will be broken if any part is changed. The unity of an artistic work is absolutely determined from within and must be bound together by logical and moral necessity. Form dominates matter; quality dominates quantity. The only unity for drama demanded by Aristotle is the unity of plot or action: it should be a single, coherent action having a beginning, a middle, and an end, such that the middle is causally consequent upon the beginning, while the end arises out of the entire plot and not as a result of a 'deus ex machina.'

He continued on through Aristotle's theory of tragedy as a catharsis or purgation of pity and fear, to Horace's Ars Poetica, *to the Renaissance revival of classicism, to Sir Philip Sidney, John Dryden, Alexander Pope, to the scholasticism of St. Thomas Aquinas, then that of Roger Bacon, Duns Scotus, and William of Occam, to Copernicus, Giordano Bruno, John Kepler, and Galileo, to Descartes, Francis Bacon, and Thomas Hobbes.*

When he eventually published his lectures on John Milton it was in an expanded version that also included a statement of his general rationale for the philosophy of literature course.

A merely aesthetical or "literary" approach to literature leaves the student one-sided or incomplete in his appreciation. The approach of the new critics (with their internalities and relativities) often results in an exclusiveness (exclusive even of all comparative intellectual or literary values—the analysis of structures remains sufficient). A factual or historical-chronological approach, period by period, viewing literature, like Taine and the multitudinous retainers of Taine, as a product just of race, place and time easily separates the student from the energy and the life of literature entirely. A philosophical or "universalist" approach is more living, more human and more real because it sees literature as involving not just *literature* or *history* but the total life of man, his whole nature and experience—in Coleridge's words, "all human knowledge, human thoughts, human passions, emotion, language." A properly philosophical approach does not disunify or disintegrate the force of art and literature. It tries to see the essential unity and depth and direction of man's life and so the unity and depth of man's work in art and literature. Art and literature have, as Aristotle suggests, a philosophical character: "Poetry is something more philosophic and of graver import than history, since its statements are of the nature rather of universals, whereas those of history are singulars." And Wordsworth, echoing Aristotle and emphasizing the philosophic quality of poetry, declares that "poetry is the image of man and nature" and that poetry can be produced only "by a man, who, being possessed of more than usual organic sensibility has also thought long and deeply."

There is, of course, no possibility of having a complete human approach to literature without reference to and use of real intellectual and spiritual values: certain, not vaporous, undulant notions of God, of man, of the universe, and of art. It should be the belief of those responsible for a genuine philosophy of literature (involving a philosophy of art and a philosophy of man and culture) that real standards and directions are provided in the Classical and Christian traditions rather than in the rationalist formulas and irrational surgings characteristic of the thought of the modern world. The Christian tradition (with its absorption of the virtues of the Classical tradition) makes available concepts of man's being, man's destiny and man's art that are more secure and realistic, more universal and illuminating than those provided anywhere else—and not merely from an academic point-of-view but in the very nature of human experience and art and the communication of values. The Christian tradition of thought and value gives constant purpose and meaning to man's life. With its possession of "the true form of the world," it gives true form to man's art and literature. Having a sense of the order and nature of things, clearly provided in the stability of the Christian-Classical tradition, the student or critic will see literature wholly and will be less capable of treating it as machinery, of making arbitrary or sentimental judgments and responses. He will be saved, it is hoped, from caprice, vulgarity or emotional escapism. He will not be made infertile of mind and imagination in his literary studies by the pursuit of the technical and the superficial. Nor will he be beaten down by "undisciplined squads of emotion." Rather he ought to be genuinely knowing, searching, sympathetic, comprehensive, *cosmological* indeed, in his study of literature, for he, above all, must know that it bears, vitally, sensuously, even mysteriously, the image of man and of man's relationship to man, to history, to nature and to God.

Within the world-view of a true philosophy of literature, I propose to make a brief and summary consideration of a great English work of art, Milton's *Paradise Lost* (with mindfulness of *Paradise Regained* and of the formal theological work, *The Christian Doctrine*), to discern—as adequately as possible within the limits set for this discussion—Milton's attitudes towards God, man and the universe as embodied there. I do not intend to look at the work as a philosopher *per se;* that is, it is not to me simply a philosophical text but a philosophical poem—a poem, an epic of its age, the age of rationalism. I am not interested in detailing or drawing out specific sources or relationships in the history of philosophy for the poem—a special task—particular studies, say, in Plato and Milton, Descartes and Milton, Spinoza and Milton. Rather I am interested in displaying the poem within its own universe of culture—a poem alive, echoing that universe, catching the mind and soul of the poet affected by his life within a particular universe of culture.

I shall not consider either the effect of the philosophy of rationalism animate in the poem upon the style or external form of the poem, although that work might be done and would be important and interesting to do: the tracing of the ways in which Milton's very art is diluted in intensity by a hollowness conceivably deriving from the "hollowness" of his concepts of God, man and nature. Milton clearly lacks the close, warm, Hopkinsesque (although Hopkins did admire the "balanced Miltonic style") feeling for a sacramentalized, Incarnationalized nature, physical and human;

and we might wonder about the impact of this lack upon a want of sensuous density, a prosiness, a vague and vasty, empty effect in the poetry itself. On this and related points, Theodor Haecker makes a remarkable general observation: "It is one of the laws of great art that its greatness is in direct proportion to the worth of its philosophy and its theology. Not that a poet need study them as a philosopher or theologian would—though in the supreme case of Dante even that did no harm—but he must either absorb them from the atmosphere of the time or learn them. . . . Even the most casual glance at the great literature of the world will show this. At the back of the decline of any great poetic talent, apart that is from personal reasons, there is always a philosophic decadence, and where the true theology has been laid aside there results not only a defective philosophy but a sick or crippled art. . . ." (I cannot help suggesting that it would also make sense to substitute in this passage the term "critic" for "poet." Then it could apply, with equal relevance, to the current "decadence" of critical efforts.)

I must note, finally, that I do not speak with any pretensions of authority on Milton. I prefer to speak as a concerned student of literature rather than as a pundit proclaiming the infallible dictum: even though I might sound definitive. Nor would I deny the presence in Milton of acceptable truths or partial truths—but I am here devoted to a general line or tendency discernible in his mind and passing over into the veins of his greatest work. I am in actuality merely offering some inevitably incomplete observations and conclusions, subject to further exploration and, if need be, correction and reconstruction. Maybe the philosopher of literature, confronted by the big, busy, highly specialized, expert-venerating industry of literary studies, has to resign himself to his status as amateur—at least to be charged with amateurism—*expert* in no particular area of philosophy, *expert* in no particular area of literature, his only field the field between the devil and God. In any event, he remains certain of his competence and of his aspirations, certain that the man of faith and thought and the man of poetry and criticism are not to be forever separated from one another, certain of the truth of T. S. Eliot's well-known judgment: "Literary criticism should be completed by criticism from a definite ethical and theological standpoint. . . . In ages like our own, in which there is no common agreement, it is the more necessary for Christian readers to scrutinize their reading, especially of works of imagination, with explicit ethical and theological standards. The 'greatness' of literature cannot be determined solely by literary standards. . . . "[12]

Our red-headed worker in the field between the devil and God then took up the specific analysis of Milton.

In the Miltonic universe of culture, there can readily be descried the new science of Copernicus, Kepler, Galileo as well as the fevered flight of Giordano Bruno into the Universe, the "self-consciousness" of Descartes, the independence of the pantheism of Spinoza, the materialism of Hobbes. There is also the perversion of the Protestant rebellion, of the divine conscience of Protestantism—and the striking fact that there is a correspondence between the rationalism of the modern mind and the illuminism of the Protestant. Consider, too, the struggle between the theological and philosophical thinkers of the Church, who could not help feeling that the new science would destroy the whole spiritual and symbolic character of existence (poetry as well as religion) and the proponents of scientism who seemed unable to view theology and "supernaturalized" approaches to experience as anything more than a stifling of the wide-sweeping movement of the natural reason. Tragically, there occurred no meeting of minds— and the theological and philosophical thought of the Christian-Catholic tradition was dismissed by "the enlightened" as non-dynamic, decadent. But the scientific thinkers did not comprehend their own terrible weaknesses, the limitations of life in the cold cathedral of reason. Man's reason was isolated and enshrined, shining "free" on all the altars of thought—and to this enshrinement Protestantism contributed in its worship of the independent, individual conscience. Indeed, Protestantism gave to the worship of reason a religious warrant and a moral propulsion.

Paradise Lost is really a colossal encyclopedia compounded of Protestant individualism and modern rationalism. To this coalescence, Milton provided, as an igniting force, the persistence, the power of his pride and the majesty, the splendor of his talent. Milton was, in fact, a man of belief but at the center of his intellectual and spiritual culture was the cult of reason: he would, with his supreme confidence in his rational powers sustained by

the intimations of his divine conscience, deal with scriptural truth
as he willed, working with "the hardest labour in the deep mines
of knowledge," delivering "his findings in all their equipage,"
drawing out "his reasons as it were a battell raung'd." In his
treatise on *The Christian Doctrine,* Milton makes clear his intention: "since it is only to the individual faith of each that the Deity
has opened the way of eternal salvation, and as he requires that
he who would be saved should have a personal belief of his own,
I resolved not to repose on the faith or judgment of others in
matters relating to God; but on the one hand, having taken the
grounds of my faith from divine revelation alone, and on the
other, having neglected nothing which depended on my own industry, I thought fit to scrutinize and ascertain for myself the several
points of my religious belief, by the most careful perusal and
meditation of the Holy Scriptures themselves." *Paradise Lost* has
been described as an answer to Hobbes's *Leviathan.* But it may
be permissable to suggest that really Hobbes and Milton seem to
live in the one universe, offering a strange, weird mixture of
Christianity and egoism. Milton grasped the order of the universe
but it was an order strictly rational, and although separate from
the mind, still to be managed by it. At the same time the universe
remained to Milton more or less unfathomable. Milton could not
deny that the universe seemed to be the product of an ordering
power, of a God. But he decided that human eyes could not see
through to the reality of God, Who must forever be incapable of
being known.

What actually does the God of Milton appear to be? His God
was a kind of bright cloud "in light and glory unapproachable"—
it seems to be the mystery of nature. Milton, I think, was sure
of and yet puzzled by this mysterious quality or character: the
godliness of being on every level, mineral, vegetative, animal, and
human. Milton was, however, practically crushed by the vast
expanse of matter and its immeasurable order. And he could not
then envision the transcendence of God, even though he realized,
as a fact of ordinary logic and observation, that the great order
of the universe must involve God. Yet Milton really dissolves God
in the universe: his view of God is essentially quantitative, an
infinitude of extension. Although Milton could not refuse to
acknowledge the personality of God in the face of the existence
of human personalities, he still poured out his personality, like a

cosmic fluid, through the whole extent of creation: "I am who fill Infinitude, not vacuous the space." God's "spread" personality, then, corresponds to cosmic necessity and regularity, stellar and planetary harmony as well as to the wonder of the free movement of the mind of man. Nevertheless, man's freedom, no matter how independent, is still caught in the "secret cloud" of God, in the universal order—and the principles of its motion are not essentially distinguishable from the principles of the motion of the universe.

Since Milton's God is forever reserved and inaccessible, dispersed yet independent of space, incapable of manifestation in the expanse of time, it should have been difficult to account for His action in the creation of the world. But Milton's unorthodox trinitarianism—a matter of modal states—proves equal to the accounting: the unapproached, silent God would create through a force or agency, here the Son, actually a kind of exertion of the power of a God Who remains, nevertheless, whole, motionless, unaltered. . . . The Son, acting from God but "plainly demonstrated to be inferior to the Father," disposes of the task of creation, ordering and giving meaning to, providing a "calm" for the whirlpool of matter. . . which is the "undeveloped" border-region of God. As for the Holy Ghost, Milton would seem to make of Him a kind of ghostly primal energy or *élan vital* of the universe; and, in any event, He is "far inferior" to the Son. Thus, for Milton, God the Father appears to be the grand, unimpaired Reason of the universe, the Son a secondary agent of the Supreme Reason, and the Holy Ghost an even further reduced catalyst. At this point, it must be noted that for Milton the Son of God and Christ are not the same. The Son in *Paradise Lost* retains a quality of divinity or at least an ability or aura of divinity. But Milton's Incarnational inadequacy is so considerable that he cannot conceive of the Christ of *Paradise Regained* except as a perfect man—a representative of man's reintegration in reason—and little else. Milton does not, in truth, realize the fullness of the significance of Christ's Redemptive action—the wondrous import of Love and Sacrifice.

Milton shows himself, in *Paradise Lost,* to be more preoccupied with the import of Satan than with that of Christ. Commonplace now is the setting-up of analogues between Milton's personality and that of the Satan of his own construction: both Milton and

Milton's Satan are rationalist rebels and content with their own tremendous reasons. Milton endows Satan with a powerful reason and with it the capacity to exercise it in defiance of the God Who is Reason itself. Still, it is in this that Milton discerns the real evil of the world: the violation of the great rational order by the Satanic will to exercise its own reason apart from the universal design . . . .

Action is the key to Milton's philosophy and his *Good*. His world is founded on action and the positive power of growth. In *Paradise Lost* it is God ordering Who is Active and so good. Satan is passive (reducible to chaos) and so evil—and must submit (actually this very subjection of individual freedom to authority is Milton's greatest horror and we may well wonder if he realized how much the tragedy of Satan is his own). To perfect himself, a person must act out of himself rather than surrender himself utterly, in the appropriate Christian fashion, to God. Apparently, with Milton, it is not the heavenly Father's will which must be done—it is man's own. Whatever God might do otherwise, it seems that man's perfection is beyond His control, for man's will hurls itself unbridled from itself. Most interesting at this point in Milton is the weird realization that man, himself monadically borne within the one reality that is God, appears, in monstrous competence, to require God's subordination to his free will. For man, through falling into evil, can frustrate the perpetual, perfective movement from *Formlessness* to *Form,* to God . . . . It would seem that God relies upon man to fulfill Himself, that man relies upon God to save himself from chaos.

However great the difficulties of reconciling conflicting attitudes in Milton's magnificent and mysterious work, one may take some comfort from the thought that Miltonism is essentially a pantheism and that in such a world God, man and the universe are all the same: "one first matter all, indu'd with various forms, various degrees of substance." It is the God of the pantheist "who fills Infinitude" and good and evil, divinity, humanity, and deviltry are all arranged and reduced to unity within the same infinite.

As the first snows of the Indiana winter began to arrive O'Malley still came for his class lectures bare-headed, seemingly warmed by an inner fire of intellectual earnestness.

The Age of Enlightenment is simply the eighteenth-century continuation of the rationalist currents of the previous century. It has as its boundaries the year 1690 when John Locke's *Essay Concerning Human Understanding* was published and 1781 when Kant's *Critique of Pure Reason* appeared.

This was a time when all that could not be justified by reason was suppressed. There was constant reference to the "light of reason"—that inner illumination shining bright and clear in contrast to the shadows of mysticism or dogmatism. There was a particular hostility to any attempt to explain the phenomena of human existence as in any way transcending the ordinary processes of reason. The effort was to reduce the problems of thought to a foundation of utter simplicity and to force a commonsense view of things to prevail everywhere—never a dogma, never a theology.

The spirit of the Enlightenment might be phrased in this way: let us not concern ourselves with idle speculation in reference to things which the mind of man can never encompass and understand. Why busy ourselves concerning the deeper significance and purpose of nature which our thought is utterly incapable of penetrating? While we may classify the laws of nature we can never look to comprehend their inner meaning which must forever remain obscure. The nature of which we are a part lies beyond our ken. The being and nature of God must remain still more incomprehensible; because He exists beyond the uttermost bounds of nature. Hence, from the contemplation of the world and of God we must turn our eyes to the more rewarding and satisfying study of the inner self. Let every man examine the phenomena of life as they unfold themselves within the inner world of his consciousness. Here, at least, is the light by which man can see. "The proper study of mankind is man."

Though this hunt after knowledge was introspective it was not reflective: it lacked penetration. It had a limited range of investigation. If no morality can be proven, man must be content with a prudent and expedient ethics. Without immortality, we must stay in the present. If there can be no appealing to the God of things as they are, there can be an appeal to things as they are in themselves.

The clue-man to this age of individual opinion and tolerance and free philosophy is John Locke. The nominalism of William of Occam had sapped the strength of the old scholasticism at Oxford, and Locke hated the decadent scholasticism which he saw. He preferred a philosophy of sensism, and this shallow philosophy got the fame of being clear and commonsense.

Locke was a self-made philosopher, picking from many systems. He was a man of many moods, depending upon which philosophy he had read last, and he contradicted himself often. He was indifferent to the necessity of harmonizing what he says at one time with what he says at another. He was profoundly affected by Descartes, but his philosophy is really a kind of eclectic medley. He was traditionally called a Sensist, but many passages in his *Essay* also suggest that he was an Intellectualist. Berkeley said that he was an Idealist. Hume said that he was a Universal Skeptic. But he himself believed that he was a Realist.

Locke's philosophy rejects innate ideas and hence innate principles. The mind is a "tabula rasa." Before examining the origin of ideas he assumed the idealistic Cartesian postulate that objects apparently external are really internal, not realities outside but inside the mind, not real but psychical. The world of direct knowledge is not without but within. This gives a slipshod meaning to "idea" by failing to distinguish between the spiritual faculty of the intellect and the material faculty of the senses. This tendency to confuse intellectual with sensuous knowledge is the characteristic weakness of English philosophical thought. Neither Plato, Socrates, Aristotle, Descartes, nor Kant was ever guilty of such confusion. . . .

Berkeley and Hume developed Locke's philosophy logically into Idealism, and yet, Locke's common sense preserved his sanity.

There have been three classical theories to explain the origin of super-sensible ideas (such as substance and cause): (1) that such ideas are not derived in any conceivable manner from sense experience—and this is the extreme intellectualism of Descartes; (2) that all ideas are on the same level with and derive from sense experience—and this is the exaggerated sensism of Locke; (3) that all ideas have their ultimate source and beginning in sense experience, that human beings have a cognitive faculty superior to sense which is capable of recognizing in the objects of sense experience other aspects of reality which are impervious to the ken of sense—and this is the moderate intellectualism or the empirico-intellectualism of St. Thomas Aquinas and Aristotle.

It has been said that Locke's *Essay* and Newton's *Principia Mathematica* summarize the learning of the time in which these men lived. They are the great figures of the period which tried so hard to order the world on the foundation of the Physico-Mathematical, Experimental Learning. Through them the new scientism spread into every aspect of human endeavor and affected every cultivated and intellectualized human being. Under them was managed the transformation in beliefs and habits of thought which has been wrongly attributed to the Renaissance in its early days. For it is not until the time of these men that the complete departure from the spirit of the Middle Ages is seen. . . .

There followed lectures on eighteenth-century empiricism and David Hume, Deism and Alexander Pope, the ethics and satire of Jonathan Swift, with finally a summary of Rationalism as a preparation for the contrasting development of Romanticism beginning with the works of Jean Jacques Rousseau.

The transition from the intellect to the warmer if darker life of sentiment is the natural reaction to the excesses of Rationalism. Rousseau's special function was his effort to reinstitute the element of feeling in the philosophical thought of the time. Extreme intellectualism was the way of life of the eighteenth century: the heart was paralyzed. But Rousseau felt that the light rising from feeling should not be neglected. By the feelings man can attain a level of truth that merely intellectual analysis cannot know. Rousseau could not take his place with those philosophers who had given life to stones but who would not give a soul to man. He believed that the human spirit transcends the bare elements of which it may be composed. The business of reducing all things to their basic terms, which was characteristic of the philosophers in his time, had brought about the destruction of the very life that these men were interested in probing. Dessication sacrifices life. . . . Rousseau protested against this; he attempted to free and emancipate sense and feeling. He was tired of frigid Rationalism . . . and he was entirely unsympathetic to this philosophy which was one of mere negation. . . . Rousseau said that by the feelings men can frequently achieve a level of truth that mere intellectual analysis cannot discern . . . for there are some situations in life which defy analysis. Therefore, the philosopher must not follow the dry light of reason alone. . . .

Rousseau believed that the world was governed by a Will, All Powerful and Wise, a Being Intelligent and Good. But he could not know the Being any better for calling it God. . . the Being escaped our senses and understanding, but even though He escaped, His existence was certain.

In his *Discourses,* Rousseau says that government, law, ecclesiastical tradition, social convention, and civilization generally have restricted the natural element of feelings in man, making morality only a surface thing. Man is naturally good, but he has been spoiled by civilization. Despite man's great mechanical advances he was in great peril of burying himself in his own monuments. With morality a merely surface thing, man had found pleasure without happiness, honor without virtue, and reason without wisdom. Like T. S. Eliot in our time, Rousseau found a shape without form in the world of his time. . . .

Philosophers only served to multiply Rousseau's doubts, answering none of them. So he finally decided to follow his own inner light which would mislead him less than the philosophers— and, at least, his mistakes would be his own. He would leave all unnecessary questions in doubt, settling by feeling only those having for himself a practical utility. With this introspection he felt that he had enough proof of the reality of the inner life and of the existence of God. . . .

For Rousseau, feeling was a function of intelligence. He felt the necessity for laws between individuals in society; but he was unsuccessful in formulating them, because his feelings defeated him. Since feelings are individual Rousseau saw man as neither a political nor a social animal. His feelings are the expression of an exaggerated, egoistic sentimentalism. He was tender at the thought of virtue but very ignoble in fact; he admired virtue but did not practice it. He never went beyond the shadow of himself in his friends, and he could not coordinate the ideal with the real. Though he never established a philosophy of living he did emphasize the need for giving feeling a place in any true philosophy. But he made the mistake of counting feeling as all, disregarding wisdom and treating reason as a foe when he should have made it a friend. When he failed, Kant tried to restore the balance between thought and feeling, acknowledging his debt to Rousseau for his appreciation of man's worth. . . .

The Romantic Movement was a rebellion against the Enlightenment, attempting to throw off the excesses of the previous century and offer a new view of life and art and thought. . . . The changes in emphasis were many: Rationalism versus Romanticism was one of prose versus poetry, reason versus feeling and imagination, analysis versus synthesis, common sense versus enthusiasm, urbanity versus nature, objectivity versus subjectivity, imitation of life versus self-expression and self-realization, mechanical empiricism versus organic form, judgment versus sympathy, emphasis on man's defects versus concentration on man's merits, a turning to the allegedly ancient world versus a turning to the Middle Ages. . . . The new spirit emphasized two elements: (1) the exaltation of feeling, and (2) the exaltation of the individual human being—elements thoroughly unGreek.

Sentimentalism or subjective emotionalism may be defined as enthusiasm for feeling, as such, or a love of feeling out of relationship with action. The sentimentalist divorces himself from actual life, from the necessary conditions of existence. Finding the conduct of life a highly complex matter, he falsely simplifies it by disregarding what he does not like. He ignores the fact that the conduct of life calls for much more than fluctuating emotional reactions, that it calls for the guidance of reason and the active energy of the will.

In the eighteenth century the tendency toward sentimentalism was greatly reenforced by Rousseau's idea of natural goodness. In opposition to the Christian idea that goodness is an achievement made possible by the effort of man and by the grace of God, Rousseau held that goodness is a purely natural possession. The emotions could be trusted. The universe and all of its creatures constitute a perfect harmony; so man needs no revelation. Since God and nature are one and man is instinctively good, man will recognize the good by being face to face with nature. The true religion of man is love of nature. Sin and evil are only appearances. . . .

Out of this Sentimentalism of the eighteenth century arose the Romanticism of the nineteenth which involved a fuller and more subtle use of the imagination in the service of a "higher reality."

The philosophical support for Romanticism was worked out mainly in Germany—probably because the Germans are among the most romantic peoples of the world. Transcendental elements in the philosophies of Kant, Fichte, Schelling, and Hegel gave support to the Romantic cult of feeling . . . .

One of the most significant aspects of the Romantic Movement is its preference for the art of music over all other arts. Sculpture seemed to be the principal art in ancient Greece, architecture in the Middle Ages, and painting in the Renaissance. But the art of music was almost a creation of Romanticism. Virtually all of the so-called classics of music were composed in the period from Beethoven to the present. Whether it is German or Russian, French or Italian, it is Romantic music, all of it. Music is by nature the least intellectual of the arts, the least ideational and the most emotional, transporting us to a realm of pure feeling. But the Greeks, for all their keen love of music, were always hesitant about entering a realm of pure feeling. They sought to cultivate a form of music that would be both ethical and intellectual. Plato in his *Laws* deplored the separation of music from words—as in the use of the flute or lute alone—for when there are no words it is very difficult to recognize the meaning of the harmony and rhythm. So the Greeks made music subservient to poetry and used it for the purpose of chanting their epics and other poems. In that way they hoped that music, essentially unintellectual by nature, would acquire a certain intellectual quality from the words that were chanted with it. Then, out of their love for moderation, for the avoidance of the passionate, the harsh, the over-expressive, the Greeks further limited their art of music by excluding from its gamut of sounds both the lowest and the highest tones of the human voice. They confined themselves to two octaves.

But the music of the Romantics was seldom concerned with such ethical and intellectual effects. It was devoted to melody and harmony, giving music a most subtle and delicate emotional power excelling that of all the other arts . . . . The literature of Romanticism, because of its emphasis on subjective feeling and upon music, constantly tends toward lyrical expression. For the first time in the history of literature the lyric becomes the most characteristic poetic form. Of course Sappho and others in Greece had written lyrics, but the epic and the drama had overshadowed the lyric until this nineteenth-century Romantic Movement with its emphasis on the individual's moods and states of feeling. Rousseau was not concerned with revealing himself as uniform with other men but as individual, egoistic. And after him literature tended to be personal, emotional, lyrical, and confessional. In turning to the ego and its emotional response to experience the Romantics explored a new world and expanded the content of literature. With the senses cultivated as never before, nature became an alter-ego— not a setting for life but an echo of the Romantics' feelings. Love became the central theme of literature: love of self, of woman, of humanity, of the divine. One loved and sympathized universally. Emotions oscillated between joy and sadness; but there was always emotion.

This gain in emotion, however, caused the Romantics to make sacrifices in other branches of human experience: without reason as a guide for arriving at moral principles they lost the power to deal with life objectively. They could achieve nothing in drama that was comparable with Greece or the Renaissance. They could write short narrative poems, but they could not tell a story. They could write long poems, but they could not write epics. Wordsworth took with utmost seriousness the impulses of the vernal wood, and he recorded them faithfully in short poems. But his long poems are nothing but short poems linked with some of the most prosaic verse ever written by a human being.

In art, expression became the supreme law. Art was for art's sake. The idea of art as imitation which had coordinated literary theory from the time of Plato was abandoned. Art was self-expression, and poetry was the expression of the poet's feelings. The classical imagination, following reason, had aimed at objective and universal imitation; the Romantic imagination, responding to feelings, aimed at a subjective and individual expression.

Romanticism, Classicism, and Realism are not to be defined in proportionate, quantitative terms: reason, imagination, and feelings are active in all of them but active in different ways, producing different qualities. In the imagination of classicism the senses stamp images on the mind, but the mind is not passive. Memory can recall these images and create abstractions from them. And so, imagination is the cooperation of the intellect and the senses. Reason and imagination were never thought of as rival paths to reality. But reason is the dominant member of the alliance, not in repressing but in using, controlling, and shaping the feelings.

The purpose of art was to reveal the universal which was blurred in actual life. The poet was to represent the concrete, the particular, and the sensuous so as to embody the universal in a way more clear and perfect than in life. He would imitate man as he ought to be. Thus, classical imagination was a humanistic one. They never saw the ideal harmony reached in real men, but by the use of the imagination they could still see the ideal and keep it as a model. The Greek did not wish to be himself, egoistic, individual. He had no sense of a spiritual infinite. The aspiration of an indwelling soul to a divine soul is a Christian development. But if the Greek was not spiritual he was ethical. The Romantic imagination, on the other hand, was merely pathetic, that is, subject to feeling.

The seventeenth century had used "fancy" and "imagination" interchangeably, but Wordsworth and Coleridge found between them a difference of kind rather than degree. They believed that fancy cannot modify or fuse images but can only associate them with each other. It is a superficial and materialistic mode of memory emancipated from time and space. But the imagination not only associates images and perceptions, it also fuses them. It is a vital and synthetic faculty, a kind of self-intuition which fuses all of the faculties of the poet: feeling, will, and reason. Fancy does not bring its images into organic unity as imagination does; it merely puts the images side by side and links them mechanically. Its effect is momentarily surprising but not enduringly illuminating. Whereas imagination gives vitality to the objects of sense, fancy leaves them inanimate. . . .

The classical imagination had pictured men as they ought to be, but the romantic imagination showed men as they wish to be. The persistence of the pastoral tradition from Neoclassical times into the Romantic period is an indication of a dream-worldliness taken seriously, giving spiritual significance to mere feeling. Romanticism regarded the indefinite as the infinite—for example, romantic, unethical music, satisfying only for the moment. Romantic poetry is flat because it lacks substance. . . . Thinking of literature as emotional and of emotion as poetic insofar as it conformed to the indefiniteness of music, the Romantics in general had little regard for form. Coleridge, however, attempted to restore the Aristotelian concept of organic form. "Mechanical regularity is form determined from without. Organic form is determined from within." This distinction is of the highest value, one of the leading achievements of the Romantic school. . . . "

O'Malley's class lectures were, of course, a tour de force, *a highly individualistic performance depending entirely upon the intuitive powers of the speaker. In private conversations he might with a shy smile express his admiration for the method of Gertrude Stein who said, "I do not explain, I insist." At any rate, he insisted upon his own choice of authors to illustrate the great movements of literature, even if this resulted in a summary dismissal of some names with a sentence or two, as in the case of Edgar Allan Poe:* "Of Poe there is grave doubt. He is the greatest fraud, the most successful faker in the whole history of letters.'

The winter months brought us what seemed an incredibly long series of lectures exploring the depths of German Transcendentalism, a subject never mentioned in our syllabus.

Johann Fichte offered a philosophy of darkness in which the ego was the only reality. He was a student of theology, but he was charged with atheism and expelled from the university. His God was not a personal Being; because every personality is finite and limited. He was a pantheistic God. . . . If reason is one in all of its operations it should be possible to deduce the categories from a single source instead of leaving them isolated, as Kant did. This source of the unity of experience is found in the pure activity of the ego. But the ego is of two types: absolute and empirical, the former being non-individual and the latter being the ego as known to itself.

Fichte was the prophet of individualism. With the world being simply a creation of spirit, the fundamental fact of the universe is freedom. Each man's complex and inexplicable ego is his chief title to truth. All of our spontaneous urges guide us toward reality. When we are most our peculiar selves then we are nearest to the absolute. By the indulgence of personality man approaches the infinite even though he cannot reach it. This indulgence of the ego, of individuality, is the only way in which man can express his kinship with the divine. In moments of carefully prepared intuition the free spiritual energy of the ego can be seen springing up within us. He assumed an infinite ego that works in us and is yet more than we are. The ego posits a non-ego, a limitation on itself, so that it may have a field of opposition against which it may contend and so develop itself.... Duty is founded in the power of self-reliant freedom possessed by every man. It is never that which is urged upon the individual from the outside.

Friedrich Schelling was another of the German Transcendentalist philosophers, and he reasoned least lucidly of all. The finite soul, he believed, is capable of building its own ideal world. The artist can be more successful and profound than philosophers.... The world-soul finds itself first in wood and stones, then in animals, and then in man and Christ. It is eternally unfolding its nature.... Nature is the unconscious side of the absolute or infinite, just as the spirit is the conscious side. The absolute is a process, an activity, not a substance, an activity which continuously ascends from lower to higher forms of development. In realizing this scheme, he used many of the new ideas and discoveries which were then affecting the natural sciences. Everywhere he saw dualism and polarity, positive and negative factors which neutralize each other and lead up to a new reality. By means of repeated steps from lower to higher potencies, the soul of nature unfolds itself. This expansion and contraction reveals itself both in the magnetic electrical and chemical phenomena of the inorganic world and in the corresponding functions of reproduction and sensibility in living organisms. Then the same process of polarity and evolution which appears in the external order of things appears also in the inner world of conscious existence. The objective and subjective sides of ourselves, the intellectual and the active, the theoretical and the practical, are brought to their harmonious union in the world of art and poetry. Art is the organ of the true philosopher, and its highest aim must be a new mythology which unites poetry and philosophy effectively....

Later in his life, Schelling felt that his system of rationalistic pantheism was too negative. He finally came to believe that some experience of a higher order—almost a revelation—must supplant rational knowledge. And so, the creation of the world became for him the free act of a supernatural, personal God. The contingent world had come into existence by a mystical falling away from the original identity in which it lived in the bosom of the absolute, divine being. This is not truly theological but merely theosophical. Nevertheless, his philosophy of nature had an immediate and potent effect in European thought, and in England Coleridge became his spokesman.

Schelling viewed nature as one vast system which had proceeded from reason and had become an unconscious form of rational life, having the tendency to generate conscious forms. Nature is intelligence in the process of becoming . . . .

Art is the finished presentation of the nature of the ego. It displays the absolute balance between the conscious and unconscious activity which is otherwise not possible in experience. It is only in art that the sensual and the spiritual, the real and the ideal worlds merge. Thus art becomes the highest instrument of philosophy, because it solves the problem which is the crux of philosophical thought: rendering a balance between the sensuous and the spiritual. Every true work of art is a manifestation of the absolute world unity expressed in a perfect form. It removes the antithesis between the impulse of thought and of will and becomes the consummation of man's worldly existence. It is the most mature manifestation of the ego which, in turn, is the fundamental basis of all reality. Thus, aesthetic force became dominant in Schelling's philosophy . . . . The highest expression of human activity is not to be found in science or morality but in art. For artistic creation is analogous to the creative power of the world-soul bound by no laws except those which it makes itself. And so, for Schelling, art actually became an act of religion. The artist assumed the way and the air of a priest celebrating Mass.

Until the Romantic Movement artists had been considered merely as artisans. They were not to be despised, certainly; but they were not to be worshipped, either. The privileges accorded them were those accorded to any successful man. They took orders for work just as tailors did. And the cause of art was often not less nobly served by this. But for the Romantic the artist was a kind of god . . . .

Georg Hegel tried to synthesize the Transcendental Idealism bequeathed to him by Kant, Fichte, and Schelling. He began by assuming that the substrata of reality are not unknowable, as Kant said, but are progressive, an active process always passing into its opposite, as spirit, as being, as religion, as philosophy. The business of philosophy was to trace this process through all of its stages. His method was to be the triadic concept of thesis, antithesis, and synthesis applied in every field. The whole truth of the Hegelian system was that something was once something else and will still become something else again. For example, this desk was once a tree. Then the tree became the desk, and some day the desk will become ashes. Thus, becoming is the absolutely highest expression of reality and of thought. We only attain the fullest knowledge of a thing when we know what it was, what it is, and what it will become: when we know the history of its development. Each stage of development has a definite name: being, life, or mind, but the only thing that is always present is the process itself. The thing changes, but the process remains. Therefore, everything which is on going is becoming and is divinely purposed....

In nature, for Hegel, the idea had lost itself, because it had lost its unity and is scattered into innumerable fragments. Studied philosophically, nature reveals itself as many successful attempts of the idea to emerge out of the state of otherness and to push itself to a fuller and richer idea. The spirit or mind is, therefore, nature's goal. For whatever is in nature is realized in a higher form in the mind which has emerged from nature. Psychology is the thesis stage of mind. Its antithesis is moral and political philosophy and philosophical jurisprudence. And the synthesis stage, the absolute mind, goes above the limitations of nature and of institutions and is subject to itself alone in art, religion, and philosophy....

The state, Hegel concluded, is mind objectified. It is something divine. The individual mind, because of passions, prejudices, and blind impulses, is only partly free. It must submit to the yoke of a state in order to attain a fuller realization of itself in the freedom of the citizen. A constitution is the collective spirit of a nation, and the government is the embodiment of that collective spirit. War is an indispensable means of political progress. It is a crisis in the development of the idea which is embodied in the divine state, and out of this crisis will arise a new and more perfect state. History shows three evolving modes of states: oriental absolute monarchy, Greek democracy, and Christian constitutional monarchy....

But Hegel found his job of weaving the modern world into meaning too tremendous a task. With his evolutionary and pantheistic divinity he could not get beyond his mere rationalism or gnosticism. His limitations show in the boldness of his philosophy of nature, his apotheosis of the state, and in the opalescence and dark shadow of his idea of God . . . .

But the tragedy of the modern soul was not limited to the disintegration or the unlimited melancholy of a few geniuses. Romanticism was in some ways the final efflorescence of a great culture which was dying and is still dying . . . . In the work of Wagner there is a further realization of the Romantic decay. All of the genuinely Romantic souls were united in their love of music, and they best expressed themselves in songs. Wagner tried to compose a music of redemption having an especially metaphysical content. But he never attained the spiritual intensity of Bach or Beethoven, Brahms or Franck. He tried to make opera take the place of liturgy . . . .

When he came to William Blake our persistent lecturer clearly found his task more joyful, as if he had met a friend, a soulmate.

William Blake was not an eighteenth-century or nineteenth-century mind or a typically modern mind at all. What I mean to say, right at the start, is that, although well aware of his time and of time altogether, he was not in tune with the *main* tendencies of his own time. Indeed time was a barrier he was forever crashing against. Blake's talent raved through the world into the fastnesses of the past and dramatically confronted the abysses of the future. His age did not confine him. As a poet he does not seem to have had real spiritual or artistic kinship with any of the Rationalist or Romantic writers of England. As a thinker he came to despise the inadequacy of the limited revolutionary effort of the political rebels of the Romantic Revolution. Blake's name is not to be seen mounted first with that of Paine or Godwin, of Rousseau or Voltaire, of Wordsworth or Shelley or Byron or Keats. With these he has, ultimately, little or nothing in common. At any rate, his voice and mood and impact are thoroughly different from the more publicly successful voices of the period of his life, older and younger generations alike. The seething Blake cannot be boundaried. He reached back to Swedenborg and Jacob Boehme, to Milton, (whom Blake would have saved from his spectre and reintegrated through love), to Pascal and Dante, to Virgil and Plato and Homer, to the Old Testament Prophets, especially to Job (Blake would say: "The Prophets Isaiah and Ezekiel dined with me"). Blake was himself, in his own way, a prophet rising out of the spiritual underworld that twists its fibres deep beneath the surface of modern civilization. He belongs with all those who lived or will live in the depths under the wasteland and who will judge the wasteland, directly or symbolically. Blake belongs with de Maistre and Kierkegaard, with Novalis and Nietzsche, with Dostoyevski, Solovyev, and Berdyaev, with Rimbaud and Baudelaire, with Bergson, with Bloy and Bernanos, with Newman, Hopkins, and Patmore, with Melville, Henry Adams, and T. S. Eliot, with Rilke and Kafka, with Joyce, Yeats, and D. H. Lawrence. For these men, too, have surged against the progress of the physical world and sought, in heaven and hell, the meaning and destiny of man-on-earth. . . .

Let it be agreed that Blake is no authentic mystic. Yet he was a religious mind, able, in radiant though involved revelation, to deal with the death of culture. Let it be accepted that he was conscious of the currents of his time. Yet he was not excessively conscious of them (I do not feel that Blake's political awareness was very obtrusive). In any event, he was not locked into them. And one who simply reads the body of his poetry by itself will not find that "the major currents of opinion of his time" were of great importance to his more searching work. John Middleton Murry, who, according to Schorer, was temerarious in boldly entering Blake's mind and in trying to grasp it "from his own page alone," has shown, I believe, more real insight into Blake than is accomplished by what Schorer terms his own "more halting approach" to Blake's genius. I am afraid that the halting approach of the academy can do little for the splendor of Blake's spiritual genius. This kind of genius is too foreign to the minor tensions and traps of conventional scholarship, which are not quite equal to allowing or holding the greatness of a true and valiant soul. The horses of instruction have never made it evident that they are wiser than the tygers of wrath. Their narrowing formulas and frameworks cannot hold Blake's fiery depiction of the infernal evil and darkness that plague modern civilization, nor can they perceive the strange, burning vision that ministers to the sorrow and savagery of the world. . . .

There is to be seen in Blake a juxtaposition of two elements that Nicholas Berdyaev found in himself: "a passionate love of the world above, of the world of the highest, with pity for the lower world, the world of suffering." Blake's mission comes forth from this combination. In his letters (and in his marginalia) the first element is given remarkable emphasis. There, with unfaltering conviction, he describes his task: essentially to liberate man and his world from the nets of rationalism, to achieve freedom from the slavery of matter through "Imagination, which is Spiritual Sensation." Out of a deep pit of melancholy, Blake says, he emerged and his eyes expanded into regions of fire and "like a Sea without shore, continue Expanding." Although he tried to chain his feet to the world of duty and reality, it was a vain endeavor. The passion of his love for the higher world, for the mansions of eternity was too great. . . .

Reflecting upon his plan to present to "the dwellers upon earth" by means of his prophecies the history of his spiritual suffering, Blake admonishes the children of man for their mockery of the prophet: "Would to God that they would consider it—that they would consider their Spiritual Life, regardless of that faint Shadow called Natural Life, and that they would Promote Each other's Spiritual labours, each according to his Rank, & that they would know that Receiving a Prophet as a Prophet is a duty which If omitted is more Severely Avenged than Every Sin and Wickedness beside. It is the Greatest of Crimes to Depress True Art and Science. I know that those who are dead from the Earth, & who mocked and Despised the Meekness of True Art . . . I know that such Mockers are Most Severely Punished in Eternity. . . . The Mocker of Art is the Mocker of Jesus. . . . "

The Mocker of Art is the Mocker of Vision. Blake abhorred Bacon and Reynolds and Burke, because they mocked inspiration and vision: "Inspiration & Vision was then, & now is, & I hope will always Remain, my Element, my Eternal Dwelling place; how can I hear it Contemned without returning Scorn for Scorn?" For Blake *Art* was the creative means of liberation from the stranglehold of reason and matter. And the action of Imagination was holy, divine. Christ the Saviour became in Blake's sight the Creative Imagination: "A poet, a Painter, a Musician, an Architect: the Man or Woman who is not one of these is not a Christian." Blake knew that there existed "a Class of Men whose whole delight is in Destroying." But to be a Christian, one had to be a Creator: "You must leave Fathers & Mothers & Houses & Lands if they stand in the way of Art," If men, Blake declared, remain just and true to their Imagination, they shall have the world of Eternity where they "shall live forever in Jesus Our Lord.". . . .

From such beliefs it is easy to see why for Blake the mocker of art became the mocker of Jesus. It is likewise easy to see why he set such great store by the extraordinary products of his own Creative Imagination, the Prophetic Books, why he could rejoice and tremble in his own creations, why he could say that his heart was full of futurity. . . .

Blake's pity for the world of suffering no less than his special vision is marked throughout his poetry, from at least the *Songs of Experience* onward. He was conscious, like T. S. Eliot, of the wasteland into which modern civilization was being transformed, of its denial of light and life, love and hope and faith, of its impoverishment of the body through industry and mechanics, of the soul through science, "the Tree of Death." The images, tones, and rhythms of his language become the forms of his lamentation for a lost world, a world without love, which has neglected or perverted the practice of divine arts. The freshness of his enthusiasm for the creativity of the formal revolutionary causes of liberty darkens into portentous voices of anguish. The poet's simple, uncomplicated lyrical pleasure in the innocence of the world is blasted in the furnaces of human affliction. Man has created his world—and it has fallen back into waste and void. And there is darkness again upon the face of the deep. . . .

But Blake did not need to be localizing the miserable conditions of man in London or in England. In his being there was response to the universal withering of man's personality in the midst of murderous rocks, the shattering and smashing of the unity of man's spiritual, intellectual, imaginative and emotional energies. In the disruptive life of modern man there was no chance for synthesis, for the closing and healing of wounds. Blake had a deep feeling for the loneliness and lost way of man in the wilds of a progressive civilization, the loneliness of man's endurance of the hard and sterile disintegration of life. In the countless passages of the Prophetic Books, he explored the wasteland with an art appropriate to his task. . . . Blake expressed such anguish and fear as were aroused over a century later in the soul of T. S. Eliot when he contemplated the triumphant civilization that seemed to him, as to Blake, capable of generating only limitless mediocrity

and misery and war. . . . Blake's land is a land of black storms
and dark valleys and dreadful ruins. . . .

The progression through Blake's wasteland is similar to that in
T. S. Eliot's. At the very end of Eliot's central poem, *The Waste
Land,* the thunder, no longer dry and sterile, speaks with the voice
of redemption: after the agony in stony places the winds bear life-
bringing rains and the poem ends with "the Peace which passeth
understanding." Into Blake's wasteland, Jesus finally comes and
stands by Albion as "by the lost Sheep that he hath found, &
Albion knew that it was the Lord". . . .

This final resolution of Blake is, as Dawson comments, "less
Christian than it may appear at first sight, for Blake not only
assimilates the Savior to the Creative Imagination and the Prophet
to the artist, but asserts the substantial identity of God and Man
in terms that seem to exclude any belief in the divine transcendence." Nevertheless, Blake's attitude is fundamentally religious,
full of wonder, love and awe. As Blake himself put it: "I speak
of Spiritual Things, Not of Natural." He detested the Spectre of
the extreme and sterile rational power that had come to haunt
and stupefy man, the Spectre that taught experiment and doubt
rather than belief and eternal life and symmetry, the Satanic
Accuser that, lacking love and sympathy, had laid waste the world.
Here was no water but only rock. . . .

The Christianity to which Blake came was life-giving for him
and for the decayed and groaning world he had constructed. But
it was, naturally, a Christianity of his own composition, baffling,
gnostic, theosophical, in the mode of St. Martin and Lavater and
of the Lutheran mystique of Jacob Boehme. Even at the end he
kept his antagonism (based upon his feeling that faith eliminates
obligation) towards the dominion of authority and the moral duty
imposed by it. Authority remained repressive and fearsome. It is
certain, however, that his pantheistic direction and antinomianism
did not compel Blake to ignore the implacable presence of evil,
its menace to human life and culture, and the importance of the
moral struggle against the power of evil. It is also clear that
Christianity was no longer the enemy, no longer embodied, as it
had in his earlier thought, the calamitous, curbing force in the
world of freedom. Christianity now turned the furnaces of affliction into "Fountains of Living Waters flowing from the Humanity
Divine." The real enemy of humanity and universal nature, Blake

wrote in the Preface to the third book of *Jerusalem,* is the deist, the preacher of natural morality and natural religion. . . .

Whatever Blake's contact, adequately investigated by Schorer, with the currents of his time, he remained essentially "an isolated figure." But he is still a great clue-figure in the spiritual and intellectual history of the modern world. He reveals, in his odd, unclassical and unorthodox ways, as Dawson notes, "the spiritual conflict which underlies the social changes of the age and which resulted from the insurgence of the spiritual forces that had been repressed by the rationalism and moralism of the Enlightenment." In Dawson's view, this spiritual revolution had a dual realization: first, as "a movement of return to the tradition of historic Christianity" manifested in the Catholic Revival on the Continent and in Newman and the Oxford Movement leading to a renewal of Catholic life and culture in England; secondly, and in contrast, as "a movement of innovation and change" resulting in new religions of humanitarianism, nationalism and liberalism. . . .

Blake is not, however, a witness of the prevalent modern mentality, but rather of all those who have, in one shape or another, fought valiantly in the underground of history for the power of the spiritual as opposed to the success of the material which is enough for the surface-dwellers. . . . Yeats, like Blake, was fascinated by occultism and spiritualism and created in his poetry his own mythological system. Just as Blake managed to encompass, in one phase of his work, the spirit of the French Revolution and the liberalist uprising in the world, so did Yeats draw into his mythology the heroes and events of the Irish Rebellion. As he grew older, Yeats, much like Blake, became more and more dubious about the new tyrants enthroned by a society devoted to commerce, science and the liberal point-of-view, the new tyrants that spat upon the pride of the people. But Yeats never seems to have gone down very deep into the inferno—and, in any event, was quite fluid in dreaming it out of existence. Likewise, the making of analogues between Blake and D. H. Lawrence is, at first sight anyway, a quite easy thing to do. Blake, however, is not so one-sided or obsessed as Lawrence in urging the mind to come down from its eminence. And Blake does not stop, like Lawrence, with the dark passional, physical powers. Blake comes closer, as Saurat asserts (even though unconvincingly), to a synthesis of the human spirit, a synthesis of "reason, imagination, passion and instinct."

Blake comes toward, I am convinced, many minds whom one might, without reflection, separate from him entirely. Blake is an enduring, unconquerable and universal witness because, despite his faults and confusions, he understood and assailed the evils which upset and will always upset the great, serious, most worthy thinkers and artists of the present and future, those particularly who find it impossible to take it easy and relax when they are braved by the demons of indifference or compromise, of mediocrity or venality in man. And, as S. Foster Damos recognized, the evils damned by Blake "are even stronger now than when he wrote, and at last the world, beholding the errors, searches for solutions."[13]

O'Malley's extended consideration of William Blake was published in the Review of Politics *in 1947, but it still contained the marks of his classroom delivery, especially in the recurring rhythm and roll of his triadic statements where the elements are joined by "and's" to give, as he might have said, a montage and a stricture and an urgency to his meaning.*

William Wordsworth never reached an integral philosophy. In his early period he had rejoiced in the possibility of man's communion with the infinite through nature. But in his later years he was oppressed with a feeling of human finitude and came to believe that man must seek aid from his sense of duty if he wants to be saved—and here, probably by way of Coleridge, he was influenced by Kant. He saw man's aesthetic faculty of imagination and his moral faculty of will becoming one in the human soul's "imaginative will." He turned towards a belief in a future life as a compensation for the evils of the present. He was not interested in speculation for its own sake. Contemplation appeared ultimately of value to him only insofar as it answered man's needs, gave him hope and helped him to do the right. Pure speculation was almost a sin; for the universe did not exist just to be examined and criticized. Kant had taught that nature did not intend man for happiness; for if it had it would have entrusted his happiness to instinct rather than to reason. Since man has a reason nature intended him to live rationally rather than happily. The value of our acts lies not in their actual results but in the will and sense of duty that prompts us to try our utmost for the good. Without the sense of duty the will moves in confusion. And so, Wordsworth wrote his *Ode to Duty*.

Somewhat also under the influence of Rousseau, Wordsworth in reacting against the sterile Rationalist philosophy believed that one movement of the heart's inspiration may be worth more than years of toiling reason—which is active but also more liable to error. Nature never did betray the heart that loved her. In Wordsworth's nature poetry, nature is a kind of substitute religion, but in his later years he came to suspect the inspirations of nature and to depend more and more upon the prescriptive admonitions of duty. In the apex poem of his poetic imagination, "Tintern Abbey," these two tendencies are maintained in balance. Very important to any explanation of his later tendency was his sense of horror at the excesses of the French Revolution and his sense of reverence for the tranquility of the English countryside. . . .

Shelley had a different surface philosophy every six months, sometimes two at a time. But his real philosophy rested far down under the foam of his mind in an enduring faith in man's natural goodness. The high purpose of poetry was to redeem from decay the visitations of divinity in man. He was by nature uncommonly high-minded, and he never sank to the level of utilitarian mediocrity. He had avidly read Gothic novels in his youth. But through his priggish and pedantically self-centered complacency there do shine the admirable potentialities of his uncontrolled and impulsive generosity. He thought that poetry was the salvation of the world, the legislator of the world. The subject matter of his poetic experience was ideas, abstractions. But his whole self did not act in a harmonious coordination of the faculties as they should converge in the poetic experience. As a result, his work fails in spontaneity. It strains. His ideas are too high for his faculties. He tried to voice them, but he sang falsetto. In his last days he became disillusioned with himself and with others—especially with others. He seemed to be trying to transfer from the emotional to the intellectual level. He did not try to answer questions but sought peace away from thought, in flowering islands or divine music. "Prometheus Unbound" is an idealization of Shelley's own encounters with the furies of doubt, but the effect is one of frustrated disintegration. He was often forced to the darkest visions of himself, of the world and of man. And when this mood of utter disillusion fell upon him he temporized in the way of the nostalgist or the escapist with a vision of a place where moonlight and feeling and music were one. He directed his poetic vision chiefly to subjects involving moral issues, but the quality of inevitability that marks the greatest art is lacking in his work. His anxiety to present life in terms of the beauteous idealization of moral excellence, a creed upon which his most important poetry was founded, is inharmonious with human truth. His romantic idealism is simply a decoration, leading him often to fatalistic visions of mankind, of himself and of the universe. He felt that he had to be a teacher, a saviour, a legislator. But this purpose often prevented him from expressing completely any human truth, and it often caused his language and tones to be dead, dead, dead. . . .

Eventually, sometime in the winter, O'Malley introduced a few American authors.

When Ralph Waldo Emerson went to Boston it was a small town; when he died it was a cosmopolitan city. It was the primary turning point for America from an agricultural way of life to technological industrialism. Emerson saw this physical expansion and the immigration of the Irish—whom he defended. He became the critic and the judge of expanding America, wanting American wealth not to be misused or to become a curse. Because he wanted to see men achieve greatness and to see American culture survive he wrote "The American Scholar." He was obsessed with the characteristic American philosophy of self-reliance. He wanted to see the sluggard intellect of this country look out from under its "iron lid."

Emerson was not a rich man, and he could hardly bring himself to speak with others, like Longfellow, who were men of wealth. He was not a New England Brahmin. He predicted only delusions for a society built upon property and exclusiveness. He believed in self-reliant poverty, relying not on possessions but on principles. To him, Napoleon was an agent of the middle classes, an imposter and a rogue but never a gentleman, a man of the world but egoistic and without principle or purpose. . . .

In his religious and philosophical thinking none was more cloudy than Emerson. In his early days he was a Unitarian minister believing in the natural goodness of man, even though he could see the evils about him. He loved American life, but he criticized its ruthlessness. The Bible had an enormous influence upon him, but when he was invited to give the commencement address at Harvard's Divinity School in 1838 he turned against the Bible, preferring not the "dead God" of Christianity but a pantheistic God of the present in every star and every pool. His most mature religious expression was the emotional essay on the "Over-Soul," a concept taken from the emanation theory of the Neo-Platonists, particularly Plotinus. It made God a reservoir of spiritual energy, metaphorically presented as divine water or an ocean of light. But Emerson was not really a philosopher and did not claim to be one. Instead, he relied upon his own experience, upon the facts of his observation, and he would utilize the laws of science for philosophical purposes. He would, in short, Americanize metaphysics. . . . His unsystematized philosophy is best described as a pragmatic mysticism. . . .

In Walt Whitman were linked the Romantic Idealist and the American Realist, the Romanticism of the past and the materialism of his time. He accepted many philosophies most uncritically, including Emersonism, and he had a profound belief in the philosophy of progress and in the natural goodness of man. He idealized physical and human nature and had a great regard for the German Transcendentalists—with whom, however, he was but superficially acquainted. His particular yen was for the Hegelian doctrine of a cosmic consciousness unfolding through conflict and contradiction to divine ends.

The purpose of his *Leaves of Grass* was to show how man might manage for himself the most full freedom obtainable within the boundaries of natural law. This freedom could be gained for the body through democracy, for the heart through love, and for the soul through religion. He was a kind of universal poet of physical, emotional, and religious freedom, singing primarily and violently the features of his own character which were egotism, sensuousness, and sentimentality. The "Song of Myself" is a complete and amazing realization of the Emersonian doctrine of self-reliance and the Romantic philosophy of Rousseau, the German Transcendentalists, and Coleridge. . . .

His formula was that style should have no style: it should merely reproduce the rhythms of nature. He had an extremely vivid and potent Romantic mind: he was Romanticism materialized. His natural theology was a kind of eighteenth-century Deism modified by the metaphysical Idealism of Emerson and the others. . . .

He believed that Hegel was the philosopher most fit for America, especially in his political theory linking politics, ethics, and metaphysics. For the universe is essentially moral and rational like man himself. One must never consider any person or object separately. Everything must have its roots and be related to the whole ensemble of the world, being the apex of a long, upward movement . . . "The Song of the Open Road" is a religious poem, but it is absolutely unChristian in that nothing is said of sin or of discipline or of faith. He had an absolute confidence in the evolutionary theory but no faith in anything except existence itself. Everywhere he sees man and things progressing, but he cannot determine the end of the progress. Nevertheless, he does not doubt that the process is good. Without any summons to penance or absolution, his only summons is to activity, to struggle, and away from apathy. The open road is a sign or figure or mark of the universe from which souls evolve. . . .

Whitman's singing of the sexual impulse is an aspect of a kind of sensual mysticism akin to that of D. H. Lawrence, realizing an affinity with the lower orders and material processes of nature. Although he feels that sex is central to all human experience, the stimulant to the truest affections, he is not a man morbidly preoccupied with sex. It becomes almost a minor, secondary theme or strain in the whole mass of his poetry. Despite his earthy sensualism he is less naturalistic than Emerson, in the philosophic sense, since he is so much less concerned with the formulations of science. His evolutionary concept is Hegelian rather than Darwinian. . . .

As O'Malley turned to consider the philosophy of the Victorian humanists he clearly enjoyed the opportunity to outline the thinking of Newman and the Oxford Movement.

The Romantic dreamers had separated man from God, but Newman and the other leaders of his group felt that what modern man needed to conquer was not so much the lusts of the flesh as the lusts of the intellect, a habit of mind generally known as liberalism . . . Froude's ideal was a kind of mental chastity, a freedom from the harlotry of philosophy. For him a Rationalist was simply a man who could not think farther than the evidence of his senses. The faithful, on the other hand, could throw their minds forward beyond such limitations, could embrace, maintain, and use truths that were beyond the intelligence. Newman and the thinkers of the Oxford Movement asserted that God was not only to be found in a still, small voice but also that the Divine Presence had made Himself visible in His extension of Himself in the Church. The ceremonies and institutions of Christian worship are not mere aids to piety. They are the exclusive source of salvation, the channels of Grace. The worshipper sees, hears, and feels the Divine Presence; he does not merely think it. Therefore it becomes so important to know the authentic ceremonies of Christ. Mystical does not mean figurative. Outward forms are appointed to be a kind of lather between our spirits and the Spirit of God. It is the action which speaks, not merely the words of the officiating priest. The ceremonial rites of the liturgy absorb our individual weaknesses into the community of a common idea and purpose. . . .

The Oxford Movement was more than a theological controversy. It played upon man's interests and enthusiasm, his instinct for progress, his sense of duty; it aimed at all that was most spontaneous and creative in the oldest and most sacred of England's religious institutions. It was the spiritual awakening of spiritual wants, and Newman gave as much as he received from it. He firmly believed that it was inspired by God. But the religious atmosphere of the nineteenth century was not congenial to the disinterested search for truth. There were too many sentimental associations, vested interests, appeals to self-importance, to inherited prejudices and to personal resentments. Religion was entangled with home life and class loyalty. And so, Newman had all too little influence upon the masses of Englishmen in his day. His conversion stimulated Catholic arts and letters and philosophy, but it did not affect the main current of English thought. Newman would not have man, in spite of a beneficent God, forget that He was a righteous God, also, that there was a devil and that man was liable to sin and was responsible for it. But the nineteenth century had convinced itself that the devil was dead. He had died in the Romantic era, and evil did not exist any longer. The over-

grown and prematurely bourgeois society with its increased pop-
ulation, increased wealth and poverty, had maladjustments,
excesses, and irregularities, but these were blamed on economics.
Man needed only confidence. The conviction of human weakness,
the belief in original sin, the acquiescence in Providence, these
things might do as sentiments, but they were absolutely ruinous
as a way of life. So the Oxford Movement which had originated
in an appeal to a nation's sense of religious responsibility ended
in theological technicalities, controversies, and perplexities. In
fact, it helped to disintegrate the Anglican Church which it had
hoped to unite. Newman and a few others had accepted the truth
where they found it, but many recoiled from leaving the Anglican
way of life; for that would have destroyed the old order. Newman
saw like Dawson in our time that the real forces which rule the
world are spiritual ones. He was the first and the greatest of those
anxious to establish a new concept of man. . . .

Whereas Newman had turned away from the movements of the
world, Tennyson turned toward them. He was religious in his way,
but he found nothing but a pantheism which Newman loathed.
From the example of the Romantics Tennyson was stimulated to
study himself. He looked inward and found more than his portion
of defects. So he was not only an artist and an aesthete but he
was also a hypochondriac, spleenful, morbid, and bitterly imaginative. External events in his early life may have served to darken
his vision: he wandered like a tall, lion-maned pirate. The Romantics had shown him that the urge to create might come out of
self-dissatisfaction and discontent. He scoured the literature of
the past to find out how other mentalities had resolved quesitons
similar to his own.

He deplored Goethe for brooding too much on his own self-
culture. Tennyson wanted more humility and self-forgetfulness in
love for human nature. He found some help in the Greek and
Latin writers, but his own classical poems are full of characters
who are like archers shooting without a target. Searching for some
value that would render life worthy and yet being frustrated in
that search, Tennyson was always dreaming of destroying himself.
However, he was always mindful of man's insistent aspiration
towards the infinite, so he held on to life. . . .

He needed a religion more than anything, and his poems were a search for it. But looking for the God of nature among all of the deprivations and struggles of the Victorian world brought him only a tinge of naturalism, and he learned to console himself with such notions as, "Wise nature will work her will."

"Locksley Hall" was a self-revealing piece offering devotion to man's marvels of progress and attempting to leave the storms of doubt. Tennyson, however, was not really preaching to the men of his time but to himself. He was full of the head and not of the heart. Spontaneity in the nineteenth-century was not to be found among the intellectuals....

"In Memoriam" began haphazardly but then was dominated by a single idea: that one cannot think of the dead as he thinks of the living. Tennyson is mourning the death of Hallam, a friend who died young and unripened. Even after Hallam's burial Tennyson believed he could feel the presence of his personality. He felt that Hallam's disembodied spirit was still living and advancing toward divine perfection in a fourth dimension free from the restrictions of matter.... At death we do not so much say goodbye to this world as goodbye to all that confines the spirit. After death one is above the world but within it ... In some parts of the poem Tennyson develops imaginatively the scientific and psychological arguments against immortality, and he never attempts to refute this materialism so much as to appeal against its conclusions. He asserts that science has ignored the most convincing evidence, that of our own mental and spiritual experiences.... And so Tennyson seemed to be a humanizer of the spiritual. No one need any longer fear materialism.... And yet, the influence of Tennyson constantly diminished.... He had failed to see the broader inferences induced by Darwin, and he failed to face the crisis ... He degenerated into an experimenter in words rather than in ideas ...

"Maud" is good evidence that Tennyson had lost his grip on his times: it is his least moral and intellectual work. He protests a fear of "mammonism," but all of his old discontent and misanthropy and skepticism are revived. He turned in completely upon himself and remained only a confirmed egoist. He was more concerned with the significance of words than with science. From then on he turned away from man and tried to build a hope on the past. But his "Idylls of the King" were a kind of escapism...."

O'Malley's high seriousness of purpose carried him intensely through all of his lectures. He rarely offered any humor, but occasionally his very intensity caused a little self-consciousness to break through. In his lecturing performance he might find himself suddenly at the end of a high-pitched and indignant denunciation of some author—only to pause, blush a little, and then quietly laugh at himself before going on.

Robert Browning was the poet of optimism. Rather than express the world in which he lived he went back romantically into the past. . . . He saw man as a microcosm, under God, full of many energies and faculties which are blended into harmony by personality. This individualized intelligence composed of will power, insight, and reason gave the microcosm its purposiveness and was guided by a higher light. . . . There is nothing here of scientific naturalism. . . . There is a certain timidity in this vision: the cautiousness of the optimist. Browning had to hold on to some kind of religious attitude toward life; because he wanted to discover a faith by which personality could fulfill itself. . . . In "Paracelsus" Browning is at peace with everything, satisfied with contemplation of his own soul and his own way. But Browning is simply preaching. His characters reiterate those phases of spiritual failure through which the poet himself had passed. They do not show men anything of themselves. They do not make us realize in a flash that the truth must be so. They do not reveal how the purposive and happy life may be led. . . .

In his dramas Browning tried to visualize character in relation to conduct. He tried to realize his great doctrine of God's influence on His creatures, especially man. But he only learned how to make his theories articulate. The dramas themselves are not good theater. . . .

"Pippa Passes" contains no preaching, and it has some effective lyric moments, dramatic contrasts, and visions of patient, tortuous, and tortured lives. But in the final analysis it is effective only in the way of an exotic romance. None of its episodes persuade the reader that all is right with the world. . . . In many of his poems the characters are fascinating to the imagination only if one does not advert to the fact that these persons give no light to the complexities of one's own life.

The dramatic monologue became the favorite artistic form adopted by Browning. He loved the idiosyncracies of men and devoted himself to explaining why and when the divine urgings were concealed.... His later monologues became tortuous and labyrinthine because he tried to trace the prejudices and obsessions of men's minds, the tricks of the understanding which obstruct the influence of the divine omnipresence. He devoted himself to the conflict in the knight's soul rather than, as Tennyson did, to the castle and the sky behind it.... He appeared to reconcile the past with the present, to blend ancient experience with modern consciousness, to make a vanished epoch live again. He anticipated realism, because he was deeply interested in his characters' imperfections. But he had no confidence in creeds which pass all understanding: he trusted God only as far as his own eyes and intuitions would take him. He introduced the ultra-modern spirit of character dissection into literature, each of his monologues being an ethical problem. Historical heroes and statesmen were his interest, men of the past who could shame our banality. In short, he suffered from primitivism. The motives with which his characters wrestle were not those of later times. Browning did not show the men of his own time how to live more intensely; he only showed how intensely the men of ancient times had lived. The world for Browning was simply a boarding house where people come and go in a confusing sort of way. The clatter is life, joy itself, but nothing more. He had learned to believe in the personality of Christ from his father and mother, but there are no Christian forces in his poems.... He searched for God within human beings alone....

O'Malley was so uninhibited in his lectures that occasionally (some would say continually) he would even toss in a personal prejudice, as in the comment about the profession of law in his Carlyle lecture.

If Browning could be called an optimist, Thomas Carlyle was a pessimist looking for optimism. He was a peasant transplanted into the world of intellectuality. His father had been a master mason and a Calvinist, believing that peace was a byproduct of honest labor. And so, because of his ancestry, Carlyle lashed on ideas in the same way that men do the material out of which boots are made. But he found it more difficult to be an artisan of ideas. . . .

Thomas Carlyle at first set out to be a lawyer, but he quit because he thought it cheapened the intellect. And it does.

He next turned to reading Goethe who taught that it was necessary to acquire and perfect in the intelligence a sense of beauty and fitness which could be imposed upon life. Goethe believed that the deity was an august mystery whom men could grasp as they progressed in the scale of intelligence. But to discuss God apart from nature was as difficult and dangerous as thinking separately of body and soul. He believed in a power not really understandable by man's intelligence but who manifested Itself in the shuffling of events. From this Carlyle took his conception of revolution. . . .

The man penetrating and rising above life must be fused with spirituality and become oblivious of the evils about him. Rebellion is futile. The whole external universe is nothing but the clothing of God. Whatever the defects and criminalities of civilization it is the vesture, the means by which God humanizes society, and man's infinitude can be reached only in society. The ordinary wage-earner should live a transcendental poem, not commanding reason but only obedience. Carlyle loved to study history because he believed that by doing so he could discover how men had succeeded and how they could again succeed in modeling life according to their inward and heaven-suggested ideas. He saw even the French Revolution as a revitalizing and reanimating of divine energy, an apex of the human spirit's will to outgrow its clothes. . . . Man has a hidden, secret source of superhuman spirituality on which he can ever depend even when he is operating the guillotine. Might must be right; because it is God's will made active on earth.

Carlyle saw the unequal distribution of money in his time, the physical poverty of the working classes who are the creators of wealth, and the spiritual poverty of the wealthy who would not use their money for their own betterment or for that of their fellow men. So the majority of his contemporaries were utterly wretched mortals fit only to be dominated and, if necessary, enslaved by the few leaders who, from time to time, became competent to grasp the purposes of God. Such thoughts made him a kind of precursor of totalitarianism. He felt that we should pay honor to the hero, the man initiated into the supernatural Everlasting

Yea. . . . In Frederick the Great he found a hero who tried the impossible and was sincere enough to persevere to the end. But he had to conceal half of Frederick's unscrupulous, two-faced truth even from himself. He paid too much for his Everlasting Yea. . . .

Carlyle had a most savage and most clawing mind and tongue. Few ever escaped his hooks. . . . He called Newman a man with the brain of a rabbit. . . . But like the other Victorian humanists, Carlyle articulated a yearning but not a realization. . . . He feared, towards the end of his life, that he would become himself what he had described his contemporaries as being—destitute of faith and terrified at skepticism.

There were occasional exams, of course, always of the essay type, and sometimes entire class periods were given over to O'Malley's dictation of possible topics for papers that we were expected to hand in periodically. For Carlyle the list of topics numbered more than thirty, including "Carlyle's Philosophy of Work and its Puritan Sources," "Carlyle's Attack on the Mechanization of Modern Life," "The Concept of Infinitude in Carlyle," "Carlyle's Attitude to Deism," "Carlyle's Conception of the Hero's Cosmic Purpose," and "A Crevice in Culture: The Incompetence of Victorian Humanists to Harmonize Insight with Experience and the Resultant Distractedness and Lack of Wholeness in Nineteenth-Century Culture."

John Ruskin came from a family of very wealthy and bourgeois Victorian Calvinists in which life meant only the management of money and the study of the Bible, a smug and hypocritical merger of profits and principles. They gave him the traditional Grand Tour of Europe, and then Ruskin faced the dilemma of whether he should break away from it all or become a hated dilettante. In the end he did neither but became a crusading art critic defending the work of an unpopular painter named J. M. W. Turner whose work seemed savage to the general public. But Ruskin felt that Turner's slashings put the human spirit in contact with the infinite, giving an insight to the Divine Will. When Turner taught Ruskin how to grasp atmosphere and a star at night, he also taught him how to possess himself of the splendor and calm and blessedness of such things. Art should be expression, not imitation. An artist like Turner desires not to deceive the eye but to suggest the yearning and desire of the artist for reality. Ruskin conceived art as the aesthetic concentration of the mind, including in a moment the whole emotional and intellectual history of the artist. Proust was later to say that Ruskin's artistic writings taught him the secret of life: that happiness lies in discovering the spirituality beneath appearances. . . .

With a sense that great buildings represent a national rather than an individual artistic experience, Ruskin wrote his *Seven Lamps of Architecture* and *The Stones of Venice*. He concluded that Gothic is the supreme architecture because its builders were content to symbolize their hopes. . . . However, the men of his time did not want an art of architecture so much as an art of life, and Ruskin was left finally with a futile, utopian hope of converting modern industrialism into medieval expressiveness. His aestheticism could not endure the trial of association with human activity and experience. . . .

When the class lectures came to the topic of Matthew Arnold there were robins and spring buds on the campus outside our windows.

Of all the Victorian humanists, Matthew Arnold was the most impressionable and responsive—and he is also the most difficult to study. He had a deeply religious instinct, and he also had the art of percipience: taking apart other men's ideas and making them part of himself. . . .

In his effort to gain a classical serenity in the modern environment he was influenced by Goethe, Wordsworth, and Newman. There is a dualism in Arnold: between the scholar's seclusion and the anxiety of the man of action. It was Goethe who had insisted upon life as action, the assertion of personality over nature. So Arnold became an inspector of schools. . . .

Arnold was instinctively a Hellenist, but he found Hellenism no buttress against the multitudinousness of modern life. He found the stresses of modern civilization sweeping over men like heavy seas, and he felt himself exhausted mentally and morally. Victorians seemed to lack flexibility and resilience of mind, and Arnold believed that these qualities could be restored by reading the saints as well as the poets. He was not interested in solitary self-study. Intellectualism must become social. But society is filled with bar-

barians and Philistines, and it can only become perfect in the perfect state. Man cannot perfect himself until he becomes a citizen. . . .

Perhaps the root of English anarchy and demoralization was to be discovered in the way that the English worshipped God. So Arnold criticized the abuses of religion in his day and found much good in Puritanism. What England needed was to fuse the Hellenic spirit of beauty with the Hebraic spirit of sublimity. Perhaps if he could elevate, spiritualize, and Hellenize Puritanism he might become the reformer of the Reformation. He admired the universality of the Catholic Church, but he felt in the end that he had to reach the mind of the Briton only through the Bible. . . .

After his summary of Victorian humanism there was a point at which O'Malley's personal religious position was stated very clearly.

Humanism will succeed only when the true humanist realizes that Christ in the Church is the only power Who can regenerate humanity by uniting organically the whole of man, body and soul, with the higher spiritual principle, making of him a new creature. Most of the humanists of the nineteenth century saw before their lives' end that they had failed; because theirs was not the true humanism which is theocentric, not anthropocentric. The creature will neither be belittled nor annihilated before God. Newman's conversion marks the triumph and the failure of Victorian humanism which only deserves to be called a humanism because it tried to reconcile man with the divinity within himself and within nature. But Newman's time could not follow him, although he had found the true basis of humanism. . . .

Sometimes after a summary there would be a projective statement giving a framework for many lectures to come.

Science cannot tell us the value of values. Those in the nineteenth century who believed that all things could be founded on science left small room for Christianity. They found other solutions in the materialism of Marx, the evolutionism of Spencer and Darwin and Huxley, and the utilitarianism of Bentham and John Stuart Mill.

There was a lecture on George Eliot as an artistic concretizing of the ideas of Herbert Spencer. She was credited with starting a kind of fiction destined to become very notable in the twentieth century: characters who are fascinating for what they think and not for what they do. But much of the following lectures were devoted to a conceptual clarification of modern Realism as a reaction against Classicism and Romanticism.

Realism offers a world of experience regarded in the spirit of modern science. Many realists might more accurately be called actualists; because they are like photographers. But the human mind is fundamentally unphotographic: it is unavoidably selective, and it makes its selection according to the artist's philosophy of life. Therefore, in studying modern literature our attention must be fixed upon the view of life held by modern Realists. . . . They are cool, curious, disinterested, exact, rational, constantly guarding against the distortions of emotion, imagination, and personality. Modern Realism collects its data in the manner of science, and it reaches its inductions and is objective in the manner of science. This is equivalent to saying that the Realistic point of view, in the main, is restricted to what is ascertainable by the senses and by logic. . . . Realism has expressed itself to some extent in poetry, to a large extent in drama, but most of all in that relatively recent form of literature, the novel. The method of Realism is one of infinite patience and detail—which is that of science, as well—and the novel has been well adapted to this method. For the Realist who seeks depth and penetration rather than breadth and completeness, the novel offers an opportunity to present a searching analysis of human passions in the spirit of modern psychology. . . .

Some have used the term "Naturalism" as being synonymous with "Realism," but there is a difference in tendency and emphasis between them. Naturalism adds crueler and more bestial touches to Realism. Unlike supernaturalism, naturalism has no place for a spiritual order transcending the natural. The natural is taken to be simply the life of organisms placed in an environment and acted upon by the environment and by the promptings of instinct. Man is such an organism, and he is not free; for he is subject to the environment from without and to pure instinct from within. Man instinctively seeks his own advantage and pleasure and deludes himself with belief in a soul and in such ideals as loyalty and love. Such naturalism has never flourished in England and America to the same extent that it has in France and Russia—for example, in de Maupassant, Émile Zola, and to some extent in Dostoyevski. . . .

Closely related to the development of Realism and Naturalism is historical criticism: they all have their sources in natural science. . . . Sainte-Beuve is the greatest of literary historians. His writing has all or most of what was good in Romantic criticism: sympathy, love of beauty, emotional and poetic qualities, perception of the personal and a loathing for pseudo-classical formalism. To these qualities he added some of the best elements of the new scientific spirit: simple honesty, boundless curiosity, a passion for truth, patient accumulation of facts or evidence, power of analysis, and a methodical relation of cause and effect. He neglected nothing in his criticism. He searched for biographical data on the men that he wrote of, and he could convey all that he perceived. Then, having understood the author and his background, he felt that he could understand his work. But he did this so much that his criticism seems to be heading away from literature and towards portraiture and history. . . .

As a contrast to this historical criticism O'Malley next turned to a description of impressionistic criticism, especially in the works of Walter Pater and Oscar Wilde.

Literary scholarship, under the influence of historical criticism, eventually became a kind of technology. The literati were the scientists of literature. The reaction against this was Impressionism in which critics sought to make their way through all periods and types of literature by a certain temperament, seeking to know beautiful things intimately. This was a late manifestation of the Romantic theory of criticism which stressed sympathy. Rousseau had said, "I am made unlike anyone I have ever seen." The Romantic critic turned from the universal to the strange and novel. So also the Impressionist was impressed with himself. In his view there was no abiding reality in the mind but only a series of fleeting impressions. The truth was what each man saw. Life was composed of many momentary impressions none of which we should lose. In the Preface to his *Renaissance,* Walter Pater believed that these impressions are a means of knowing real objects, but in his Conclusion he found the impressions purely personal, subjective and changing, true only for ourselves and not reaching out absolutely to any object. The work of art is to be seen through a temperament which gives all value, degree, and intensity. Oscar Wilde believed that the work of art is for the critic a suggestion for a new work of his own, a critical creation which bears little or no connection with its starting point. . . .

Impressionistic criticism had some very real values: it recognized that there must be a response between the artist and the critic, an intuitive understanding of the artist's intention; it recognized that the critic must be interesting and show expressive power, persuasion and stimulation; it recognized the values of the subjective experience, even if it came close to the pit of utter relativity; and it recognized the importance of personality in criticism which can become creative in its own right.

However, the defects of this type of criticism are to be seen in the showmanship by which many critics degenerate into being merely enthusiastic pedagogues, giving up all efforts to judge by standards which go beyond the artist and his work. Also, as the critic becomes unsure of discovering the uniqueness of an author and turns instead to showing his own uniqueness he is no longer really a critic. In the end the critic stands or falls by the stability of truth. Fanciful inventions will delight only for a while. Skeptics have as their tradition only the tradition of delusion, but this does not explain away real tradition which is the element of permanence remembering remote times and places and which is hostile to fundamental alteration. . . .

After some brief attention to the English realists, George Gissing and George Meredith, he returned to American authors.

At the end of Mark Twain's life he was in the despair of mechanism, disbelieving in all human values. His position was somewhat like that of Henry Adams, that disillusioned wanderer between worlds, gifted with poetic sensibility and yet forced to endure a bourgeois society. However, Adams saw in the end two possible integrative forces for the world: the dynamo and the Virgin of Chartres. For Mark Twain there was only science and the dynamo. He dabbled in telepathy and dreams and psychology, but he ended up affirming that man is essentially a machine in mind and body, without free will or spontaneous thoughts. Man's life is determined by environment acting on his inherited structure, and choice is merely an illusion. The differences between the minds of men and the other animals is only in the degree of efficiency. The mind is simply a function of the physical organism, and thought is the association of external stimuli with instinct which is petrified thought. For Twain, man was a pitiable thing, the only animal that is morally degraded. . . . And so, Victorian natural science was concretized in Twain.

Henry James, on the other hand, was definitely not a mechanist. His novels are always studies in problems of choice. His animating notion is that there exists a moral sense, a sense of decency, that is inherent in human beings at their best. This sense exists somewhat precariously. It may become confused and hysterical in moments of crisis, or it may be enriched by a certain environment. It might be cultivated by association with European civilization, but it might also be dissolved by an excess of such association. The primary European qualities are those of civilized superiority, while those of America are of moral superiority. However, in his later years James also came to see that there could be a corrupting influence from American financial life. . . .

Since James thought of fiction in terms of plot and of plot in terms of ethical choice by the characters, his writings elevated plot into a significance which it had never before had in American literature. His main theme was the influence of cultivated sensibility upon the moral character. He knew only intellectual Americans and those who lived abroad, but he loved to deal with Americans uprooted from their native ways and confronted by the workings of an older society—the American enriched by European influence or suffering from a dissolution of moral character or betrayed by a representative of the old order who has been ruined by over-culture. . . .

Henry James seems finally to have lost his imagination in an experiment of nuances. He invented problems of upper-class ethics and psychology and worked them out with great complexity, but his interest stops with the techniques of the intellect. There is in him no full or complete understanding of the forces of human

nature but rather a certain sterility, a technological intellectuality. . . .

Joseph Conrad was qualified to give leadership to a new generation of writers precisely because he was not hampered by class
distinctions and was interested in men of action. His material was
human nature stripped of its civilized accretions as he examined
life in the steamers serving the money mart. He is not so much
interested in all that human life can be as he is in the problems
of inverts. His characters may be interesting in their adventures
and exploits, but they are also ironically disinterested. For Conrad
narrows his focus onto the debased strangeness of human life. He
offers psychological problems in the deterministic frustration of
volition. He was much influenced by Turgenev and Dostoyevski
who had advanced the techniques for portraying the abnormal. . . .

*After lectures on George Moore, Thomas Hardy, and Samuel
Butler O'Malley came to a French writer, Henri Bergson, who
clearly engaged his personal interest more than most. And this
was because of Bergson's theory of intuition, that process which
O'Malley loved to use most often in his own work. He carefully
dictated to us a key passage of Bergson's* Creative Evolution *and
asked us to submit written comments on it.*

Instinct is sympathy. If this sympathy could extend its
object and also reflect upon itself, it would give us the key
to vital operations—just as intelligence, developed and disciplined, guides us into matter. For—we cannot too often
repeat it—intelligence and instinct are turned in opposite
directions, the former towards inert matter, the latter towards
life. Intelligence, by means of science, which is its work, will
deliver up to us more and more completely the secret of
physical operations; of life it brings us, and, moreover, only
claims to bring us, a translation in terms of inertia. It goes
all round life, taking from outside the greatest possible number of views of it, drawing it into itself instead of entering
into it. But it is to the very inwardness of life that *intuition*
leads us—by intuition I mean instinct that has become disinterested, self-conscious, capable of reflecting upon its
object and of enlarging it indefinitely.

This is the most essential and important statement of Bergson's vitalism. He believed that men have not trusted enough to intuition, that we have undiscovered depths within ourselves which science cannot explore. And yet, he made a mistake in putting intellect and instinct apart. As St. Thomas Aquinas and Newman have maintained, they both act in the same direction, although not in the same way. Certain truths, although self-evident to some, demand a discursive reasoning process to reveal their significance to other minds. Intuition—or what Newman called the "illative" sense—is an operation of the mind itself by which the intellect perceives a truth as immediately evident. Intellect and intuition do not act at variance and in opposition to each other but rather act harmoniously. Instinct spontaneously serves the intellect. Man can no more think with his instinct than with his tongue, but the instinct can telescope and reduce intermediate intellectual processes. . . .

This put O'Malley in position to bring the course to a conclusion by taking up two authors whom he greatly admired.

D. H. Lawrence always searched the depths of his consciousness for something deeper than thought. He hated Proust's soundproof walls and tried to get away from modern society as something dirty and unreformable. He hated not only science but even philosophy, despising all things of the intellect. He insisted on the primacy of the Dionysian, emotional, unconscious, instinctive life. Intellectualization seemed to him to kill vitality, diminishing the sense of wonder and sensitivity. The flesh, he thought, is wiser than the intellect. Sex was a mystic concept for him, the symbol of and the gateway to the outer darkness, the force that gets men out of their small conscious selves and merges them with the vital principle of life, uniting for a moment an individual's jet of flame with the immortal flame that is forever flowing. Much of his criticism is directed against a machine-burdened, science-directed civilization. He wanted a primitive culture built upon a religion of the blood beating in the pulses of our arteries and in the tom-toms of a pristine universe. . . .

James Joyce in his *Ulysses* has extended tremendously the realistic technique of fiction and has uprooted it, too. In a mock-epic form based upon the Homeric classic he has tried to gather together the totality of human experience, showing the present in the past, and the future implicit in the present. In an ordinary day of a befuddled poet and salesman of Dublin, Joyce offers a miniature of the universe and a symbol of mankind. He invents new ways of expression, splendid for the size and minute particularity of their working. His immense talent and overwhelming virtuosity serve a steady realism and the diabolic insight of the Irish. No one can deny the tremendous vitality of his concrete handling of experience. His vulgarity and depravity are sublimated by the universal submission of his work to the comic spirit. *Ulysses* is neither moral nor immoral, neither blaming nor praising: it simply records while Joyce seems to be paring his fingernails. It is probably impossible to align Joyce with any definite philosophy. Some feel that his portrait of a tedious day in the life of the modern world is intended to show pointlessness, absolute negation. He seems to offer the ceaseless flux of sensations as his sole end. It is a greatly and expertly elaborated world, but it is a static one. *Ulysses* offers us as we have never been offered before the materials for valuable action. But in the end he declines to dispose his materials. There is no important action.

Joyce in his education had known the philosophy of scholasticism but had recoiled from it. His sight was always weak. Dublin was to him a city of sounds and smells. He is concerned with words for their own sake, the contemplation of an inner world mirrored in a single phrase. He came to have a fanatical fondness for words as having a life of their own. Language is for cooperation, but Joyce is not interested in cooperation, only in language. This is a dangerous and unphilosophical confusion of means with ends.

One critic says that Joyce's blindness is not the cause but the effect of his work. However, T. S. Eliot sees Joyce as the most Christianly ethical of all modern writers. Perhaps Joyce can be viewed as a traditional mentality, most influenced by Catholicism. Perhaps *Ulysses* is only a brooding sense of sin, the blasphemies being the protests of a man doomed to accept inwardly what he hates outwardly. Perhaps *Ulysses* is a philosophic work tormented by a Catholic conscience.

But Joyce also shows a pagan gusto and a Rabelesian intensity. However, he suffers less from the mediocrity of his age than from its disintegration. Especially in *Finnegan's Wake* he goes from the world of concrete reality to his own individual, inner world. Partly responsible for this may have been the collapse of the values that he once trusted. In retreating into himself he becomes morbid and introvertive. He shows much of pure Dadaism, refusing even the possibility of universal meanings and standards. His indifference to his readers is symptomatic of a profounder indifference to cooperation with man and reality....

By the end of the 1947–48 school year he had added, after D. H. Lawrence, an extended lecture on Franz Kafka and a restated conclusion for the course.

We have concluded from our study of literature that the modern artist is on a search, that art has been one at least in its quest for unity. Various artists in different times and places have arrived at different concepts of the nature of man and have developed these concepts as if they were the final reality. Thus, while the object of art is one the results achieved by individual artists and exemplified and embodied in their art are not one. They have been distinctly different in their philosophical implications.... There is only one basically true concept of man—the Christian one. But the Christian concept will depend largely on the object with which it comes into contact. If that object is vital, the Christian artist can, in his representation of it, reach great art. If it is sterile, the artist's success will be less, not because of a weakness in his own powers, but simply through defects in that object. Thus, modern naturalism is less satisfying than other art because of the sterility of its object. In today's age Christian standards seem strange, and yet today they are needed more than ever before. Today's artist views man as a purely natural creature, and his art can never rise above naturalism. For a higher art, a higher concept of man is a prerequisite. Man in the fullness of his being provides the greatest subject matter for art.

The Christian concept of man is that of a natural and supernatural creature—natural in his being and supernatural in his destiny. Man is intellectual and spiritual, as well as body and blood. The Christian concept would make man a figure of Christ— an Incarnational man elevated by Divine condescension. In his immediate relationship with the Infinite God man is raised above himself and made more than he is in himself and in his natural state—a new being. This man is innumerable degrees above the purely natural man. The art, then, that takes this man as object— if it succeeds in realizing his being to the utmost—is infinitely greater and more satisfying than other art. . . .

Today's artist must himself be vitalized before he can revitalize his art. . . . Literature, as we have maintained, has no specific content except that of existence itself. It cannot be delivered over to philosophy, but it is concerned with philosophy. We have not been concerned with the techniques of art and not with any narrow criticism. . . . We have seen in our study of the works of artists the search for values, the problem of man in modern civilization. . . .

In this moment of crisis we must abandon ourselves not to dissolution but to Providence. And this submission will make man free of the whole creative world and will let him adhere to the One. . . . Attempts to reach a new life on rationalist or humanist lines cannot long last. . . . This is the dead world, crying for life. . . . The Catholic thinker cannot by pious slogans transcend today's disaster and misery. He can, though, be confident of the presence in the world of justice and charity, even today. His value will lie largely in his hoping; for hoping he will work and strive. And having courage, he will go where no ordinary artist or humanist can go.[14]

The Conclusion

The last meeting of the class before the final exam period was pure O'Malley. Having disposed of all the writers that he had intended to include, in this last session he concentrated entirely upon his own views and hopes.

It is very certain that there is a great and rather inexpressible sadness about doing for the last time what one has been accustomed to doing daily, monthly, yearly. We will meet today and I shall speak today as we have done . . . but we will not meet and I shall not speak tomorrow or in the days thereafter, and never again certainly to the group here as it now is. There will be no *regathering*. And that reflection summons and excites a necessary nostalgia, a poignant, sorrowful kind of feeling. And I do not say this with any sentimentality. I merely acknowledge what is a great fact for me and possibly for some of you.

Some of the people here—indeed, a good number—I first met as freshmen, in Freshman English, the classes of which course always interest me and please me almost without fail. And others I have gradually but surely come to know. I do not have any sense of strangeness or remoteness from the ways and works, therefore, of the people here. I have tremendous interest in you as human beings, and, of course, as students. . . .

[You have come in these hours as] intelligent, anxious, concerned people, hoping for truth and wisdom and spiritual and intellectual understanding. To [you] I am *profoundly* grateful. To [you] today I must acknowledge a debt which I have no means to pay adequately. And I shall always, *always* be grateful to [you]. . . . [You are], in some ways, the great and terrible tragedy of our academic world: we can give [you] so little, because our own view of things, unfortunately, is so often out of focus, even when we want it to be sure and fine and helpful. We owe much, though, to [you]; [you] save us from despair—and we must be eternally remorseful because we give so little to [you]. . . .

I have been troubled by what I know must be your distress in the face of and thought of this frightful world, of "the sorrows of this savage world." This sorrow I cannot look upon without sometimes questioning the *relevancy* of the academy. And yet those very sorrows make it necessary to go on finding and teaching the *truth*—even when men pervert it and try to destroy it. Because to the men of truth the future belongs; if it is not theirs, there is no future. The world just ends! I have been personally tormented by this time in our life—to the point of terrible darkness, even. But yet men must go on, as long as they are permitted, searching for and articulating the notions of truth and justice and love and freedom.

Yes, I have kept on speaking and explaining and interpreting. And I hope that I have not erred too much. You, I know, have heard me through with deference. I have seen plainly, though, that some of you hardly got my drift, hardly got my MORAL. And sometimes you will understand that I have felt chagrined like one indeed "who has defined the colors of the sunset to a friend born blind."

I shall have to say, though, at the last that I shall remember you always without dismay and that I hope this terrible time and this chaotic world will never spoil you or trap you or triumph over you.

And now let us turn to the *Finalities*: the *last words* I shall say about our life and our culture—and our hope.

This century of ours is undeniably one of the most potent in the history of civilization. But where its potencies and energies will take it—is the gravest, gloomiest question that presses us, pierces us, perplexes us. Undeniably, this twentieth century is dissipating its energies, spiritual, philosophical, literary, social, economic, political. Its efforts, in all fields, seem to be so utterly diffuse rather than patterned, centrifugal rather than centripetal, explosive and tumultuous rather than quiet and well directed. The twentieth century seems to be self-destructive, indeed, because really it is stimulated by no uniform *idea* or ideal; it is sprung from and rooted in no common belief; it is set upon no common purpose, none at all. Individual effort has always been notably competitive, "unsocial when not antisocial." Men in our time still incline to take extremely individualized rather than communal points-of-view; many men practically ignore men-in-society, in-the-group, many work hard to be *utterly different* from their fellows (and I do not deny that there may be some good reason in it).

Collective effort is limited to changing, shifting groups and to confused and conflicting systems and plans, programs—there is, indeed, a welter of conflicting fidelities. The *Communal* is, as yet, in this century, but dimly understood and rarely practiced (but better practiced in our own land than elsewhere). Of course, we have many immediate problems, problems of operating decently a hugely complex scientific-technological civilization constructed without consideration or design or teleology—a creation of destruction.

The more pragmatical, utilitarian thinkers of our society, the socially successful, the business men, are not much concerned about a philosophy. But nevertheless all cultures and societies are rooted in some philosophy; and inadequate, defectible, spurious philosophies bring about such horrifying disturbances as wars, and, of course, depressions—and, indirectly, imperfect, defective philosophies may be responsible for physiological confusion, as in the case of epidemics, and physical confusions like floods and dust storms. Think it over! No society can take onto itself a philosophy, plaster it on, *clothe* itself in it; a philosophy cannot be so external, so inorganic, so patented. A philosophy has to root, to grow, to pervade, to penetrate, and, finally, to integrate. But it must be organic.

Now the critic of art and letters in our society must not be just a popularizer or exhibitionist or impressionist, but one who integrates principles, one whose work is integrally worked into the whole of thought and life. His effort as a critic, as a judge, must be founded upon a philosophy large enough to comprehend and to underlie this vast civilization, and definite enough to offer a coherence, a schemed, designed set of values and no mere nattering, muttering, plastering of preferences.

And, wanting the completeness, the definiteness of a true philosophy revealing the nature of this life and the ultimate principle of all life, and anxious to escape the glimmerings and gutterings and half truths of much contemporary thinking and judging, some critics have chosen to follow what they consider the fruitful way of the New Humanism (Americans More and Babbitt).

Men who believed in the New Humanism felt that it was "the most inclusive, the least biased" and, consequently, the most desirable philosophy in a culture of mechanics and specialists. Humanism, they felt, could comprehend the discourses of scientists, grasp all the values in the work of modern specialists, as well as all the richness of our past heritage. It might have seemed a bit blurred in places, but that was because it gathered a multitude of perspectives and dealt with a multitude of imponderables and immeasurables. It could not give the completest exposition of all its values, and it could work no astonishing miracles perhaps. But they felt that humanism was wealthier in values, more responsive to the profoundest demands of human life and spirit than any techniques or material methods or other philosophies. Humanism, they felt, would restore a decent concept of humanity in a naturalistic society, weighing down the human spirit; it would give the artist the fullest, freest choice for his rich talents; it would give the critic the integrals, the principles, the essentials dimmed and closed, hidden in uncertainty. The New Humanists felt that they would come closer than their contemporaries to final meaning, to ends, to purposes.

But even though the New Humanists were and are sincerely desirous of preserving spiritual values and recognizing "man-ness" and saving the earth from intellectual and spiritual aridity, they employed criteria that were, and are, from our point-of-view, irrelevant and inadequate.

They have a way of talking cloudily and remotely about the demands of an era of "hard, bitter, bruising fact"; and they seemed and seem more concerned about saving their sort of thought without rooting it into our busy and shifting culture. Indeed, they do discuss genteelly the GREAT TRADITION, flowing down from Greece, just as if it were "a hothouse plant and not an organic . . . growth," just as if it could be kept going in a vacuum.

Notably dubious and mysterious is the ethical absolutism of the creed of the New Humanists. Babbitt talked always of the "inner check," P. E. More urged the "inalienable authority" accruing to a "law within nature but not of nature in the naturalistic sense." But they and their kind are unable to demonstrate the authority of this moral law—and, of course, they never tangibly define it. In some measure, actually, they do "substitute verbalization for (true) vision."

The most definite principle of the New Humanists—and one with which we can have our sympathies—and one on which the Humanists condemn many of our important novelists—is their detestation of Naturalism. But the standards or bases upon which this principle rests are vague and nebulous, and, really, just missing. For the New Humanists, most of them, reject a genuine religion or, at least, give it a reluctant attendance as a decent yet needless ally; for the New Humanists actually do not acknowledge the sanctions of religion, the sanctions which could save them and save their creed. The question comes to mind: if they decline to admit the authoritativeness either of divine revelation or of "naturalistic" science, whence comes their ethical will? T. S. Eliot once wrote so rightly of them, however admirable their intentions,"I cannot understand a system of morals which seems to be founded on nothing but itself," and Eliot offered the inescapable dilemma: "Either everything in man can be treated as a development from below, or something must come from above. There is no avoiding that dilemma: you must either be a naturalist or a supernaturalist."

The New Humanists cannot get enduring sanctions for any concepts of man, society, or creation, unless they recognize that man, shifting, vacillating, transient, myopic, cannot be the source of changeless, permanent, real values. The New Humanists cannot answer these questions: Why must man live? Whom does man serve, if nature serves him? Why are men on this planet? What is the function of man? And who sanctions his function? Who sanctions his art, his culture, his life?

In our twentieth century, too, one of the notable forces to be dealt with in any real contemplation of life and literature is Communism or Marxism. Now despite Marxism's warrants of economic security, it cannot, by automatic management, produce a rich and glowing culture. "The citizens of the perfectly regulated classless society cannot lead a full life simply by the ecstatic contemplation of all the wheels going around" [Muller].

More recent devotees of Communism as a philosophy, like Waldo Frank and Edmund Wilson, have been objecting to the technological emphasis of the first champions of Communism, who neglected the whole man for the economic man. Frank and Wilson and such are trying to fit Marx's thought into a better frame, trying to make it truly organic, trying to adjust it to spiritual needs. Indeed they seem to be trying to integrate it with a sort of humanistic tradition. (This has been a tendency of Marxism generally.)

There is further the problem of science and the critic. We cannot categorically condemn science, repudiate its facts and findings, its intellectual integrity. Still, once one has *realistically* accepted modern science, realistically recognized its value and its necessity in this way and culture of modernity, he has to go beyond *natural* knowledge to *supernatural* knowledge (or to subnatural knowledge, like D. H. Lawrence and Joyce). It is undeniable that science has been so preoccupied with understanding and controlling all nature that it has neglected or ignored the nature of the human being it is supposed to serve; it has forgotten man and his origins and his destiny. Scientism has offered the notion—long prevailing—that man is simply a perfectly rational creature who can exist solely on his knowledge and his techniques (Spengler). But this is not adequate, no finally wholly adequate definition. Man is more than a rational animal. He is also a spiritual creature. He recognizes his dependence, his tentativeness; he craves God—he craves that which neither his mind nor his body can fulfill.

This judgment just passed does not signify a repudiation of science. It suggests simply that scientific rationalism alone is not sufficient. Today, of course, you find a secular critical mind like that of I. A. Richards trying to achieve a corrective philosophy. Richards recognizes the good man of science—but he also sees that the truths of science are ultimately *limited*—and must be submitted to the needs of an ethical-spiritual-rational animal to whom *purpose,* ends, *God,* teleology, and theology are more important than *facts.* Now the so-called "mystical tendencies" in modern letters are also recognitions that scientific rationalism must be *supplemented,* sustained by deeps and heights it cannot reach. Consider the "intuitionism" in the thought of Nietzsche, Butler, Bergson, in the work of D. H. Lawrence, Thomas Mann, Huxley, Wolfe; and in science itself, the positivist no longer feels quite so complacent in the world composed by chemists, physicists, biologists, and astronomers—the physicists are not determinists.

A few artists and critics in England and the world have found an integrating principle in the philosophy of Catholicism and in Catholicism itself. And we are most interested in their effort, in their success. Their philosophy has real supernatural sanctions, unlike that of the New Humanists and Marxists. T. S. Eliot comes close to this philosophy, Aldous Huxley and John Middleton Murry are enticed by it—and others. Some have gone all the way; and it is interesting to consider that Hopkins, Claudel, and Sigrid Undset are to be listed among the greatest names in modern letters—and their art is underlaid by the sacramental life of Catholicism. These writers can be called the True Humanists, the Integral Humanists. Man lives in the sight of God, and man's universe moves in His shadow. Man's meaning for them is not man-given—it endures because it comes not from fallible man, but from infallible, ever-doing God.

They realized the real problem of man and his position, as human creature, before God and his destiny: they are Christians. They know, like the thinkers of medieval times, that (as Maritain puts it in *True Humanism*) "man was not merely an animal endowed with reason, according to Aristotle's famous definition, which truly can be regarded as a 'naturally Catholic' one—and this commonplace concerning the nature of man already goes a long way, for, in making man a spirit in his principal part it shows that he must have aspirations that go far beyond our human life;

and also, since this spirit is that of an animal, that man needs to be the feeblest of spirits, and that in fact he most often lives, not by his soul, but by his senses."

Maritain continues: for medieval thought, that is, Christian thought, "man was also a person; and one may observe that this notion of person carries a Christian hallmark, so to say, since it owes its evolution and its definition to theology. A person is a unity of a spiritual nature endowed with freedom of choice and so forming a whole which is independent of the world, for neither nature nor the state may invade this unity without permission. God Himself, who is and who acts from within, acts there in a particular way and with such a supremely exquisite delicacy, a delicacy which shows the value He sets on it; He solicits it, but He never compels."

Maritain also notes that in his actual historical existence man, for medieval thought, for Christian thought, was "never simply his natural self. He is a being out of joint and wounded—wounded by the devil with the wound of concupiscence and by God's wound of love. On the one hand he carries the burden of Original Sin, he is born dispossessed of the gifts of grace, not indeed corrupted in the substance of his being, but wounded in his nature. On the other hand he is made for his supernatural end: to see God as God beholds Himself, to reach even the very life of God; he is traversed by the calls of actual grace, and if he does not turn against God by his power of refusal, he bears within him even here below the truly divine life of sanctifying grace and of its gifts. Hence, in point of existence, we may say that man is at once a natural and a supernatural being."

This, says Maritain, is, in general terms, the Christian conception of man, and this is, indeed, the conception suffusing the performance of the greatest modern English poet, Gerard Manley Hopkins, and the fiction of Sigrid Undset and the drama of Paul Claudel.

I recommend to you the reading of such a poem as "The Caged Skylark" to find the Christian conception of man: the suggestion that man is at once a natural and a supernatural being. It is indeed a poetic realization of the philosophical idea of the nature of man, the substantial unity of body and soul; the natural, the body and senses cannot be rejected, cannot be cast off, but must be disciplined and purified since "man's spirit will be flesh-bound when found at best." (See Gerald Vann, *On Being Human.*) Man may be natural, but he goes *above* it; goes *super,* goes beyond.

> "As a dare-gale skylark scanted in a dull cage
>   Man's mounting spirit in his bone-house, mean
>   house, dwells—

And Hopkins's Felix Randal, you will remember, had had his natural self, had had his sins, had had his glory on earth that Hopkins could admire. But Randal was an image of Christ.

Maritain, also, in *True Humanism,* suggests the three planes of activity of the Christian: "the spiritual plane, the temporal plane, and the intermediate plane which joins the temporal and the spiritual. And it is in the Christian community, borne of Christ in his Body, that the nature and significance of integral Christian living, of integral Christian society is to be found. The Christian religion suggests the reality of a cohabitation of the two principles, Christianity and life, which must intermingle, coexist, if an integral life for man-in-society is to be realized. Christ came into the world, became incarnate, and died for all men. All men have Christ for their Head, all men are born to Christ: incorporation into the Mystical Body of Christ is the literal and exclusive source of salvation. St. Paul suggested this, Karl Adam, Guardini, Claudel—and Hopkins also express the relation of the individual to the Mystical Body of Christ—the community of men and saints."

Hopkins also manifests in his poetry that response to reality which Dawson has termed "the sight of the whole universe as the shadow of God," having its being in the contemplation or reflection of the being of God. For Hopkins, all creation is a manifestation of the Divine. And Hopkins views the falcon, the Windhover, not simply as a bird, but as a sign, a symbol, truly a microcosm of creation in all its beauty and power and animation, confirming and professing and celebrating faith in a personal and lovable creator. The world is charged with God's grandeur. Through our variegated, transient, natural beauty, pied beauty, we rise to absolute, immutable beauty: "Give beauty back, beauty, beauty, beauty, back to God, beauty's self and beauty's giver."

> I kiss my hand
>   To the stars, lovely-asunder
> Starlight, wafting him out of it; and
>   Glow, glory in thunder;

Kiss my hand to the dappled-with-damson west:
Since, tho' he is under the world's splendor and
                wonder,
His mystery must be instressed, stressed;
For I greet him the days I meet him, and bless when
                I understand.
                [The Wreck of the Deutschland]

Regrettable it is, I feel, that many of the poets whom Hopkins today influences technically are lacking his tremendous religious attitude-to-life, living as they do outside a Christian philosophy and most inexpert in the sacramental life, not aware, like Hopkins, that this world is Word, expression of God.

We cannot, of course, expect many poets like Hopkins to live and labor in this century. His view of man, society, and creation, the view of Christian philosophy and theology, would be the sustaining, integrating, peace-bringing view for all the writers searching today. But it is hard to expect many to come to this light, this glow, this glory; still, the fact that some have come, achieving great peace and great art, Hopkins, Undset, Claudel, indicates a way, indicates the salvation of this century, if it is to be saved. The only philosophy and theology that can satisfy is that pretty much neglected and ignored during the seventeenth, eighteenth, nineteenth, and even in this twentieth century. It is the completest, it is the firmest, it is the least temporal and time-spoiled; to it great artists in the past have come and, *Deo volente,* the artists of the future time may take to it and, through the human eyes of St. Thomas, under the divine head of Christ, may construct man, construct society, construct Creation.

But we who do accept a Christian philosophy and theology cannot expect this miracle too soon—and we must be sympathetic to those who strive, to those who are confused, desperately confused. We cannot be smug or complacent or cruel. We must be sympathetic to attitudes and artists who exploit the values and elements we deem worthy. But we must be sympathetic critics and readers of creators who in whole or in part wrench or ruin our values. We must be ready to understand always the worth and even the necessity for the artists of "dimmer" understanding than that of a Claudel or a Hopkins or an Undset. We will be looking for the D. H. Lawrences and the Theodore Dreisers, the Gides, the Thomas Manns, and the John Dos Passoses. We shall stand ready to mark their failures, in the light of what we know; we shall recognize their complexity and their bewilderment and imperfection—but we will understand their existence and what they try to contribute to a decent way of life, to art and to culture.

The questions that ring in your minds and ring in mine are those that cannot be answered here; but in your time you will know in part the answers:

Will the world rediscover and reestablish a genuine culture, uniting the temporal and spiritual? Will authors in general succeed in rediscovering, in reestablishing in the boundaries of this culture the highest virtues and values? Will the men of this century be able finally to work out, to trace a spiritual community beneath the flash and flutter, the swaying and smashing of modern men and modern experience? In our crowds, in our streets, what will be found to be final?

We ramble, we gamble so with the resources of men and of society. And more than ever now the outlook is darkened by the deviltry we are experiencing—but in which we must engage heroically to beat down the devil. Today, I know, the world is embattled and bloody, immersed in a flood of errors, errors of all kinds— and the Catholic critic and the Catholic philosopher cannot by any piously uttered slogans transcend them or overwhelm them. But, at least, the reader who is a Catholic, the philosopher who roots himself in a Christian philosophy, can be hopeful, can be confident that justice and fidelity and Redemption and Charity have not departed forever out of the world, and that our own struggles of these days may permit their renewal. And his constructiveness will lie in great measure in his hopefulness that value and virtue can be reasserted in this world, in the universe of men. For in hoping, he will work, he will strive—and darkness will not entirely overtake him. Such a man, who has not abandoned Christ, can go where no ordinary humanist, no ordinary mortal, can follow him. For he will have courage, the courage to keep his soul composed, his mind free in the face of danger. He will feel himself stronger than the death he does not fear; he will know his manliness, his manness, know what the miserable ones, slobbering with fear, can never understand: mortality leads to immortality. He will be the Christian humanist—the Christian humanist of this century, turning his face upwards, climbing again, as most of us must, "in blood and filth the flowery slope that Erasmus and Montaigne descended so long ago." He will make the proper entreaty for a Christian: "My heart is hot within me and my meditation sets me on fire. Sorrow and joy—Lord, show me my destiny. Tell me what is the number of my days that I may know what remains to me. Thou hast measured my time and my being is as nothing before Thee. Truly all that lives in the world is but vanity; man passes like an image that fades. But Thou, Thou art my Expectation, O Lord. Thou art the hope of those who have no other hope."

Man seeks forever in God the understanding of his being, the illumination of his darkness. Man forever calls upon God's infiniteness. But man-of-earth is too small to contain it, and man-of-earth breaks under the burden of divinity; yet he will be of the Church as a member and his voice will echo the voice of the Church:

> And God will recognize in us His Love
> And henceforth our heads shall wear no other veil
> than the dazzling light of Him who is our judge.
>
> [Gertrude von Le Fort][15]

It was the end of the most sustained and intense intellectual performance that any of us had ever seen. We stood spontaneously and applauded as he stepped down from the podium, blushing, smiling, bowing slightly on his way out of the room. We knew that he was in many ways arbitrary and capricious, perhaps even presumptuously self-confident, but he was also a man of high seriousness and sensitivity. He had created and sustained for us over nine months a vision of how one man could confront the culture of our time and achieve his personal integration with validity and power. Every gesture and prop, every lifted eyebrow and tab collar, every fine suit and rhythmic sentence, every tone of voice and tap of finger had combined to weave the spell about us. None of us would ever forget it. We might later discover others who were perhaps greater scholars, as such; but they would all sadly lack that final integration of personality, that performance.

4
Modern Catholic Writers

The Philosophy of Literature course, designed to include the major post-Renaissance writers for consideration of English majors, necessarily included a great many authors with whom O'Malley had no great personal sympathy or interest. Yet he had to deal with them because they were there. His lectures on them contained many negative comments.

But there was another course that he developed early in his teaching career which allowed him to focus more on the positive, on those authors whom he personally admired and delighted in. He called it "Modern Catholic Writers," and it was intended as an elective course for any student at the university, not just English majors. It exhibited what Garrett Bolger has called "his sacramental vision of life and grace and his open view of the Church."[1]

In the opening class he would hand out mimeographed sheets containing an outline:

English 237, *Modern Catholic Writers* by Professor O'Malley

I. The Problem of Religion and Life and Religion and Culture.

A. Karl Adam, *The Spirit of Catholicism, Christ our Brother*

B. Romano Guardini, *The Church and the Catholic* and *The Spirit of the Liturgy*

C. Christopher Dawson, *The Making of Europe, Enquiries into Religion and Culture, Medieval Religion, The Modern Dilemma, Religion and the Modern State, Progress and Religion, Beyond Politics*

D. Jacques Maritain, *Freedom in the Modern World, Three Reformers, The Degrees of Knowledge, True Humanism, Prayer and Intelligence*

     E. Etienne Gilson, *Medieval Universalism, The Spirit of Medieval Philosophy, The Unity of Philosophical Experience*

     F. T. S. Gregory, *The Unfinished Universe*

     G. G. K. Chesterton, *Heretics, Orthodoxy, St. Francis of Assisi, St. Thomas Aquinas*

     H. Hilaire Belloc, *Europe and the Faith, The Servile State, The Crisis of Civilization, Essays of A Catholic*

     I. John Henry Newman, *Idea of a University, Apologia Pro Vita Sua, Grammar of Assent, Development of Christian Doctrine, Sermons and Poems*

     J. Orestes Brownson, *The Convert, Literary, Scientific and Political Views, The American Republic*

II. The Problem of the Catholic Critic.

     A. Jacques Maritain, *Art and Scholasticism*

     B. Eric Gill, *Art and a Changing Civilization*

     C. E. I. Watkin, *The Bow in the Clouds, Men and Tendencies*

     D. G. M. Turnell, *Poetry and Crisis*

     E. Thomas Gilby, *Poetic Experience*

     F. Gerald Vann, *On Being Human*

     G. Karl Pfleger, *Wrestlers with Christ*

     H. Theodore Haecker, *Virgil, Father of the West*

III. The Problem of the Catholic Poet.

     A. G. M. Hopkins, *Collected Poems, Letters* (three volumes), *Journals and Notebooks*

     B. Francis Thompson, *Collected Poems, A Renegade Poet and Other Essays*

     C. Coventry Patmore, *Poems, Religio Poetae, The Rod, the Root, and the Flower*

     D. Alice Meynell, *Collected Poems, The Colour of Life and the Rhythm of Life*

     E. G. K. Chesterton, *Poems*

     F. Hilaire Belloc, *Poems*

     G. Paul Claudel, *The Tidings Brought to Mary, The Hostage, The City, The Satin Slipper, The Book of Christopher Columbus, Ways and Crossways, The East I Know*

     H. Gertrude von Le Fort, *Hymns to the Church*

     I. Charles L. O'Donnell, *The Rime of the Rood*

His opening lecture is reproduced very fully in an article that he published in 1954.

For many reasons it is regrettable that we have to be at all agitated about the problem of the Church and modern culture. Certainly, had the lives and works of modern men been naturally and vitally integrated with the life of the Church, it would be quite unnecessary now to write or talk about the vitality of religion, of the world of worship, with respect to man's life and action in every field. It is most evident today that we are self-conscious about the truth and values we possess as Catholics. We do not take them naturally, we are not easy with them, since they are not, as they ought to be, the sustaining rhythm of our existence. Therefore, we feel the need of making them the objects of discussions, conferences, symposia, lectures, and articles; and, as a result, what was and is natural and easy, in the rhythm of existence, may become artificial in effect, may sound complex and academical, large questions for forums and organizations and special movements created to consider them. The life of the Church, of course, is not to be dealt with or disposed of as a problem, a formula, or even as a philosophy, for the Church is a total existence, a living reality, a true "consciousness" that involves man and all mankind, one not to be reduced merely to the motions of dialectics or the abstractions of exposition. Yet our self-consciousness today is vastly more desirable than the state of death, the almost complete "unconsciousness" in which Catholics (and non-Catholics alike) have lived for too long, blind, somnolent, petrified, with only the rarest shattering of the composure of the liberal-bourgeois generations. And our very self-consciousness helps to make us aware and to convince us that the voice of the West can still be heard among the men of our irreligious civilization, that the spirit of the Church is still strong at least in the spiritual underground of this embattled and explosive universe.

The Catholic intellect and art of the modern world have enjoyed a tremendous source of power in the liturgy, the cult of the Church. Many Catholics all over the world are experiencing the relation between the world of worship (the cult) and the world of human experience (our civilization). And many important movements of Catholic life and action in our own country regard the liturgy as their right and necessary root or incentive and as the heart wherein their various efforts will be refined and resolved (although the liturgy is never to be thought of as a means simply to practical solutions of individual or social difficulties or as an instrument existing only to construct a brilliant aesthetical or intellectual "culture"); nor is the life of the Church at any time to be debased into a stamping ground for blundering activists and reformers. Such efforts verify what has been termed the resurgent wonder of the faith now at work, at work clearly beneath the confusion and horror that blight the surface of man's life in the twentieth century. There were the first easy-flowing, peaceful ten years; and then came the terror: the first World War, followed by a lush and riotous aftermath issuing into the economic depression of the thirties, which closed in the disaster of the second World War, raging into the forties. Now well within the brink of the fifties we look out, with a certain fear and anguish, upon a more or less desolated civilization and brood about the possibilities of universal catastrophe.

A great modern poet provides us with an appropriate phrase and a figure by which to describe vividly our present age and our present state of existence: "There are the noises. But there is something here that is more terrible: the stillness. I believe that in great conflagrations there sometimes occurs such a moment of extreme tension: the jets of water fall back, the firemen no longer climb their ladders, no one stirs. Noiselessly a black cornice thrusts itself forward overhead, and a high wall, behind which the fire shoots up, leans forward, noiselessly. All stand and wait, with shoulders raised and faces puckered over the eyes, for the terrific

crash. The stillness is like that" [Rainer Maria Rilke]. Nevertheless, in this turbulent century of terrible noises and terrible still-
nesses, this century of extreme tensions, there has re-emerged—
in the depths indeed—a real and wonderful "consciousness" as
dynamic, diverse and universal as the Church itself, a life that
has expressed itself in great achievements in art and literature, in
theology and philosophy, in sociology, economics and politics, and
in education—all of which, for their authority and effectiveness,
draw in some measure at least upon the liturgy of the Church
defined well as *the public and corporate worship of God.*

When one considers the mangled and mangling "progress" of
the main events of modern history, this renascence and capacity
for renascence—everlasting in the Church—become all the more
impressive and comprehensible. Indeed, for many years, Dawson
has been saying that the present, overwhelming crises of Western
civilization are due, precisely, to the disjoining of culture from its
proper religious motivation; and he has been insisting that the
center of culture is cult or worship. This insistence is one that
Catholics especially should appreciate and grasp. For the Catholic,
above all, ought to realize that the meaning of the world is to
give God, in Gerard Manley Hopkins's language, "praise, reverence, and service, to give Him glory," that religious experience
has, as Romano Guardini puts it, "a unique relation to life . . .
that it is itself life," and that its effects must be the springing-up
of all "vital forces and manifestations." So requisite and so important is this acknowledgment of the heart of Christian culture as
cult that we are ready to accept the judgment that any Catholic
expression or effort, in the interest of the attainment of Christian
culture, lacking the sense of corporate worship ignores reality and
denies to itself "the special apprehension of Catholicism proper
to the twentieth century" [Gerald Ellard, S.J.]. As a consequence,
it cannot sufficiently distinguish its cause or character from the
nation that is not holy.

Thus we come to the central matter: what can or what must
every Catholic today understand or derive, as he moves through
time and civilization, from the liturgy, from the cult of the Church?
Guardini, with exceptional brilliance, acuity and force, has provided us with the answer to this question. As he sees it, we are,
whatever to the contrary we must witness, also the witnesses of
an event of enormous significance:

That stupendous Fact that is the Church is once more becoming a living reality, and we understand that she truly is the One and the All. We dimly guess something of the passion with which great saints clung to her and fought for her. In the past their words may sometimes have sounded empty phrases. But now a light is breaking! The thinker, with rapture of spirit, will perceive in the Church the ultimate and vast synthesis of all realities. The artist, with a force that moves his heart to the depths, will experience in the Church an overwhelming transformation, the exquisite refinement, and the sublime transfiguration of all reality by a sovereign radiance and beauty. The man of moral endeavor will see in her the fullness of living perfection, in which all man's capacities are awakened and sanctified in Christ; the power which contrasts uncompromisingly Yea and Nay, and demands decision between them; the determined fight of God's Kingdom against evil. To the politician...she is revealed as that supreme order in which every living thing finds its fulfillment and realizes the entire signficance of its individual being. It achieves this in relation to beings and the whole, and precisely in virtue of its unique individual quality combines with its fellows to build up the great Civitas, in which every force and individual peculiarity are alive, but at the same time are disciplined by the vast cosmic order which comes from God, the Three in One. To the man of social temper she offers the experience of an unreserved sharing, in which all belongs to all, and all are one in God, so completely that it would be impossible to conceive a profounder unity.

It is in the wisdom of such utterance that we can comprehend the true strength and meaning of the cult of the Church. We know that for too long a period the idea of liturgy was reduced to signify the aesthetics of worship or the ceremonial rules, the externals. Today, however, we are able to know the liturgy in the fullness of the Pauline and Patristic meaning and with the complete value given it by the Church. The liturgy, holding all creation as signed by God's excellence and goodness, orders everything in existence—man, things, nature, civilization—to God, with grace and through prayer: "Creation as a whole embraced in the relation with God established by prayer; the fullness of nature, evoked and transfigured by the fullness of grace, organized by the organic law of the Triune God, and steadily growing according to a rhythm perfectly simple yet infinitely rich; the vessel and expression of the life of Christ and the Christian—this is the liturgy. The liturgy is creation, redeemed and at prayer, because it is the Church at prayer." [Romano Guardini]

The liturgy, expressing "a community of spirit and spiritual life, involves at once the Mystical Body, Christ and all Christians at prayer." It is the acceptance of this truth, with its wealth of personal and communal meanings, that today characterizes all those persons anxious to reveal and to live the profound and total life of the cult of the Church.

To those who do understand the grandeur and reality of the Church at prayer and who live in the greatness of the perspectives of corporate worship, no Christian will be seen, in reference to God or to the world, as a lonely and solitary creature. This was very clear to Cardinal Newman: "Socrates wished to improve man, but he laid no stress on their acting in concert in order to secure that improvement. . . . " Contrastingly, with the Incarnation, with Christ and the Christian order, there comes the reality of community, making the fellowship of Christians an unmistakable object and duty, and arising "out of the intimate relation between Him and His subjects, which, in bringing them all to Him as their common Father, necessarily brings them to each other." And Karl Adam has also stated what we mean, that with every Christian there is the complete Christ, the Head and fullness of His members composing one Body: "Consequently we do not face God in isolation and loneliness; we come before Him in Christ, united in a profound union with His only-begotten Son. Just as breathing and feeling and thinking are functions of our natural being, so living in Christ is a function of our Christian being. Christ is the new sphere in which our whole religious life is to be lived. . . . And even our natural activities, which must at bottom be controlled by religion, are exercised within this sphere: our daily work, our achievements, our struggles, our suffering and our dying. The Christian never toils and suffers and dies *alone*, that word is absent from his vocabulary. Christianity is a living and dying in full membership with Christ and His members." Hopkins, it may be

added, has beautifully recreated this theme in the poetic experience
of "The Blessed Virgin Compared to the Air we Breathe":

> Men here may draw like breath
> More Christ and baffle death;
> Who, born so, comes to be
> New self and nobler me
> In each one and each one
> More makes, when all is done,
> Both God's and Mary's Son.

Catholic Christians, as worshippers then, cannot be isolated
individualists. It is required of them to be persons, new selves and
nobler ones, in the community of persons. Appropriate to mention
here is Jacques Maritain's now famous distinction between personality and individuality, made in a number of places in his work.
In Maritain's viewing, a Christian is a person—and was a person
in medieval culture, a culture organically informed by the Church.
With the rise and advance of the modern world, the person
became, it seems, strictly an individual. Yet the core of personality,
Maritain declares, is the subsistence of spirit, of soul, whereas,
for men as for all other things in nature, the core of individuality
is to be found in matter: everything, whether mineral, vegetable,
animal or human, is an individual of a species. Man alone has
spirit, man alone dwells in the community of spirit, is personal.
So a Christian city, as Maritain defined it, remains as essentially
and fundamentally anti-individualist as it is personal and communal. There can be no place for unbridled individualism in the
Mystical Body—and when we have stripped our civilization of
unbridled individualism and all the selfish brutality it suggests,
when we are dominated by the communal idea, the deep consideration and reverence for our fellowmen, then we shall begin to
live in the spirit of community that receives its pattern from our
community of worship, our community of sacrifice, love and
order. We are aware, however, in modern civilization of a strained
state in the relationship between the community and the individual
personality and even between the Church and the individual personality—a ruinous condition contrary to the nature of things.
On this point Guardini has spoken of the special task of our time:
"To see how the Church and the individual personality are mutually bound together; how they live the one by the other; and how

in this relationship we must see the justification of ecclesiastical authority, and to make this insight once more an integral part of our life and consciousness is the fundamental achievement to which our age is called." To be successful in such a task, we must reject the common and repressive philosophies around us, like individualism on one side, and communism or any form of totalitarianism on the other: "Once more we must be wholeheartedly Catholic. Our thought and feeling must be determined by the essential nature of the Catholic position, must proceed from that direct insight into the center of reality which is the privilege of the genuine Catholic."

The privileges and truths of the Mystical Body are, of course, best taken, best made into objective reality, by genuine participation in corporate worship. It is said that the law of prayer clarifies and instills the law of belief; and we may append that it clarifies and instills as well the law of action. So if the people who throng the churches in unaccountable numbers actually seized upon the truth that as worshippers they enfold the entire Christian fellowship, that they are living and moving (in the words from the Mass, itself a completely communal act) "through Him and in Him and with Him," as His Body and His members—they would of necessity distinguish their cause from the nation that is not holy, carrying over into the currents and cross-currents of their day-labouring this wonderful consciousness of which they have repossessed themselves. In any event, the liturgical movement, the great protection of the culture of the Church, with all its social, political, intellectual and creative manifestations, is a sure sign that the spiritual life and the community of the spirit are growing, even though they are not roaring, among the people. Despite all the weaknesses, waverings and imperfections inseparable from human works, there is today, as Don Sturzo has discerned, "a reassertion of the character of Christianity as responding to all situations and all needs, influencing by its teaching and its spirit every society, even those as refractory as ours of today. Nor should we pass over the great contribution made by the Church to the sciences, to letters and the arts, the modern growth of universities all over the world; the ever-expanding number of missions, the continuous increase of institutions, especially among women, for education, relief, charity, of which the most outstanding as examples of sacrifice are the leper settlements in

Asia, Africa, and America." And Don Sturzo considers that, in the three great battles against the endemic naturalism of our time—the first against totalitarianism of whatever sort, the second against any economic system that preys upon the whole of society and the poor particularly, and the third for a universal construction of justice and peace making war impossible—it will be the spirit of love and of community that must provide the form for the action. This form is forever available to us in our corporate worship and instructs us as members of Christ's Church in our responsibility to be new witnesses to God, the persons who will "bear witness to Him among all peoples and in all ages to the end."[3]

No matter what changes of emphasis he might make in the course from semester to semester there was always a lecture on that favorite German author with the Italian name.

Romano Guardini is a Newman type of thinker in the twentieth century. . . . Certainly the range of his concerns is reminiscent of Newman's: literature (for instance, his studies of Dante, of Dostoyevski, notably the legend of the Grand Inquisitor, and of Rilke's *Duino Elegies*): history (particularly revelation as history); subtle reflections upon theological questions as well as the critical problems of the contemporary political and social scene. More important to note is that he is, like Newman, a *spirituel*; to use Newman's term, he is *spiritually minded*. Guardini himself uses the phrase *spiritual consciousness* to describe what he centrally means and desires. In his *Prayer in Practice*, he declares that in the presence of God there awakens spiritual consciousness: "Man does not live by the use of his conscious faculties alone; his many and varied needs and aspirations can be satisfied only by drawing on sources lying much deeper in his being." He points out that "the answer to a routine problem or anxiety over a professional difficulty; the feeling engendered by some great work of art or the devotion to a beloved person; all these reactions rise from equally varied depths which lie close to our essential being." But Guardini knows and says that these sources cannot be tapped at will: "each one will respond only to the need or the object appropriate to it. Many of us do not know what dwells in us and of what we are capable until the right call reaches us. This same condition may be said to apply to spiritual consciousness. . . . "

These statements constitute a clue to the intellect of Guardini, to his spiritual thought, enabling him to penetrate more deeply into the mystery of human history and destiny, into the awesome movement of the events of our time, than the regular run of scholars and analysts. . . .

There is everywhere today some feeling that the life and works of man, of all that is most fully and freely human, are threatened. Many have been brought perforce to believe that our culture has lost the features we long saw in it or thought we saw in it. . . . Nevertheless, while considering the breadth and depth of this twentieth-century world of power and danger, Guardini dares to hope and says that his trust is not founded on "optimism or confidence either in a universal order of reason or in a benevolent principle inherent in nature." Rather his is a Christian hope, a Christian optimism resting forever "in God Who really is, Who alone is efficacious in His Action," trusting, simply in the truth "that God is a God Who acts and Who everywhere prevails."

Some may think that Guardini resolves the perplexities of the modern world of power and danger by uttering eschatological statements. There is ever the element of the eschatological in his thought and words. He can concern himself about death, purification after death, resurrection, judgment and eternity, as he does in his work, *The Last Things.* There, however, he makes crystal-clear that there is no denial of the values of the world and history: "nowhere is man looked upon as so great a being as in the Christian Gospel; nowhere else is the world of such serious importance; nowhere else the temporal order of creation so elevated toward God and in God as by and through Christ. . . . " In *The Spirit of the Liturgy,* emphasizing the liturgical roots of human and Christian culture and the primacy of the *logos* over the *ethos,* he asks us to reconsider the nature of our too often purposive pursuits and professions in the midst of a struggling and plunging civilization. . . . The liturgy, he emphasizes, is "a universe brimming with fruitful spiritual life, and allows the soul to wander about in it at will and to develop itself there." And he argues that the liturgy, the world of worship and contemplation, cannot be regarded as purposeful: "it does not exist for the sake of humanity, but for the sake of God." Within the liturgy "man is no longer concerned with himself; his gaze is directed towards God." The experience of liturgical worship will help a person to understand that he doesn't always have "to *do* something, to attack something, to accomplish something useful." Rather it will give him the chance "to play the divinely ordered game of the liturgy in liberty and beauty and holy joy before God." This does not mean, Guardini notes, that those who live in the liturgy will be removed from and unperturbed by the thunder and tumult of the actions and efforts of men. The liturgy expresses an extraordinary knowledge and reality: "those who live by it will be true and spiritually sound, and at peace to the depths of their being." So much so that "when they leave its sacred confines to enter life they will be men of courage."

So the Christian today, a man of his time, will be, spiritually formed, a man of courage, incapable of dissociating himself from social and historical changes and capable of alleviating the anguish accompanying them. . . .

Let man, in his endurance, Guardini urges, realize that the bearers of the power of evil and disorder in the world are primarily man himself and the disarrangement of his nature and, beyond, the broken communications among persons in such areas as language, customs, law, economics, and science. Having this endurance and realization, he may be able to construct the Christian life, the whole of life, in the twentieth century. . . . Redemption guarantees to the Christian that no essential harm can befall him. This warrant, however, should not lead him to recklessness, the careless and defiant dissipation, in the interest of cheap victories, of his talents and endowments. The Christian consciousness of inner invincibility, Guardini affirms, has ever to be "restrained, simple, not given to extravagant gestures, humble in the purest sense, and for that reason truly unconquerable."

What does it mean to be unconquerable? For Guardini it means to be *free*. . . . He acknowledges that the word *freedom* has become shop-soiled; yet he insists upon its nobility as a term, a royal word, and urges us to take it unto ourselves to develop it and to practice it. . . .

First he says that man is free when living "in complete harmony with the divine idea of his personality," when he is "what his Creator willed him to be. . . . " A person is free "when he sees everyday life with all its rough and tumble and all its shortcomings, but also what is eternal in it," when "he can gaze upon the stars, but find his way through the streets."

Guardini assures us that the Church paves the road to freedom as it daily opens the gates of the prison of environment and individual psychology, that regardless of its historical shortcomings, the Church reveals to man "truth seen in its essence, and a pure image of perfection adapted to his nature." For the Church involves "the whole of reality, seen, valued and experienced by the entire man." The Church is "co-extensive with being as a whole, and includes the great and the small, the depths and the surfaces, the sublime and the paltry, might and impotence, the extraordinary and the commonplace, harmony and discord." In sum, Guardini states that the Church is "the whole of reality, experienced and mastered by the whole of humanity," and that, to think with the Church, is truly "the way from one-sidedness to completeness, from bondage to freedom, from mere individuality to personality.... *Man is truly free in proportion as he is Catholic.*"[4]

The course lectures were always O'Malley's expression of truths lived and breathed.

How is man to bring his life into vital relationship with God? This is not a specifically Christian problem. It is faced by Plato and the religious traditions of the ancients as well as by Catholicism. The answer is an attitude of mind which will not be content with finite or sensible good. Our primary religious instinct is dependent upon a super-human power....

T. S. Gregory shrinks from the idea of progress. He believes with other sensitive souls that the nineteenth century was an epoch of cultural decline, evidenced by the building up and organization of civilization.

Primitive agriculture was a kind of liturgy. Ancient philosophies of religion such as Brahminism and Taoism identified the cosmic principle operating behind the world with the spiritual principle viewed as the source of being and as the source of ethical order. This desire to go beyond the normal categories of human thought and the ordinary circumstances of human experience remained the end of religious life. Merely rationalistic or deistic religion which proscribes the chance of any vital relationship between man and a higher order of spiritual reality does not fulfill the function of religion at all, and it finally disappears as a religious force.

Christianity agrees with the great oriental religions and with Greek Platonism in its goal of spiritual intuition. Religious knowledge is the highest kind of knowledge, the coronation of intellectual effort and advance. Orientalism, Platonism, and Christianity in this attitude towards religious knowledge are utterly antithetical to what may be called Europeanism—the conceptions of religions and of religious experience that have been offered by modern European minds.

Modern man has refused to accept the possibility of the objective value of spiritual knowledge. This was not characteristic of former times. The whole tendency of Western thought since the Renaissance and especially since the eighteenth century has been to deny the existence of any real knowledge except that of rational demonstration which has been based upon phenomenal or sensible experience. Intuition is something wholly irrational or emotional in the view of the modern mind. Modern civilization has become thoroughly secularized.

Western Europe once had civilization and even grandeur, but spiritual writers like Dostoyevski condemned the new rationalistic, materialistic, and commercial tendencies arising there as destructive of the image of man and as a betrayal of European tradition. Man cannot live by reason or by material well-beng alone. His spiritual life starves, dries up in the aridity of rational consciousness. So when the rational does not satisfy him completely he turns to the non-rational, whether it be romanticism or animalism. . . . [5]

An author much in vogue in intellectual circles during the period of this course was T. S. Eliot, and O'Malley did not neglect him.

T. S. Eliot is a modern man, a powerful poet, who has a distinctly religious mentality . . . and who is one with Dawson, Maritain and Gilson, in regretting the decay of religion in our society and in our world. *The Waste Land* symbolizes the decline of modern culture as a result of spiritual drouth. The images of the poem, dark, dry, agonized, and bewildered, enforce the theme of the sterility and confusion in contemporary civilization. . . .

Once, however, men find "the arid plain" behind them, they will discover that the Church is the salvaging force, the spiritualizing agency that will revitalize the dead world. Eliot offers us the way of Christianity, a Christian society, against the way of the world, a secularized society. Eliot, like Dawson and Maritain, is certain that Europeans cannot succeed in shaping an effective but non-Christian mind and culture. And he has given us, like Dawson, but in poetic actuality, a whole history of our culture, of our world, in *The Rock,* a magnificent indictment of the irreligious world.[6]

Then there was always also a lecture on Eliot's contemporary fellow countryman.

Christopher Dawson was born in 1889 and became a Catholic while attending Oxford in 1914. The primary work of his life has been the composition of a history of culture. He believes that the source and root of human thought and action in civilization is the life of the spirit. Nevertheless, he gives proper place to material forces which have affected the development of civilization and of thought. He believes that it is only when we become aware of our culture that we begin to lose it. For as long as we possess a living culture we are not aware of it. Happy is the people that has no history! . . .

Dawson believes that the society which has lost its spiritual roots is a disintegrating society or culture, however prosperous it may appear externally. He examines all forces and features that have gone to the composition of European culture and deals with them carefully: (1) Roman Catholicism, (2) the Roman Empire with its political traditions, (3) the Classical or Hellenic tradition, and (4) the influence of the barbarian races. . . .

Dawson shows that the moral forces of the tribal societies in Western Europe were much higher than their material standards of life. The ideal of loyalty to a personal leader found in these societies led to the foundation of feudalism. . . .

Another important factor was that Western Culture grew up under the more advanced civilization of Islam. It wasn't until the thirteenth century that the West began to become equal to the Islamic civilization, and it was only in the fifteenth century that Western Culture acquired that leadership role which we, in our time, have always looked upon as being more or less a law of nature.

A mechanical and industrial civilization will try to reduce all waste effort in work and will try to make the operator complementary to his machine. But a vital civilization will make every function and every act partake of beauty. Dawson asks why a stock broker is less beautiful than an Homeric warrior or an Egyptian priest. And the reason is that he is less incorporated with life. He is not inevitable but accidental, almost parasitic. When a culture has proved its real need every office becomes beautiful. . . .

Dawson recognizes that even in its highest forms, culture is to some extent conditioned by physical factors. Man is the creature of environment, heredity and function. But [Dawson] is not a determinist, like Spengler. He believes that man's development, intellectually, is from the confused to the clear rather than from the lower to the higher. . . . [7]

Among the poets and novelists considered in the course O'Malley especially loved to include "three whose accomplishment is famous and influential and whose power is unquestioned": *G. M. Hopkins, the Victorian Jesuit whose work was not released, however, until 1918, Paul Claudel, and Sigrid Undset.*

Hopkins genuinely and completely offers us in his poetry that response to reality which has been termed "the sight of the whole universe as the shadow of God," having "its being in the contemplation or reflection of the Being of God." For Hopkins all life is a wonderful revelation, a wonderful gift of the divine: "all things counter, original, spare, strange," God, Whose beauty is changeless, "fathers forth"; the flight of the falcon in "The Windhover" is significantly dedicated "to Christ Our Lord" for the very "mastery of the thing" is a sign of the loveliness and the life that rests forever in the being of God; and constantly he urges, "Give beauty back, beauty, beauty, beauty, back to God, beauty's self and beauty's giver." Hopkins is conscious of the Incarnational Fact, of the descent of the supernatural into the world in the reality of Christ: "Christ plays in ten thousand places, lovely in limbs and lovely in eyes not his," and through the features of a man we may come to the Father of men. Hopkins's thought is beautifully intense and alive. Hopkins, sensitive, impressible, is aware of the universe, close to it and its processes, and this perception brings him closer to God Who built and sustains the universe, God Who floods it with light, flushes it with color, fills it with splendor, with all the "things that give and mean to give God glory." "God's Grandeur" articulates, as well as anything else, his criticism of the industrial, urban devitalization he saw in his time and, very explicitly besides, his own grand insight. . . . No one can experience Hopkins without being given a real view of the "dearest freshness" that lives "deep down things." His work is animated with warm, breathing Reality. Lamentable, I feel, is it that many of those whom Hopkins today affects, in matters of technique anyway, are wanting in Hopkins's tremendous religious knowledge, working as they are apart from the spirit of the liturgy, unaware, unlike Hopkins, that man's world is "word, expression, news of God." *The Word* has been made flesh indeed in his mind and poetry.[8]

On the days when he took up Gerard Manley Hopkins in detail he would bring to class with him his thin, black volume of the Hopkins poems in the Robert Bridges edition of Oxford University Press. Many of its margins were scrawled with his notes. Opposite "The Starlight Night" he had written that "Hopkins tries to precipitate in words the intensity of his experience. The words are not quick enough to hold his intuition." *Opposite the opening lines of "Spring" there is a note about "synaesthesia":* "Here H. describes the sound first in terms of touch and taste, and then in terms of sight and touch at once."

There is also a note about his beloved "Pied Beauty" which says, "consider as expression of the philosophical idea that through variegated, transient, natural beauty we rise to absolute, immutable beauty." *Below the first part of "Hurrahing in Harvest" there is another note: (he would read the poem aloud first in his carefully attentive voice, then explain that "stooks" meant shocks of corn, and finally read it all again). The note:* "Some readers resent H's spareness, say it is private poetry, puzzling, not popular. Now H. wanted his poetry to be popular. 19th century poetry was so unconversational, so literary, so far from the natural ejaculations of the Englishman that H. resented it. H's poems should be *spoken,* as people speak, he said. H. wanted to be nearer the people, to be direct, unliterary, and colloquial." *The note on "The Caged Skylark" says,* "consider as the poetic expression of the philosophical idea of the nature of man, the substantial union of body and soul according to which the body and the senses cannot be rejected or cast off but must be disciplined and purified since 'man's spirit will be flesh-bound when found at best.'"

In spite of his tremendous enthusiasm for the beauties of Hopkins's work, O'Malley was not blinded to occasional defects in those works, also. His hand-written note at the end of "The Bugler's First Communion" was: "This poem is tainted by the offering of one image after another, doing nothing more than startling, images which will not integrate themselves with the pattern of the poem, but persist, protruding and lumpy." *There is an unfinished poetic fragment entitled "Margaret Clitheroe" which ends thus:*

> When she felt the kill-weights crush
> She told His name times-over three;
> *I suffer this* she said *for Thee.*
> After that in perfect hush
> For a quarter of an hour or so
> She was with the choke of woe.—
> It is over, Margaret Clitheroe.

O'Malley's note on the margin includes the sentence: "I do not choose to comment on the absurd last line."[9]

The Modern Catholic Writers course, being oriented more toward the Catholic sensibility of poets and novelists than philosophers, usually included substantial attention to the writings of the Frenchman, Paul Claudel.

For Paul Claudel, as for Hopkins, "all creation seems to rest with God in a profound mystery." Claudel is fascinated by all that God has created. When the magnetic, patriarchal, "supernaturalized" Anne Vercors, in *The Tidings,* comes back to his own land after his journey to Jerusalem, he contemplates the place of which he has been the master, saying:

> And all the aromatic odours of exile are little to me
> Compared with this walnut leaf I crush between my
>   fingers.

And Claudel looks upon the world as Vercors looked upon his land. The world speaks to him of God as it does to Hopkins. As

Pierre de Craon puts it in *The Tidings,* "That which was hidden grows visible again with Him, and I feel on my face a breath as fresh as roses. Praise thy God, blessed earth, in tears and darkness." We can see that relation between things and God, between men and God, only when we know that God became man and was crucified in this world, only when we know that Christ came into the universe. The knowledge of the Incarnation, the knowledge of the wonder of *the Word,* for Hopkins, for Claudel, is the knowledge which gives the universe its meaning, which gives man his freedom to understand. By this knowledge man will conquer.

Whatever one may say about Claudel's political career and political opinions, his literary life has been set upon the recreation of "a Catholic imagination and a Catholic sensibility which have been parched and withered for four centuries." Previously he had remarked: "The examples of such men as Poe, Baudelaire, Rimbaud, Verlaine and many another should be enough to warn us." Claudel has attacked the modern European conception of the universe with "God's world on one side and our world on the other and nothing to join the two." Once he wrote: "Who would know from Rabelais, Montaigne, Racine, Moliere, Hugo, that a God had died on a Cross? There is no such impassable distance to be put between this world and the world of God's dwelling, for it is said of them that they were created together. Out of the two of them is made the Catholic oneness, with its different aspects like a book that is written within and without." It is this Catholic oneness that makes Christian art and civilization. "It is this which once made Europe something more than a stupid empire of the average."

That time when Europe was at its best O'Malley found concretized so well in the medieval novels of a modern Norwegian writer.

Sigrid Undset achieves notably the Catholic oneness. Her novels fuse magnificently the world of sense and the world of the spirit. There is certainly in her work no gap between this world and God's world. She affirms everywhere her faith in the redeeming God, in man's tremendous freedom and its tremendous responsibilities, her belief that the central struggle of every human being is the struggle of the Seven Capital Sins, the struggle for Salvation, through the Sacramentalism of the Church.

In her masterworks on medieval life and culture, *Kristin Lavransdatter* and *The Master of Hestviken,* religion is the most vital element. For the extraordinary people in these works, damnation or redemption are real possibilities: their misdeeds involve far more than social or legal penalties, far more than the vengeances of men. All their long lives, their relationship to God is never lost, never diminished, no matter how sin and passion may assail them. And I know of nothing more tragic or more effective and beautiful in the literature of the twentieth century than the persons of the blundering yet grieving man and woman whose characters were fundamentally religious: Olav Audunnson, the master of Hestviken, and Kristin, the mistress of Husaby. In particular the section called "The Fruit of Sin," narrating Kristin's pilgrimage of repentance to the shrine of St. Olav, gives a poignant picture of the importance of religious faith to Kristin and to the people of a Christian society, in contrast to the casual dispositions of the men of the modern world: "Kristin crouched in a heap over her child. . . . She looked upward toward . . . the golden-grated doors of St. Olav's shrine [which] gleamed in the darkness. . . . [and she] shut her eyes, sick and dizzy. The King's countenance was before her—his flaming eyes saw to the bottom of her soul— she trembled under St. Olav's glance." Now she understands that she needs God's help, the king's sustenance, and she prays that she may not turn from God again. Her prayer is the simple, sad, single, fearful prayer of every religious mind: *God, do not thrust me from Your sight.* Such a prayer is that of all men-in-time who believe in the existence of a supernatural order and who know the dependence of human kind and human society and law upon the divine society and law of the supernatural order, who know that separation from the Godhead must mean loss of being, loss of living, must bring "drooping, dying, death's worst, winding sheets, tombs and worms and tumbling to decay" [G. M. Hopkins].

The perspectives of the course were almost totally European. Although a few American authors were listed in the outline, the lectures usually made mention of Americans only in brief passing comments.

The enfeebling of religion and religious knowledge in the modern world is the most terribly tragic experience that our world knows: a wonderful, liturgical reality has become, for the millions, a hollow, dead formulation. This devitalizing and degrading of religious knowledge and experience goes far to explain the blazing, gnostic prophecies of William Blake, the Asiatic "mystery-mongering" of William Butler Yeats, the anti-Christian attitudes of writers like D. H. Lawrence and Robinson Jeffers, the apostasy of James Joyce, the fragmentary vision of Virginia Woolf, the vigorous propaganda of Stephen Spender, the vacant interiors of Marcel Proust, the disharmony of Andre Gide, the torture and tumult of Thomas Wolfe, the pathological virulence of William Faulkner, the "broken images" of Ernest Hemingway, and, in general, the desperate sociological consequences of American novelists these twenty years between the wars—for example, John Dos Passos, whose work runs the gamut from bitter criticism of contemporary American culture in the trilogy, *U. S. A.,* to finding in the Fathers of this land and its people *The Ground We Stand On.*

The spiritual and religious confusion of our culture has also compelled such figures as Aldous Huxley and Thomas Mann to a new search after values and to the achievement of new syntheses and evaluations of twentieth-century experience. Aldous Huxley has passed his years in a somewhat self-conscious search for a faith, of which his most recent book, *Grey Eminence,* is a fine example. Sub-titled *A Study in Religion and Politics,* it is, in considerable part, an analysis and evaluation of contemplative experience in contact with a world that spoils it, and it reveals Huxley as slipping more and more into the abyss of Buddhism, leaving us to wonder if, after all his flirtations with the Christian ideal, this will be his final resting place. Thomas Mann has not been satisfied individualistically just to save himself, nor has he been satisfied by the flimsy stopgaps which some of our most admired artists have used for salvation. Mann has confronted without fear the greatest difficulty of modern culture: how to reintegrate genuinely human and communal values in modern society. *The Magic Mountain,* negative as it is, is actually an attempt at a synthesis of the whole range of modern experience. The ordered revitalizing of human and communal concepts, the drawing together of the remotest past and the dissipated present, and the vivifying of these efforts in the measures of literature—such are the finest aims of Thomas Mann. I believe that it is not at all fatuous to say of him, as one student of values in modern letters has observed, that he has tried to be the thinker for his time, and to achieve for it, in his own way "what St. Thomas Aquinas and Dante together did for theirs" [H. J. Muller]. In a civilization in which the religious man has been repudiated, the man of letters deems himself a spiritual and intellectual substitute and offers to men the integrating power of art for want of the integrating power of religion.

Yet in the work of the great Christian thinkers and writers of the modern world, thinking and acting, as they must, against the currents and crosscurrents of their times, living, as they must, in a kind of spiritual underworld, the integrating power of faith pervades. In this world, of course, it is possible, as Etienne Gilson has noted, to be a philosopher and an artist without a knowledge of religion, but it is impossible without such knowledge to become a Christian philosopher or a Christian artist. Writers like Sigrid Undset, Claudel, and Hopkins owe to their Catholicism the religious character of their writing, and such work, naturally, suggests the concepts and channels by which Christianity will renew our thought and letters and culture. Even as the wonderful Thomas, they are the true humanists, the integral humanists. Man lives in the sight of God and man's universe moves in His shadow. Man's meaning for them is not man-given. It endures because it comes not from fallible, non-during men but from infallible, ever-during God.

They realize the real problem of man and of his position as human creature before God. They are themselves Christians, they know like St. Thomas and the medieval thinkers whom Maritain has marked in *True Humanism* that man is "not merely an animal endowed with reason, according to Aristotle's famous definition." Christian minds know, like St. Thomas and his modern interpreters, that man is also "a person, and one may observe that this notion of person carries a Christian hall mark, so to say, since it owes its evolution and its definition to theology." To the Christian thinker and artist, man, in his real existence, as described by Maritain, is "never simply his natural self. He is a being out of joint and wounded—wounded by the devil with the wound of concupiscence and by God's wound of love. On the one hand he carries the burden of Original Sin, he is born dispossessed of the gifts of grace, not indeed corrupted in the substance of his being, but wounded in his nature. On the other hand he is made for a supernatural end: to see God as God beholds Himself, to reach even to the very life of God; he is traversed by the calls of actual grace, and if he does not turn against God by his power of refusal, he bears within him even here below the truly divine life of sanctifying grace and of its gifts. Hence, in point of existence, we may say that man is at once a natural and supernatural being." Inevitably this is the Christian conception of the nature and destiny of man and this is, indeed, the conception, as we have just seen, suffusing the performance of some of our most effective modern writers.

Having this conception of the person, these minds likewise have the proper conception of the community, of all humanity together. These minds have the *wholeness* of vision. They know that anxiety to reach and maintain religious knowledge has been that of all good men in all the world, explicitly or implicitly: Plato and Virgil no less than St. Augustine and St. Francis longed for such wisdom. Since there can be no fundamental alteration in human nature, all "kneeling-men" may not be denied the grace of the fact that Christ came into the universe, God Incarnate, and died for all men. "For God is the God of mankind as a whole," writes Guardini, but the distinguished contemporary liturgist is only restating the words of St. Paul: "For in one Spirit were we all baptized into one body, whether Jews or Gentiles, whether bond or free; and in one Spirit we have all been made to drink." Thus the great Christian minds understand that all men, ancient and modern, primitive and civilized, live under the headship of Christ and find that they must turn to Him, as Gertrude von Le Fort reveals in so much of her work.

Understanding this, men can understand well how inclusive is "the banquet of wisdom" to which all "poets, artists, scholars, philosophers, ay, and the man in the street. . . . as well as priests and theologians" are summoned from "the whole universe of culture" [Maritain], coming by grace to truth and order. The great spiritual minds, in every age and place, have, like St. Thomas, looked beyond earth's wisdom to Love. And the cosmic wisdom of St. Thomas is fixed upon the Host, the miracle and mystery of *the Word, the Word made flesh.* In words alive with *the Word,*

St. Thomas himself, making "no exception to persons," speaks his vision, his own language here rendered by one who more than others grasped the grandness of its beauty:

> O thou our reminder of Christ crucified,
> Living Bread the life of us for whom He died,
> Lend this life to me then: feed and feast my mind,
> There be thou the sweetness man was meant to find.
>
> [G. M. Hopkins][10]

Amid all the religious seriousness of the course there were also moments of comic relief, as when some naive student would venture a question about Sinclair Lewis only to be told that he is "a pure and unadulterated propagandist for a different industrial system. He is a preacher but not an artist. He does not know the meaning of art and of history and of man and of society. Art cannot be expected to survive on vulgarized preaching of a world on fire. We don't have to have truth concealed in a dung-hill."[11] *Or, in another connection,* "Hemingway has struggled in the cruelty of the wars, and he cannot free himself from the surface meaninglessness. . . . He can admire nothing except courage."[12] *Someone who asked about the Christophers was told that it was* "a Catholic Dale Carnegie movement, very pathetic and possibly even tragic—precisely because it does not see the profundity of the problem and the fact that thinking about first principles must precede the Christian revolution." *His opinion of the South Bend* Tribune *newspaper:* "a collection of garbage dumped in a clutter." *The Book of the Month Club showed* "ghastly contempt for the intelligence of the American people . . . in making us, under the name of cultural opportunities, more mediocre than we already are."

Such comments were a kind of game that he played, partly out of wry wit and partly in self-dramatization. He had always extolled sharp and succinct criticism, such as that of the famous drama critic, George Jean Nathan, who wrote after attending a production that had been hastily put together for the Broadway season: "The most significant action of the evening was that of the paint drying on the backdrop." O'Malley knew that students sometimes baited him just to see how succinctly he could demolish some figure of popular culture. And he clearly enjoyed having a go at it.

O'Malley eventually developed other courses as well. One called "Western Civilization and Culture" was offered for several years, based largely on the work of Christopher Dawson, but he eventually dropped it.[13] "Modern Catholic Writers," on the other hand, continued to be offered throughout his teaching career, both in the long session and in the summers. It was listed for graduate credit during the summers and became a very popular course with the nuns who came in great numbers for many years to work on their masters degrees. This audience also rewarded O'Malley over the years with a large number of honorary degrees from small Catholic colleges founded and taught by nuns.

The last lecture of the course attended by Michael T. Meaney in the spring of 1950 resulted in Michael's note that "A bird is learning to fly outside, and he is proving to be a great distraction. . . ." But there is also recorded O'Malley's closing statement: "A Christian Literature can only arise from people whose Christianity has turned to blood within them. These write not from a desire to [please] but from inscrutable necessity, an anguish sometimes terrible and troubled but always magnificent and holy."[14]

5
Blood on the Bricks

During its early years of poverty the Notre Dame community made its own bricks from the local clay in the lake beds. Many of the oldest buildings are constructed from these home made bricks: the Main Building, Sacred Heart Church, the Old Presbytery, Washington Hall, the Old Science and Architecture buildings, St. Edward's, Corby, Sorin, and Badin Halls. They are not fancy bricks by modern standards, but they are cherished for their link with the hardworking pioneers of the place who put their sweat and blood into them. Frank O'Malley loved the place and all of its bricks, both old and new, but he was not always entirely happy there. During some administrations whose policies he resented he was often heard to sum up his frustrations with the sentence: "There's blood on the bricks!"

Ed Murray, a university staff member and long-time friend of O'Malley's, recalls an exchange of remarks between O'Malley and then president of the university, Father John Cavanaugh. "The main building should be replaced," said Father Cavanaugh. "But there's blood on those bricks," said Frank. "We can get new bricks and smear new blood on them," replied Father Cavanaugh. O'Malley was horrified.[1]

At times even a good many of his colleagues on the faculty contributed to O'Malley's sense of depression. There was once a crowded faculty meeting when O'Malley came clattering in breathless and very late to take a seat and was heard to mutter a line from Dante by way of T. S. Eliot: "I had not thought death had undone so many."[2]

Christ College

Sometimes he got so frustrated that he thought seriously of leaving Notre Dame, but he apparently never went so far as to apply for a faculty appointment at any other existing college or university. Instead, he began to think about the design of a utopian institution where the faculty around him would be mostly his own "children of God" discovered over the years at Notre Dame.

During the summer of 1947 he had been corresponding with a group of his former students in California. One of them, Joe Lanigan, a partner in the small printing firm of Berliner and Lanigan in Nevada City, had drafted a statement describing an ideal small college which he called "Christ College." He even felt that there might be a possibility of founding such a college in California. O'Malley went out to discuss the matter. Lanigan recalls that "O'Malley did visit with Harold Berliner and myself in Nevada City . . . where we had a printing shop . . . and we did look at some possible sites and also discuss the nature of the College. Also involved were Bill Madden . . . J. H. Johnston . . . Bill Dougherty . . . and Ed Meagher."[3]

John H. Johnston still has copies of letters that he wrote during those days to Agnes Haney, his future wife, at St. Mary's College in South Bend:

> Tuesday, 9 September
> Nevada City, Cal.
>
> I got off the bus in the main street, feeling very Eastern (South Bend now feels very East, just outside of New York City) and uneasy. As I followed out directions to get to the Nevada City News, home of Berliner and Lanigan, I ran into Mr. O'Malley and two N. D. students, Buck Madden and Bill Dougherty, who have been here for some time. Mr. O'Malley was completely tie-less, which shows you what the West can do. He conducted me to the building in which I slept last night, in which I now sit—the parish house of the local Catholic Church. It is a run-down and ramshackle affair, but it houses us all—Joe Lanigan, Buck and Bill. Mr. O'Malley has a room over the Nevada City News. He soon told me about the situation here, which is pretty bad. It seems that the people on whom he had relied have not come through with the material support and there is no one here who knows the region and the people well enough, and who is influential enough, to make any kind of start. He is somewhat discouraged with matters here, and plans, with others, to go

ahead in another section of the country, most likely in the
midwest, possibly around Cincinnati—where Grailville is
located. I have never personally felt that Nevada City was
the place for a school—too remote, too much of a "frontier."
So: Mr. O'Malley and the others, except, of course, Berliner
and Lanigan, are leaving by the end of the week.

Thurs 11 Sept.
Nevada City

I am over the initial disappointment of having all of these
plans come to an impasse—and so, apparently, are the others,
even Mr. O'Malley. He is leaving Monday for South Bend
(classes begin Wednesday). . . . we are living a primitive life
in a building known as the parish house. Bill Dougherty is
really supporting the group: he works in the nearby Grass
Valley radio station as an announcer, and in a late musical
program broadcasts quotes from Leon Bloy. The printing
firm of Berliner and Lanigan is, of course, too small to give
all of us employment. . . .

I am sitting at a card table (which accounts for the unstead-
iness of these words) in a peeling room with a propped-open
window and a pile of rubbish in the corner. Below me lies a
part of Nevada City and beyond are those gold-bearing hills
covered with cedar, pine, and fir. . . . Mr. O'Malley brought
his recording of "Anna Livia Plurabelle" by Joyce, and I
have listened to it many times.

Saturday 13 Sept.
Nevada City

I wish you could be here to see Mr. O'Malley seated in
the Union Bar among these rough prospectors and lumber-
jacks (all more human, somehow, than the people who inhabit
the Oliver) [a South Bend hotel]. The proprietor of the Union
Bar, Glenn Roscoe (one of the two "most spiritual" people
in Nevada City, according to Mr. O'Malley), gave "the professor" five gold nuggets—worth $350—to carry around over-
night. Mr. O'Malley seems to enjoy unusual esteem here,
even among people who are certainly not cultured or refined
in the ordinary sense. But they have human qualities and

Mr. O'Malley is quite human too, more so than ever before, now.

Friday 19 Sept.
Palo Alto, Cal.

I have not yet told you about Mr. O'Malley's remarkable departure from Nevada City. To avoid the long bus ride to Sacramento, where he had to make connections for the flight eastward, Mr. O'Malley decided to fly. The Nevada City airport is on top of a flat mountain, and there is nothing available larger than a Piper Cub—those tiny yellow planes. On last Monday afternoon Mr. O'Malley turned out immaculately in a tan tropical suit, and we took him up the mountain in a taxi. I think he was somewhat taken aback by the smallness of the Cub, but nevertheless he gravely shook hands with us and squeezed himself and his baggage in. The Cub took off in a cloud of dust, straight into the setting sun. What a picture! O'Malley rising from the top of a mountain into the sun! My admiration for that man's mind and spirit is enormous, as you know, and it was quite seriously that I said to Joe Lanigan: "You could almost believe that he wasn't going to Sacramento at all." It was "Ascension Monday" for us, and we all returned to Nevada City bereft and disconsolate."[4]

Johnston also recalls other details of the meetings: "Glenn Roscoe, with reddish hair and moustache, was a true son of the West. His vitality was overpowering as he sang and played the guitar for customers at the Union Bar. Frank O'Malley's customary drink was Bushmill's Irish Whiskey, and every third round or so was on the house, courtesy Glenn Roscoe. . . . Joe Lanigan never participated in these nightly missions, and I suspect he disapproved strongly of our drinking. Not present in Nevada City, but somewhere in the background, was Ed Meagher; he thought our venture was impractical and perhaps foolhardy."[5]

The firm of Berliner and Lanigan were the printers for the "First Annual Directory and Guide to the City of Nevada." J. H. Johnston still has a copy of it in which there is a listing of "O'Malley, Frank, Tribulation Trail."

His ascension from Nevada City was the first and only recorded incident of Frank O'Malley taking flight. The railroad always remained his favorite means of transportation.

A copy of the untitled collaborative statement of the college outline, revised in O'Malley's own hand, is to be found in the Notre Dame Archives.

> The Catholic College, as a College of Christ, should be a community of students and teachers centered in Christ; made a society then not on the ground of temporal or local juxtaposition, nor on the ground of a dutiful submission to the social convention of higher education, nor even of a certain real concern for knowing and for the promotion of knowledge, but made a community precisely as Christians, as worshippers, living, praying to the Father through Christ in the unity of the Holy Spirit. And so, the Catholic College as a college of Christ should have evident from the beginning characteristics very profoundly different from those of a school of the Hebrews, trapped in the letter and in external forms, or from an academy of the Greeks, tragically removed from history and from the humble concrete lives of human persons, or especially from the educational establishments of this day, structures without souls, drained of the vital sap of fundamental intuitions and, in the suppression of all determinate differences of intellectual position or at least of the actual relevance of such differences, rendered purposeless, meaningless, occasions at best of a certain dubious social conditioning. For the word which the College would know and to which it will be conformed and which it would proclaim is not just any word, but the Word Who exhales the breath of Love. (The Word then is no longer a mere sign of the actuality; it is in some way the actuality itself: the marrow of a Catholic College is not a system of thought, but a saving personality). And so the life of the Catholic College must proceed from within, from the quiet of the soul with God in liturgical and mental prayer, must seek to make actual all the resources of nature and grace, reverencing everything that is, for "Everything that is, is holy," and "Everything that happens is something to be adored," and, seeking to rehead all things in Christ, must finally become *involved* in the here

and now, the situation of man and of human things, the precarious, the changing, the dying. The community of a college of Christ must have sustenance in the liturgy and must in some way overflow into the apostolate, the uttering of the word to a city and to the world.

The Catholic College must be characterized by inwardness, an intellectual largeness and intensity, a descent to sources from which the universe of thought and love proceeds, a meeting of the mind, of man, with the mystery of things. Its concern with realities must begin with intuition (the primal, immediate contacts of intelligence and sensibility with the inner secret of these realities) and, proceeding through exposition, analysis, criticism, etc., return to the total insight, to a keener, more fully released knowledge in which the conclusion is seen in the principle, the developed work in the formative fire of the germinal idea. The rational elaboration of thought, the prudential ordering of life and action, the artistic qualification of the material are meaningful only in terms of origin and termination at the experience of existence, which is the act of acts, the form of forms. When the rational elaboration of thought is not a sign but a screen, a separate enclosed system, a sort of autonomous mental artwork; or when the acquisition of virtue and the development of institutions and organizations and techniques are pursued without the sense for that which alone quickens discipline, the pull of the determining good; or when art seeks beauty in design, when the splendor of meaningful form is forgot in the gratuitous refinements of integrity and proportion: then there is dry death. For Christian thought, as well as Christian love and Christian making, must open onto existence, the act of the real tasted with the mind and thought with the fingers. (Thus, for the school, the progressive qualification of knowledge should not mean a parcellation, a fragmentation of the real into inert and ultimately unintelligible masses called art and life, or the sacred and the secular, or the contemplative and the active, or the heroic and the ordinary, or the theoretical and the practical, etc. It should know diversity in order to enter into unity.)

And so the college community must be full of reverence for everything that is, and, so, characteristically interior,

non-violent, full of peace, waiting, watching the slow working out of things fully from within. In the awareness of the
people of the school the descent of the Word into history
will not have shrunk and shriveled the universe, narrowing
all to the fearful slit-view of duty and purposefulness, but
all will have been transfigured, recreated in the depths. He
said that He, if He be lifted up, would draw all things to
Himself. And it is for the Christian intelligence and sensibility
to cooperate in this restoring, reheading all things in Christ,
the Son of God, Who would not crush the bruised root nor
quench the burning flax, but Who sees His Father's Will
worked in the world not by violence, or by imposition, not
by intervention or regimentation, not by working charismatic
signs and wonders, but by allowing, with wonderful *respect,*
the orders of His Creation to act, each according to its own
being and the measure of its causality—most of all, man
whose freedom related to God in utterly unique, secret, delicate immediacy is never violated, never exploited, but is
touched with tenderness superbly from within.

At least on the level of intuition, of an immediate knowledge (indemonstrable because prior to all demonstration) the
Catholic College must achieve an integration of knowledges,
but not, as is proper to a college of the natural reason, under
the ordering principle of metaphysics—although surely that
would be a wonderful thing and possibly only a Catholic
college would have factually sufficient respect for reason, for
the order of the naturally intelligible, to seek to actuate such
a synthesis. The Catholic College as a College of Christ must
not be simply a secular, natural, metaphysically-determined
college, although under Christian inspiration. It must be a
specifically Catholic college, a college ordered and vivified
by theological wisdom. And this does not mean the setting
up of theology as simply a crown to a structure already fully
integrated and inwardly differentiated by metaphysics. It
seems that the acceptance of theology as wisdom means a
most profound reordering, reactualizing of all the knowledge
and experience of man; a system of knowledges integrated
by theology is removed by a distance qualitatively infinite
from a system of knowledges integrated by metaphysics. The
truths of revelation cannot affect the objects of knowledge

whose concern is with the eternally necessary laws of possibilities. So far as the order of knowledge, the order of pure
specification, is concerned, the shadow of the Cross does not
seem to fall across mathematics. Nevertheless, in Christian
wisdom mathematics is a part in an entirely different organism. Of course, in the order of exercise and of intention as
the chosen operation of a Christian man, the spirit in which
it is taught and studied will be different. It is not that theological knowledge is alone Christian; mathematics and philosophic knowledge reaching a truth through reason are to
be wholly saved, restored in Christ; in philosophy, for example, revelation may help reason to reach perfection in its own
order. And in those knowledges whose first principle is the
end—ethics and the sciences subordinate to it, politics and
economics—there is (with revelation) a profound change in
the character of the object itself, for man has been called to
share in the inner life of God, an end utterly surpassing the
end which determines his nature. And in the knowledge concerned with "the coexistence and sequence of existential positions" and in the knowledges—including the knowledge of
poetry—concerned with the interpretation thereof there has
been the greatest change. The unique, unrenewable, concrete
point of existence, the here, the now, the hodie, has a new
and revolutionary meaning, an unsuspected depth and richness. For the Son of God has descended into history and the
Holy Spirit moves within the souls of men, and the life of
man is a dialogue with the Father. Men like Léon Bloy and
Georges Bernanos have recognized that in the choice, in the
word, in the making of a man in a moment of history, there
is at least a similitude to what St. Gregory says of the words
of Holy Scripture, "while it tells of an event, it reveals a
mystery," all meaning, the deeps of all thought and love. It
seems that the point of existence is simply infinite, utterly
mysterious, that all senses—literal and spiritual—are there;
that everything that is is present and operative, that the
moment of choice at least is a reactualization of all the possibilities of history; that those which for the natural man are
but signs of mysteries are now for the Christian, because of
Christ, the mysteries themselves. Because of Gethsemane all
remorse, all loss, all the sadness of fading and failing things

and the bitterness of our own betrayal and that of our brothers is here right now.

The curriculum of the school should proceed naturally according to two ways, the order of knowing, in which the man is measured by things and the order of making, in which the man measures things.

In the order of knowing we would distinguish four developments, or perhaps one integrative development with three subordinate exploratory members.

First, a development, historical, total, intuitive, whose focus of intelligibility should involve an approach to a sense of the inner secret, the spirit, the style, the character of a man—and to the spirit of the cities or communities of men and to the spirit of moments, cultural wholes, in the history of man, a study involving religion, thought, art, etc., as of a time and of a place and then and there involved, as taken up and integrated in the whole of the wisdom of a man or of a community, as made actual in the living of men. Most immediate are the men and cultures of our time and these are also to be the most carefully penetrated, so the study may perhaps begin with and culminate in an investigation of modern man and communities of modern man in modern situations.

Second, a study of whatness, the eternal necessities of things: natural science, mathematics, philosophy, theology, all beginning with and terminating in intuitions. This consideration should be sharply speculative, but scientific only within a measure proportioned to the state of minds emerging from the dominance of imagination and not yet fully articulated as rational. Where necessary it should proceed—and without apology—through recourse to a belief substituted for rational argumentation, rather than through a discursus which would overburden the young intellect and stifle its creative synthesizing or through a watered-down show of argumentation or exposition which would reach the conclusion or seem to illuminate the principle, but not by the right way, and which would, in fact, prostitute the fundamental awareness involved.

Third, a consideration of the autonomous universes of artworks (these, as well as the matter in two and in four, should be studied in one, but there rather as revelations of a cultural moment) recognizing the work of art as a world of its own which, though uttered out of a man in a time and a place is not immersed in or exhausted by the man in the time and the place but which moves through all men, times, and places and reaches for the infinite. The works should be seen first of all and last of all as things of splendor, but they may be related also, without patronizing and without profaning, to the student's own call to express his experience. Works of literature, as the type art, may well be the special concern of this study.

Fourth, Holy Scripture, to be studied in integration with the Year of the Church.

The private work of the student in the order of knowing should be intensive and unpretentious, a close careful investigation of a significant aspect or phase through which the reality of the whole is approached in an actual way, by really participative thought upon it. This work must be conceived as an integral part of the knowing process and quite distinct from making, although surely it may quicken the poetic resources of the soul and may condition an artistic grasp of media.

While knowing should have a priority over making, for the soul of man must be formed before forming, yet—and although the soul is not formed simply in order to form—making seems to possess an importance equal to that of knowing in the education of man. The total integrated vision is not accomplished on the level of a knowledge merely scientific in mode. And the intuitive energy of a speculative investigation often demands to go beyond the barriers of formal objects to seek completion in a work or in a deed. For the knowledge is the knowledge of man—it does not exist in a separated way as a subsistent department or field; it exists only in a knowing subject—and in man by a most natural and primary movement what is known passes into love and love overflows into making.

The students will express their own personal experience of men and of the places of men and of the things of their using. This experience should not become less close and fresh and mysterious as the student grows to see things more and more within the self-awareness of a moral and rational being. We speak chiefly of making on the level of the beautiful, and autonomous creativity, a creativity unsubordinated to considerations of utility. But the students should develop also, each in his own measure, a sense for crafts, through instruction and through serious exercise—an exercise measured by the requirements of personal growth in practical knowledge, rather than exclusively by considerations of immediate productive efficiency.

Man knows particular material things through his use of them and, finally, through his love for them: at first he may see them merely as means for his survival or gratification but then, through working upon them and with them, and through a certain community of suffering, he will come to see them as human things, as fellow creatures with a wholeness of their own. This sense for the form of created things helps engender integrity in dealing with forms in imaginative and spiritual worlds.

But servile work is not at all to be conceived as replacing the necessary creative leisure to which it is opposed as a purposeful discipline to a free play. Time and space to be, to germinate thought, to enable the knowledge however genuinely acquired "to distill from its bookish and didactic forms and to become a living substance," to allow conceptions to fructify unwrenched by violations through academic regimentation, is an absolutely necessary condition for the growth of intelligence.

We think that the primary qualities to be sought in students are those of an open, reverent, spirit rather than those of cleverness or inquisitiveness or even of an intellectual keenness (although a good measure of intellectual power is certainly presupposed in any of the desired qualifications). These desired qualities are not of course discernible through an ordinary college entrance examination or through any examination of the candidate in which information-content has primacy over style or even indeed entirely suppresses style. By style is meant the person's basic attitude toward the real, his way of moving among things and through things and beyond: a sign of his character; the mode of operation and of utterance that is him. We do not think we are looking for ageless youth splendidly equipped with hyperthyroid instruments of science and scholarship precisely in those areas where science and scholarship may be most inhuman; people with the narrowness and smugness necessary for prodigious and undeviating works of mental drudgery. We are interested in men. And while it is true that the college is not to develop the philosopher, or the literary critic, or the biologist, but the man, it is also true that the only person who will develop into a decent thinker or artist or teacher or father or lover or saint is the intuitive man. A large trouble in "contemporary metaphysical thinking" is not so much the lack of carefully trained minds but the lack of intuitive souls. A large trouble in contemporary literature and criticism is not so much the lack of widely read and conscientiously developed talents, but the lack of intuition in the soul. Maritain says "you will understand what kind of man the Thomist metaphysician should be. He should possess a sensitive body, be like St. Thomas himself *mollis carne*. Most certainly he must not be exclusively an intellect. His equipment of senses must be in good order. He must be keenly and profoundly aware of sensible objects. And he should be plunged into existence, steeped ever more deeply in it by a sensuous and aesthetic perception as acute as possible, and by experiencing the suffering and struggles of real life, so that alone in the third heaven of natural understanding he may feed upon the intelligible substance of things. Is it necessary to add that the professor who is nothing but a professor, withdrawn from real life and *rendered insensible* at the third degree of abstraction is the diametrical opposite of the genuine metaphysician? The Thomist philosopher is dubbed *scholastic,* a name derived from his most painful affliction. Scholastic pedantry is his peculiar foe. *He* must constantly triumph over his domestic adversary, the Professor."

The qualifications for students and teachers should be in root the same, although it is of course to be expected that the teachers possess their knowledge in a more highly qualified mode and, liberated by the truth, be free to utter it for the liberation of others.

And more, teaching belongs to the active life or, rather, to that activity which is the overflow of thought and contemplation.

It is the utterance of the truth to men who will grow upon the utterance as mystery and rebel against it as formulation. So it involves as well as a concern for the inner requirements of the object, a concern for the way of growth of man. As the teaching function becomes exercised in a more and more immediate and present way, in a family or in a school, it involves a selfless, dedicated concern for the unique working out of manhood of each soul, a delicate sense for the peculiar needs and aspirations of each, for the peculiar partaking of knowledge, the peculiar way with knowledge, that is each one. This sympathy, this capacity to appreciate the requirements of another's fulfillment because that fulfillment is desired even as one's own, seems formal in the teacher. It seems a function of prudence, perhaps an extension of the prudence of the father. The teacher must respect the delicate sacred interiority of each student, he must encourage the timid efforts at genuine utterance and integration. And it is this prudential discernment and decision which seems to set off the teacher, as such, from the thinker, as such, or the scholar, as such, and which intimates a conflict between the way of the teacher and the way of the thinker or scholar as they exist in one man. Students and teachers must form a community and thinkers, scholars and artists have a place in such a community; nevertheless, the functions of these others seem quite distinct from that of the teacher, so much so that an efficacious union of these functions in one person would seem extraordinary. Surely thinkers and artists could and should be present, could give occasional lectures, converse with students, etc.; but they are not the proper, close, abiding ministerial agents of this most delicate process. There are very few teachers, and few of these are college teachers. It is a most finely determined and most wonderful vocation: one does not become a teacher simply through intelligence, good will, and hard work. In the beginning the faculty of the school must be small—it will never be large—and entrusted with the most difficult formative responsibilities; it had better be composed exclusively of true teachers.

It would seem that we will need some people who are analytically, and perhaps one may say, scientifically minded, but nevertheless men liberated by knowledge and not enslaved by formulae. It would seem difficult to get hold of a metaphysician who would be a sign of the object of metaphysics (a most central and a most demanding study), who would reverence the utterly fundamental analogical intuition of being, who would not stand in the light, who would not smother minds in the Scholastic professor's syllogistic trap. Likewise, it would seem difficult to find a man who would be able to teach mathematics with care and with mastery and as a realist, without submerging himself and his class in that romantic ocean, or without treating mathematics as a mere measuring instrument toward practical domination over the physical universe.

We do not believe it will be at all adequate to have mathematics and the experimental sciences of nature taught by those who have merely dutifully studied these out of the urgency of the occasion, read the interpretive judgments of various competent critics but who have really no feel for, no habituation to, the science in question and who can at best speak of the study from the outside without the advantage of any of its living intuitions, without communicating to the student the intention, the intelligible concentration, the life beneath the dry constructs. Now we do not expect and certainly do not recommend a highly refined investigation of mathematics or physics in college; the student is to get a sense of the nature of mathematics, its place in the order of knowledges, its modes of procedure, and one very natural, free aid to the acquisition of this sense is the experiencing of the presence of a live and functioning mathematician. And even if the resources of knowledge of the mathematician or physicist are never called into full explicit play, even if much of their science is simply strange and unassimilable even to the understanding of other teachers, it must be present and operative in the school's natural and necessary determinations regarding, for example, modern culture, many of whose themes derive from findings in physics and mathematics and biology, perhaps in many instances misinterpreted, perhaps in many instances given a scope of relevance which does not at all belong to them and which can be fully explored only with the aid of an intelligent man who is a physicist or biologist or mathematician.

The work of restoring, reheading all things in Christ, of permeating with the leaven of the Gospels the reluctant paste of history, the sanctification of the secular, seems a work proper to the Christian laity. And the education of the man, and of the Christian man, which is basic to any such mission, seems also a work peculiarly proportionate to the state of the Christian who is in a full sense a member of the temporal community. For of course it belongs to the family, to the Christian community living in the earthly city to bring men and Christians into being and to assist them to the fullness of growth. It is true that for centuries the work of education has been taken over by those in the religious state, but we think that this function of religious communities of men and women has been simply substitutional, necessitated during the long formless dormancy of the laity. At first, of course, only clerics were formally educated anyway, perhaps the teaching of potential clerics and clerics by clerics was right and proper. But the religious state is not proportioned to this work of understanding and respectfully assisting the way of growth, intellectual, social, and—to some extent—spiritual, of those who seem destined to be Christians in this world, those called to confront with all the resources of nature and grace the antinomies, the tensions, the terrible lacerations of the modern world which is not simply an area irreducibly pagan and so to be abandoned, but which must indeed, in the fulfillment of the mission of the Church, be transfigured by Christianity. Beginning with Leo XIII and culminating in the remarkable words of Pius XI and Pius XII, there has been a progressive self-awareness and positive differentiation of the lay state and, correlatively, a reassertion of the specific concern of priests with ministration of the true Body of Christ and, in their measure, with the care of His Mystical Body and the recognition of the peculiarly contemplative function of monks and nuns. A Catholic college is not, then, to be conceived after the fashion of a seminary or of a convent, not even—in an atmosphere of guilty compromise—of a somewhat relaxed seminary or convent, even as—and actually because—the layman is not to be conceived as one who is too weak spiritually or intellectually or morally to be a religious and to whom marriage and life in the world is given as a somehow conniving back door route to heaven. The Catholic college is to be conceived after the fashion of a family or rather of a community, a community rather fraternal than patriarchal or paternal—a community trans-figured, to be sure, by Christ.

The college community, a community of Christian intel-ligences, will naturally seek expression in works. Some of the works of the college community, some of the fruits of its inner plenitude, may be:

A publication, edited by students and teachers, of work of students, graduates, teachers.

A student drama, through various media.

A publication, edited by teachers and associates, of work—naturally rather more qualified, more matured—of teachers and associates and graduates.

Books.

The college might even be a college on the land, drawing some sustenance from the land, and as little as possible a mendicant college, although it seems that it is simply the lot of thinkers and artists to be beggars—and as aliens, from enemies.

It should be a small college, a community whose domestic and academic functions will be discharged by those who share its intellectual and spiritual life, a community whose char-acter may bear the mark of each of its members, a community in which each member has ontological and moral weight, in which each member will really contribute to the spiritual and physical becoming, a community whose good returns to each member. When the presence or absence of one person does not make a determinate difference in the character of the school, does not call for a redisposition of all its possibilities, that will be a sign that the school will have grown too large (or, as it may be, that that person does not belong in the community).

The character of the Catholic College will be terminated in the persons of the community, the teachers and wives and students and associates, in the men who participate in the wisdom, the community, the other Christs. The question, what is the Catholic College, gives way to the question, Who is the Catholic College. Its name, its unique inner mystery, is at last hidden in the intercommunion in this place of these people.[6]

When O'Malley returned to Notre Dame with this document—or an earlier draft of it—in September of 1947 he soon took copies of it and spent several weekends with his little group of disciples at the Committee on Social Thought in the University of Chicago, discussing revisions. Because of the density of the document he was urged to develop a companion piece that would be more in the nature of a simple and brief brochure. So his papers came to include seven pages over which were spread the following words in various clusters:

THE COLLEGE

A Community of Teachers and Students

FUNCTION:

To provide a true education
in the liberal arts, *the
humanities,* that is, the
studies that mature the
human being.

THE STUDIES:

EXPRESSION
LITERATURE
MUSIC AND FINE ARTS
MATHEMATICS
PHYSICS AND NATURAL SCIENCES
HISTORY OF CIVILIZATION
HISTORY OF SCIENCES
PHILOSOPHY
ETHICS AND POLITICAL AND
    SOCIAL PHILOSOPHY
THEOLOGICAL WISDOM

(a) These studies will be carried out over a period of four years.

(b) A principal method will be the use of "pure texts," tutorials and seminars.

(c) The degree conferred will be: Bachelor of Arts.

THE STUDENTS:

(a) Only those deemed fit—by examination of previous record and experience and by personal interview—will be accepted.

(b) Preferable age: 16 to 19.

(c) The number of students will be limited in the first years to about 50. Later the number will be increased to a final of about 200.

(d) All students will be required to be in residence.

(e) It is hoped that fees will be apportioned, so that qualified students of lesser financial means will be enabled to attend.

THE TEACHERS:

These should be men

(a) who understand the importance of a proper experience of the liberal arts,

(b) who know the great failure of American colleges and universities to provide this experience,

(c) and who have a real sense of the action of a *teacher.**
    *For this reason, Ph.D's will, in general, be undesirable, since the infertility and darkness of their usual pursuits cannot fail to blight the spirit and unfit it for the "dynamics of education." Rather, "self-educated" men, lacking all conventional academic qualifications but having a right understanding of the problems and issues involved, will be preferable. On the significance of the teacher in education, see Jacques Maritain, *Education at the Crossroads* (Yale University Press, 1943), pp. 29–57.

THE COLLEGE COMMUNITY

(a) It is important that the relationship between teachers and students be genuine and constant and that the social life of the college community grow naturally out of this association. In their own life, the students will be placed under no arbitrary, artificial rules or pressures.

(b) So that the college will be a community worthy of the name, the life of its members will be united and move within the spirit of the Liturgy. See Romano Guardini, *The Church and the Catholic* and *The Spirit of the Liturgy* (Sheed and Ward, 1935).

ADMINISTRATION:

The whole administration of the college will be in the hands of the president and of the teachers. There will be no other officers, no functionaries unrelated to the real existence of the college.[7]

The projected budget for the first year showed anticipated expenses of $35,000 which included, among other items, three married teachers at $3,000 per year, two unmarried teachers at $1,500 per year, and one unmarried administration man at $1,500 per year. The income was to be totally from the tuition payments of an initial twenty-five residential students.[8]

The group of disciples in Chicago was invited to become active in founding the institution, but none of them saw any really practical steps that they could take. And yet, they did not entirely dismiss the idea as quixotic and utopian. Had not Father Sorin and his little band of six brothers in the Congregation of Holy Cross launched a University in 1842 with even less prospect of success?

Ken Woodward writes that "O'Malley almost pulled it off, with the help of his protege John Gilligan, a member of the English faculty at Xavier University, who managed to get the Archbishop of Cincinnati to provide a recently bequeathed estate for the college's use. Gilligan also raised some $250,000 in pledges from donors—enough, in those days, to get a college started. When the two men went over the project one Easter weekend at Gilligan's home, however, the professor's reservations surfaced. 'O'Malley was to be president, dean and soul of the place,' Gilligan recalls, 'and I think being out front and center like that made him balk. Besides, I also think he hated the idea of leaving Notre Dame. We talked and drank till three in the morning. Frank broke down and cried, saying he couldn't do it.'"[9]

And so, the project was shelved as a practical matter. However, the ideas that it had generated continued to reverberate through the rest of O'Malley's life. For example, many of those ideas reappear in a 1958 paper that he prepared for the Committee on Academic Progress in Notre Dame's College of Arts and Letters. The paper was entitled "How Teaching Can Be Made Personal and Individual."

> The real question is: what must be not our matter or our method but our attitude, our disposition, our demeanor, our spirit of approach in the establishment of a true community of teachers and students? It would be sad if the new order of the college, with its accentuation of the personal and the communal significance of intellectual life, should disintegrate into so much machinery while the persons of the college simply groan and grope amidst gongs and gears. At the end of the schoolyear it would be well if we were exhausted not by the effort to manage and operate our machinery—or to disentangle ourselves from it as the case may be—but by our ministry to the welfare of our students and their minds.
>
> Teaching, like everything else in the anti-personal power-world of the twentieth century, is always in danger of being submitted to the process of massification we observe everywhere about us in the history, society, and politics of our time.... Human sorrow asks whether man is still able to be masterful, so that he may live in freedom and dignity, so that he may be generative and joyous. Often the feeling prevails that man, as he is today, is not able to be himself any more. Activities and their effects have mastered him and have even made themselves independent of him.... We must realize that the basic answer to our question is this: we, as men and teachers, have to recognize and take over the full nature and kinds of our teaching responsibilities. To be able to do this we have to regain our right relations to the truth of things, to the realities of other persons, to the postulations of our inner selves, our deepest inner selves, and finally and constantly to God. Our main problem is a *metanoia*: an examination of our whole attitude towards life and a change of the way in which we see and deal with men, ideas, things, and with our own knowledge. As I see it, our problem as

teachers (who would make and maintain our teaching as personal in the midst of the impersonal power-world) rests not in matter or method but in our whole attitude towards life and in the examination and re-examination of this attitude. Now the pressing questions come: have we tried enough to realize what happens when the average teacher teaches his students and maintains the order, character, and discipline of learning? Do we always find respect for truth and confidence in its strength? Is rule always unassailably right? Does the person dealt with always feel that there is a personal relation established, especially one of respect? Is the action really concerned with this relation and is it realized as it should be, according to its nature? Is there a true appeal to the animate, the creative faculty, the freedom in the student?

We must understand that these are not questions of private morale merely but of the success or failure of intellectual and cultural life and of the education that would nurture this life. We must realize that everything depends, for ourselves and for our students, upon the activation of a true and deep respect for truth, right, personal dignity and the "creative center" of our fellowmen. . . .

First: We must renew, in some measure, the contemplative attitude. Emmanuel Mounier has mentioned "the danger of becoming shut up in ourselves, and it is very real." But "of the majority of men . . . and of a great part of our lives, thronged as they are with worldly solicitations, the true description is that of Valery: 'We are shut outside ourselves.' From that kind of imprisonment nothing but contemplation can deliver us." And Gabriel Marcel has remarked that "a civilization which . . . finally denies the place of contemplation and shuts out the very possibility of contemplation, such a civilization . . . sets us inevitably on the road towards a philosophy which is not so much a *love of wisdom* as a *hatred of wisdom*; we ought rather to call it a *misosophy*." Everywhere there is action, everywhere activity, everywhere busyness, everywhere organization—but out of what are they directed? From an inner self which is not quite at home or at ease with itself but rather acts, thinks, and judges from its superficial spheres: mere intellect, mere calculation, mere achievement, mere impulses of power, possession, or pleasure. The depths of men have to be revived again. Man's soul has to be rediscovered. Everybody must have periods of his life and moments of his day as a permanent, constituent part, when he becomes quiet, concentrates himself and—with a living heart—asks himself one of the innumerable questions suppressed during the busy day. How a person will do this cannot generally be stated. It depends on his personal *ethos,* on his fundamental convictions. At any rate, he has to pull out of the daily chase, he has to become quiet and present to himself, has to expose himself to a world of wisdom and *pietas.* Only an attitude deepened in such a way can permit a person to take a strong stand against the powers of the time and of the world around him. And this "moment of silence," so necessary for ourselves, is equally necessary for our students. . . .

Second: We must open ourselves again to the elementary fact of the nature of things and persons. Even a cursory examination will show us how schematic or systematic we make them, how far we deal with them only on the basis of conventions, how much we handle them under external aspects of efficiency, convenience or the saving of time. The result is not only innumerable mistakes—but also a severe want of appreciation of, indeed an embezzlement of reality giving rise to all kinds of disorders and even catastrophes. We must approach the essence of being again. We must commit as Josef Pieper would say, the philosophical act; we must ask philosophical questions: what is work—and what is intellectual work—as soon as it is seen in the frame of the interrelations of life? What is learning? What is wisdom? What is thinking? What are order and discipline? What are authority and obedience? What are friendship and love? What is man? Is there a scale of values? Which are not important at all? What are the final aims of life? What are the means to achieve them? We live out of these basic realities. We live for them and with them. We regulate and reform them. But do we know what they are? . . .

Third: We must learn the meaning of that we might call an asceticism of the intellect and of its lieutenant, the will. As far as our vocations are concerned, asceticism does not mean anything other than this: that we have ourselves and our own minds and wills in hand, that we learn to master our knowledge and our powers and talents, that we learn to possess ourselves truly of our knowledge and to sacrifice the lesser for the greater, that we educate ourselves not to yield to our own power or authority but to use it with responsibility, with charity, with love. What I mean, simply, is that no form can be built or created, if he who builds it is not formed himself. This is the assumption for the achievement of our greatest aims as teachers: to create forms that have room for the spirit, orders in which personality can exist, ways of discipline that allow dignity. The asceticism I speak of should aid us in discovering what it means to command, to exercise authority, to direct as well as to obey ... too often in our schools, instead of a true exercise of authority and command, we have had force; instead of obedience, the complete surrender of personality. Inept ourselves in the exercise of our authority, we exact from our students not obedience but the abject submission of their persons. Nevertheless, by the manifestation of an intellectual and personal asceticism, we can encourage our students towards the development of the same self-possession.

Fourth: We must realize the importance of community, of the true relationship that must exist among ourselves and that must exist between us and our students. I am not, of course, thinking at all of "palsiwalsiness"; I do not mean the lack of distance, the camaraderie more appropriate to a barracks or a camp than to a college or university; and certainly not mere participation in committee meetings, whether they are hot or cold. Community is the unceremoniously and unofficially felt solidarity, unforced and unappointed, of those who do the same work and are in the same situation; it is the spontaneous readiness for mutual help and joint efforts, for joint intellectual creations. This attitude—involving sympathy and a sense of kinship—is essential. . . .

Fifth: and here I am led to emphasize *the need for us to conserve and to develop the virtues of reverence and patience.* The attitude of reverence ("belief in God's presence," Newman called it) will keep us from committing acts of aggression against all realities and knowledges and against those whom we would introduce into the mysteries of our realities and knowledges—and will help us, out of our respectful recognition of other persons (our students), to avoid the dangers of instrumentalization and depersonalization. On this point Mounier has noted that "whenever I treat another person as though he were not present, or as a repository for information for my use, an instrument at my disposal; or when I set him down in a list without right of appeal—in such a case I am behaving towards him as though he were an object, which means in effect, despairing of him. But if I treat him as a subject, as a presence—which is to recognize that I am unable to define or classify him, that he is inexhaustible, filled with hopes upon which he alone can act—this is to give him credit. To despair of anyone is to make him desperate; whereas the credit that generosity extends regenerates his own confidence. It acts as the appeal (the invocation) that nourishes the spirit."

While we know that we cannot indulge a foolish faith in the good nature of those students coming under us (for they will be capable like ourselves of a variety of sins and weaknesses), we must avoid the perils of what I would like to call *academic Jansenism* which, having too low a view of human nature, chronically underestimating human quality, integrity, and decency, crushes out or obstructs the possibilities of great life and growth in our students, deals death-blows to or ignores their often excellent sensibilities and powers of imagination. For, on the whole, our students are far, far from being worms; and we have much more to do than to observe them turn up their bellies in a just agony. We have also to be wary in dealing with our students, as Dietrich von Hildebrand reminds us, of the common belief that "everything can be acquired by taking courses in a subject, and that studying is the chief and surest way of gaining the ability to perform something well. Abilities based on special gifts, such as an understanding of art, are believed to be accessible to everyone by study. In this adulation of learning, one forgets that there are many things that are pure gifts which we cannot acquire even with the greatest assiduity: they are endowments granted to us by God. To these gifts belong, for instance, creative artistic talents, as well as profound sensitivity to art, music or literature, philosophical power, or scientific intuition." So we should beware of breaking in ruthlessly upon domains of the soul where devils no less than angels would fear to tread.

Even with those students who may seem at first inadequate though earnest (I am not thinking at all of the academic vagrants, around whom we spend too much of our time and energy building barricades, into which we finally herd everybody; vagrants, incorrigible and irreconcilable, practically irredeemable, should be sent out into history at the earliest possible moment, sent forth unanointed to their destined vagabondage), we must have patience, "for patience bears with the imperfect," as Guardini memorably puts it, "uses restraint in dealing with the defective, spares the unfortunate and surrounds them with that deep-seated concern which is not only compassion, but also a common destiny."

Sixth: So we are brought to the thought that, in our concern with teaching and with the works of the mind, *we must meditate seriously about the final relation of our existence, our relation to God.* Man is not a being sufficient unto himself who can acknowledge his relationship to God or reject it, precisely as he thinks and decides. The nature of man is essentially determined by his relationship to God. Man exists only as one related to God: "where there is no God there is no man." And the way in which he understands this relationship, how seriously he takes it, and the consequences he draws from it—all this determines the nature of his life, his work, his vocation. . . . Above all people we must keep remembering in the midst of the rush and rampage of the schoolyear that, of all our realities, God is the definite reality. If man does not do justice to Him, his whole being will be sick and all forms of neuroses will result. And it would not be sensible, in proffering these various ideas and suggestions, finally to neglect the only point at which, in trying to embody them, we can succeed or fail. Certainly through our meditation upon this final and eternally persisting relationship, we shall realize the limitations of our little creaturely worlds; we shall, as Marcel suggests, be put on our guard, in our roles as teachers and as men of art, science and learning altogether, against *hybris,* against unmeasured arrogance—and we may discover that "all pedantry and caste spirit and tin-god service" are defeated and dissolved.

... I believe that effective personal teaching is not, as I have said, so much a matter of matter or of method. ... There must, of course, be a serious matter, especially since so many of the student's experiences outside the academic are hopelessly trivial, trashy, ephemeral. But the matter, in undergraduate education, must always be submitted to the student's own development, to his own call and need to be himself and to dominate or master decently his experiences rather than to be dominated or mastered and overwhelmed by them. That is why an honest teacher, responsible to the task and anxious to do justice to the different needs and clearly indicated possibilities of his various students, may find it necessary at times to alter or to depart from an arbitrary course syllabus which can be set up only out of sight of and out of range of the living presences and pressures of students and which in the concrete situation may be, like so many textbooks, found irrelevant or untoward. I can't help saying that the souls and bodies of at least a few teachers and students tremble always somewhat in terror of smothering in the spread of syllabusification.

There may also be no absolutely sacrosanct method or practice of teaching. Indeed each teacher is entitled to his own style, his own way—and certain ways may succeed, for this reason, with one teacher and not with another. Each teacher may also use—depending upon the levels of experience, quality, and requirements of his students—a variety of methods. Perhaps the best method, especially when it is concerned with the action of the student's mind on his own work, is the personal conference. At any rate, surely unsuitable is any method or practice which does not acknowledge the student's existence and which deprives him of *his own style,* his own way with things and ideas. The truth is that no two students grow towards perfection in exactly the same way. Failure to grasp this fact can result only in standardization, if not actually in a "massacre of the innocents." I may add that very unsuitable is any method which makes the teacher's function merely presidual or which brings the teacher, in all literalness, down to precisely the same level as his students, as in some kind of game or play.

Whatever the matter or the method, effective personal teaching depends upon a disposition, a demeanor, an attitude, a spirit of approach, a development, a self-possession, a presence—call it what you like—that will ultimately and gradually transfuse and dynamize our action with our students. I guess all I really mean is that we have to be, to be allowed to be, and to recognize ourselves as persons before we can see and treat and trust our students as the persons they are. And since I could neither develop nor concretize my notes and points here, I recommend your further meditation not upon the usual and numerous works dealing with the nature, the crisis and reform of contemporary collegiate education and teaching but upon such works as I personally and others, too, have found helpful, nourishing of a spirit that enlivens the "day-labouring," that enlarges the horizons of teaching— the spirit which allows the arrival of those wonderful epiphanic moments, the joyous moments of revelation, of the discovery of some new and transforming reality in the midst of routine, moments to which every scholar, every teacher and every student are entitled.

While many of these works may only incidentally, if at all, touch upon the specific problems of teaching and education they do, in their concern for the sanctity of the person and personal life, in their acute realization that *personality is sacred,* provide a formation, an attitude, a spirit of approach towards personal teaching. They do suggest the truth of a recent remark by Robert Frost that "there cannot be anything interesting between persons unless they are persons"—and the truth also of an observation by W. M. Dixon: "To imprison the human spirit is the unpardonable sin, the attempt to make men automata, to force them into the same mold. No means will ever be found to induce human beings finally to surrender themselves, either body or soul, to a dictated felicity, to satisfactions chosen for them, whatever vulgar Caesars rule the world." The list—incomplete and unranked—follows: Romano Guardini, *The Church and the Catholic* and *The Spirit of the Liturgy, The Faith and Modern Man;* Josef Pieper, *Leisure: the Basis of Culture;* Dietrich von Hildebrand, *Liturgy and Personality, The New Tower of Babel;* Emmanuel Mounier, *Personalism;* Gabriel Marcel, *Man Against Mass Society, The Philosophy of Existence;* Max Picard, *The World of Silence;* C. F. Ramuz, *What is Man?;* Gerald Vann, *The Heart of Man;* Nicholas Berdyaev, *Slavery and Freedom;* Jacques Maritain, *Education at the Crossroads, The Person and the Common Good, Creative Intuition in Art and Poetry;* Erich Frank, *Philosophical Understanding and Religious Truth;* Christopher Dawson, *Enquiries into Religion and Culture, Education and the Crisis of Christian Culture* and other essays; Charles Peguy, *God Speaks;* Franz Kafka, *The Trial, Metamorphosis;* Elizabeth Madox Roberts, *The Time of Man;* Robin Flower, *The Western Island;* Leo R. Ward, *God in an Irish Kitchen, Holding up the Hills, Blueprint for a Catholic University.* And I can only pass over countless passages in Newman and in Kierkegaard (notably his *The Present Age*). Apart from all books (treatises, reflections, essays and creative literature, all-moving and all-important), it will not hurt us to listen to good music and to face in wonder good painting and good sculpture—personal and individual achievements quite difficult to bibliographize or to solemnize in any sort of symposium.

Consideration of such works and absorption of their meanings and values will fortify us in the ministerial as well as in the properly magisterial character of the action of teaching, will strengthen us as persons, will save us from settling down into the status of functionaries of the college, business-managers dealing with our consumers or credit-victims; and will enhance our sense of the great though still and inevitably mysterious mission of teaching, in the mid-twentieth-century power-world, the liberal and the fine arts involving as they do human integrity and destiny and the personal and individual integrities and destinies of our students—and of ourselves.[10]

This statement is perhaps as close as O'Malley ever came to admitting, even to himself, that the secret of his teaching success was simply his presence, his dramatic presence, allowing the mysterious core of his personality to be seen and heard, admired and enjoyed. His shyness may have been a contributing factor in much the same way that Henry Fonda's shyness found its solution on the stage in the feeling that shyness was no longer necessary because he had become someone else. The personality that O'Malley became on the podium was the "saving personality" of Christ College.

As Arnold Sparr writes, O'Malley's "strength lay in his ability to take a particular thinker, extract what was important in his thought, and . . . present it with passionate intensity. This was most effective in the classroom and on the lecture platform. Here O'Malley could step outside of his shyness and, in effect, become Lèon Bloy bellowing with brutal axe-edged words against Christian mediocrity, Maritain and Dawson cooly analyzing the spiritual disintegration of modern times, or Romano Guardini movingly describing the liturgical character of Christian existence."[11]

The Teacher

In a way, the idea of Christ College was simply O'Malley's teaching personality writ large, a personality that was always progressing from teacher to friend to compatriot in the City of God.

Being a favored student of O'Malley's was something like an adoption. You very soon became aware that he lived in a black-and-white universe in which the forces of light constantly clashed with the forces of darkness. And the fact that he had spotted you as one of the "children of God" made him your ally and loyal protector from then on. If you were standing in one of the boring lines during the registration process, clutching the random selection of class cards issued to you for the required courses (all showing professors that you had never heard of) O'Malley might come up and ask to see your cards. He seemed to hover about during the registration process. Suddenly he would then walk off but reappear in a few minutes with an entirely new set of cards for you, including classes with some of the best professors on the campus, many of them teachers whose classes he had himself taken as an undergraduate.

His adopted ones were not abandoned when the course was over. During the summer after my freshman course with him he sent me gifts of two books: Christopher Dawson's *Enquiries into Religion and Culture* and Karl Adam's *The Son of God*.

Then during the low ebb of the sophomore year when my lack of electives prevented me from signing up for any other O'Malley course he invited me to attend informal readings in his room, along with Burley Johnston of Little Rock and Walter Fleming of Dallas. I was from Corpus Christi, probably the only person that he had ever met from that town; and the name itself (given by a Spanish explorer when he sailed into the bay on the Feast of Corpus Christi in 1549) may have intrigued him. He would read to us for an hour or so in the evenings from some of his favorite fiction writers, such as Katherine Mansfield or R. P. Tristram Coffin. From the chair where I sat I could look out the window toward downtown South Bend several miles away and see the intense red spot of a neon sign on a hotel. I watched it constantly during the readings. It was not possible to read the sign because of the angle, so it was just a fascinating spot of beautiful red light against the black sky with O'Malley's voice in the background reminding me of Pater's saying that the purpose of life was to "burn with a hard, gem-like flame."

After undergraduate school, Edward Goerner interrupted his education with a period of Navy service during the Korean War. So O'Malley followed him up with a series of long letters as well as books, a kind of directed readings program entirely beyond any formal instructional assignment by the university:

> Dear Ed, I am sending you today the *Pascal* and the *Kierkegaard* I promised you. I am also sending you Dawson's *Enquiries into Religion and Culture,* a book that has meant a lot to me personally: you will realize that it is not a new book; I have used it for years; but I really do not need it any more, since I have thoroughly digested it, and, like most of the books I have already consigned to you, I would rather that you have them than have them gathering dust on my shelves. For I believe that you will make, whenever you get a chance, excellent use of these books and others I shall send you. There are only a few students to whom I would give them anyway . . . your career in the Navy must not obstruct your effort to know and to make sense. I think I liked especially your exceptional ability to work independently— beyond the frustrations of the academy.

As for the huge projects (offered in sincerity but also in distraughtness) I have proposed to you, I think that, for the moment, they are not compassable. The only sensible suggestion I can make to you, actually, is that, this summer, you read Parrington, Dawson, and Frank—as a sort of novitiate. With respect to the whole business I also wonder if it wouldn't be well for you to draw in some others—like Joe Scott and Ed Waters and Charles Fahy—so that, however you may all be circumstanced and however remote one man from another we could but create a community of concern and correspondence through the years of exile. Hugh Schade, I am sure I can take care of and help next year but the others, like yourself, will be gone. I got this thought too late to present to you or to anyone else. But in order to maintain yourself and the others, a real effort in this direction ought to be made. If you consider my thought to be (like so many others) impossible to execute, you ought to tell me so.

At the end, I felt desperate and melancholy, wishing I had done more when I had a *real* and living and present chance to help the many good students of this year. But in the heat of the day and under the pressure of the hour I sort of collapsed. In any event, you I shall always remember as one of the best men we have ever had here, and I shall miss, sorrowfully, seeing you and talking with you. All the same, I shall always be thanking you for the fidelity of your action and refinement of your spirit in putting up with all our goings on at Notre Dame. And, if ever I can help you in your movement through history, I shall try hard so long as I live.

Sincerely,
Frank O'Malley

Dear Ed,

I am glad that you liked von Hildebrand's Essay. It is too important a statement to ignore or to have had out of print for so long. I note that you thought I cited it in the lectures of the first semester. I didn't because I had no copy of it then—only a remembrance of it as it first came out in Kotschnig's *The University in a Changing World* (a book now very hard to come by). . . . I guess you know that I had—and still have—considerable agitation of conscience over presenting you at the end of last semester with a number of huge problems and a few direction books—apparently to send you off to float on a wide, wide sea. . . . I knew, of course, that even without further comment from me you would make sense of all our wide-spreading proposals. But I realized, too, that I should have started earlier in last semester, going over all these possibilities with you. . . . You are, however, starting off very, very well—and I like to think that you are—as is proper, putting and fitting things together by yourself. The list of books you are now gathering in stride is fine, I think, for your present intentions. I am pleased, too, that you have got hold of E. Brunner's *Christianity and Civilization:* one of the first rate Protestant theologians and philosophers known to me, he has in this work . . . attempted to establish the principles for the construction of a Christian civilization. . . . It will be interesting to see what you have to say, finally, about the shape of his mind. I have the following additional suggestions:

(1) To the books by Berdyaev, I would add his *Spirit and Reality,* which you have.

(2) I note that, in the over all, you are meditating on *Living Thoughts of St. Paul* which is, as Maritain points out, so great for his assertion of the spirit of the gospels, of the primacy of spirit over letter—I would also recommend your reading of St. Augustine's *City of God* (you can get it easily in a Modern Library Edition if you don't have it), which is the classic statement, really, of the Christian philosophy of history. In this connection, too, you should read Dawson's essay, "St. Augustine and His Age," in *Enquiries into Religion and Culture*—a very important essay. I'm glad, also, that you managed to find Cochrane's *Christianity and Classical Culture,* a centerpiece for a study of cultural synthesis in prospect and now here in the making. Dawson's *Religion and the Rise of Western Culture* will also fit in here, especially the first five chapters. It is interesting, I might add, that Dawson has considerable respect for Toynbee. Your reading of the *Study of History* may lead to some further adjustments of your judgments on Toynbee—even though your assertion that his is not an "inspirited mind in its fullness" may remain correct. At least you may come to believe that, despite his

inveterate system-making, there is, within all the systemati-
zations, a certain suppleness even if there is no reverence of
the handling of the realities. And I think you will find the
Toynbee design amazing—I note that you plan to read Butterfield's *Christianity and History*. B. was, I believe, a student
of Toynbee's at Cambridge. I shall be much interested in your
comments on Butterfield. I was, as a matter of fact, going
to suggest that you read him after Toynbee and Dawson.
You may keep the Toynbee and Dawson books I am sending
you. I would probably have given them to you before, except
that I was afraid of glutting you.

Ed, I hope you will understand that in all this spreading
of comment and suggestions I mean well.

(3) You might also want to note Karl Loewith, *The Meaning of History*. Let me know whether you can get it or not.

(4) As a final addition, I would suggest your reading
Spengler's *The Decline of the West,* a brilliant and classic . . .
show on the *cyclical* manipulation of history.

Whether you add anything or not, you will have enough
to do to encompass this first monumental problem. I would
like to indicate here a possible long-range development which,
in the exigencies of your life during these next three years,
you may be able to fulfill, with grace and heroic acts of the
will. From your first preoccupation with (1) the questions of
History and Culture, you might then pass on to

(2) The *Existentialist* concern with the human person and
the human situation: here your concern would not be with
History and *Culture,* but with *Man*—immediately in his
moment of living. The term *Existentialist* may seem to be
just a label or something . . . but I think it holds a meaning
very deep and real for us. . . . Never more than today is the . . .
fact of human insecurity more apparent. Man's whole history,
of course, may be seen as a constant struggle to secure his
existence, a struggle founded on the reality of an enduring
conviction of human insecurity—a condition which the modern belief in progress—now crumbling—by technical . . . and
organizational action has obscured from us. Here, of course,
there are involved the non-Christian existentialists, like
Nietzsche, Sartre, and others. But I am especially interested
in the position of the Christian Existentialist philosophers

(with Eddington and Pascal as the background), like the Protestants Kierkegaard, and, today, Karl Barth and the Catholics like Gabriel Marcel, Theodor Haecker, and Peter Wust certainly the Christian Existentialists have renewed our consciousness of the *insecuritas humanae* and have, beyond this, awakened us to a fresh grasp of man's responsibility for and in his human destruction. All this leads, for a Christian, to the religious realm of life where man is seen not as *homo sapiens* but as *homo religiosus,* man's deepest character being grasped only in his relationship to God, for "when there is no God, there is no man." Here the religious aspect of being is reasserted: the inherent relationship between man and God. I am drawing up the design for this.

(3) the meaning of the modern world. Here we come to the specific question of man's social and political action (in the contexts of modern history and culture)—the prospectus of which ought to be (as I tried to suggest in the special lectures I gave in the afternoons . . .) a *pluralistic* society formed by a *personalist* philosophy . . . what Karl Mannheim notes in the very title of his latest book, as "Freedom, Power, and Democratic Planning." (By the way I'm sending you the latest issue of the R of P, which contains a review of this book . . . and an article on Rationalism which should interest you). All this is not to say that these proposals depart from the main theme of *Intellect and Spirit* (*and* their estrangement) because, in the course of all your concrete examens, you will be constantly coming back to this *central* concern. I guess all I'm trying to do is create more from designs (and variations on them)—and to suggest the relationship between them.

(4) The *American Ethos*—and its possible meaning . . . to the life of man in the crises of modern civilization. I have already indicated the general lines of this problem—and the additions will come.

The designs for, and additions—and extensions for all these—I shall send you slowly but surely. Right now you don't need, of course, to worry about them. You have enough to do. You understand, Ed, that I'm not imposing any of this on you. Your present studies may lead you into different directions and further studies of your own choosing and shaping—and that will even be better. I'm trying to be long-range and may only be absurd in the effort.

I might add that as for the books I have furnished to you—all have, in my mind, bearing in one way or another on all these four major problems: (1) History and Culture, (2) Man, (3) Society, the social order (and disorder)—and (4) the *American* context. . . .

Your comments on Dawson show that you see very well the nature of his thought and work. I knew, of course, that, after reading more of him, you would have realizations of his perspective that perhaps the essay on "cycles" did not entirely deliver over. I'm sorry that I never did really get to the point in my . . . last letter: Dawson's thought is essentially *liturgical:* that is, he sees and believes—as well as demonstrates that worship is the heart and the rhythm of existence throughout history—and on every level of culture . . . reaching its highest and holiest point in the Incarnation, history's central fact and event in which every man grows and every age flows . . .

I am forced to write in something of a rush—and so may not be as *crystalline* clear as I would want—especially now with summer school drawing to a close and, with it, a great crowding of duties and activities for me. I'm afraid that you were not wrong in referring to my "mountain of projects." I'm deep in the mountains—and I fear sometimes that I may get lost. I'm being turned inside out. Frankly, I marvel that you are finding it possible to do so much this summer, while bearing with the routines of the navy school.

You're going along fine, as far as I can see. And I hope that you can maintain the strength and energy to keep on going.

Sincerely,
Frank O'Malley

Dear Ed,

Thanks for returning Butterfield's article. I would be glad for you to have it, except that in the course of editing the *Review,* I have always to be looking back into past publications—and there are no other copies of this Butterfield issue available anywhere (except in the libraries). But I am more than glad to have your remarks on the piece. Interesting to me is that your criticisms are not dissimilar from some I voiced when Gurian and I were discussing it for publication. I felt, for instance, that there was a certain *aridity* in it, a lack of spiritual or cosmical spaciousness in developing, as you say, "so momentous a topic." And I agree with you utterly that Butterfield's belief that "the basic problems would not be fundamentally altered, and would certainly not be avoided, supposing what we were confronted with at the moment were all the power of modern Russia in the hands of the Tsars, instead of the regime of the Soviet" is unacceptable. The problem is, in your words, "an *essentially* different one" today. Still, I think that, were Butterfield to read your commentary, he would have no objection to the perspectives which you—with admirably logical organization and analysis reaching always toward and fulfilled in fine synthesis—insist upon. But he would himself, in this vast issue, insist upon the *human* necessity of his own "level" of discussion. I am much impressed by your elaboration of the importance of the *universal* historical objectivity of the *ideological* and *material* causes of world-conflicts as opposed to the subjectivity of "human psychological inadequacies"— the "Hobbesian fear." But I think that you may be over-arbitrary in suggesting—and I hope that I do not misinterpret or mistake your thought that the "Hobbesian fear" remains, in historical reality, a subjective thing. In the actual movement of man through time, it seems to be a *common condition of man*—and so I would say that, as such, it acquires a very real *objective* existence—and this, I am sure, is Butterfield's thought and justification. I do not think, therefore, that he has elevated, as you judge, "a fringing issue" into the central place "properly belonging to the *ideological* or the material" or both. As for myself, I would prefer to use other terms to describe what he intends: such as *perversity*— the *mysterious* and inveterate and unaccountable waywardness of men at all times and on all cultural levels in disrupting the most ideal situations for human existence, and so, creating the terrible, bloody beastly moment of human warfare. There are other aspects of Butterfield's Essay which ought to be consistent, too: notably, the fact that he is speaking here, in a sense, to academic historians—and warning them against complacency and "security" in their establishment of facts and causes—and indicating to them the "puzzle" of history—and the precariousness of conventional historical studies. There is much—maybe there is everything—that the historian cannot account for. And you can realize withal the *temper* of Butterfield's mind in discussing the "tragic element" at all, when he observes at the end of this essay our responsibility in the universities "to enlarge the bounds of understanding; for though our enlarged understanding of the problem will not necessarily prevent war, it may remove some of the unwisdom which has made victory itself so much more disappointing in its results than it otherwise might have been." Very seriously, your own brilliant little essay on the problem presented by Butterfield enlarges the understanding of the problem and helps to remove the unwisdom. I like very much, too, your observations about "false impartiality" in the face of theological conflict: such impartiality is perilous—and more often"perfectionist"—and that is why I find discouraging today the political neutralism of some great French Catholic thinkers, like Gilson, Mauriac and the crowd around *Le Monde*. The implementation of such a view could easily plunge us all to an unimaginable hell: however beset by wickedness, injustice and disorder, we can still live and have the chance to live as *persons* in the non-Soviet society and with the non-Soviet world-view. And I am equally admiring of your emphasis on what you describe as "another aspect of the tragic in human conflict. In the very battle to preserve a higher form of culture and its inner dynamic or world-view, this very dynamic may be destroyed in the heat of battle by its own defenders who betray it to necessity and to the thirst for the external victory."—This is a statement excellent in its succinctness and its understanding. I can't help feeling that in our country today there are frightening *signs* that our own world-view is more than endangered by, as you say, "our very attempt to preserve it." In any event, I shall be interested to have your appraisal of B's Xianity & History whenever you get around to reading it. I do not want in any sense to prejudice your reading—so I shall say nothing of the book now. But I do wonder if it will not alter your present outlook on Butterfield's historicizing. I have commended to you another book of Butterfield's, *The Origins of Modern Science*. It is an attractive and stimulating performance in the history of modern ideas. But I confess that I found it disappointing in this: a lack of sufficient *emphasis* on the true significance of the developments of modern thought; the sad despiritualization of the intellect, the estrangement of intellect and spirit. As for our attitudes toward history, we realize as Christians that the solutions of history lie beyond history: only after history is over will we know really its meaning. And even though we may see the historical legitimacy of the "Hobbesian fear"—or perversity—we also know as Christian—and indeed experience as Xtian, in the events of all real, human, historical existence, another deeper, vaster quality in the life of man. . . .

24 August, 1952

Dear Ed,

Far from being "fumbling," your comments on von Hildebrand and Cochrane are truly incisive—and altogether excellent. In describing von Hildebrand's notion of the *classical* in reference to the liturgy, you make a remarkably cogent reduction of the whole book. And I like the way you put your experience—so far—of Cochrane's *Christianity and Classical Culture* into the focus of your reflections on von Hildebrand. It is important—and certainly a sign of genuine maturity of mind—to be able to see how one experience—or as in this instance how one book, specifically the ideas of one book—bear upon and illuminate another. I appreciate your excitement over von Hildebrand's *Liturgy and Personality* (and I think, too, that you can now realize perhaps even more vividly the depth and direction of his thoughts on the nature of the Catholic university). Quite a few students in the past—and a number last year—have told me that they considered *Liturgy and Personality* to be even more potent a revelation than Guardini's *The Church and the Catholic and the Spirit of the Liturgy*. And I noted that some of the graduate students (particularly one priest, a seminary professor) I had this summer seemed more attracted to this work than to Guardini's. In the long run, though, from my experience it is evident that Guardini wears better. The sad thing, however, is that both books have been out of print for ages. My own copy of *Liturgy and Personality* is broken down to pieces. To me the central chapter of this most central book is the one on "The Spirit of Reverence in the Liturgy." I think I made something of this chapter during the first semester—last year—of Modern Catholic Writers, although everything in the book is appealing. Von Hildebrand's recognition that the *classical* man—that is, *the personality*—will be free from one-sidedness is not different from Guardini's. Both men see that what will make us *classical,* that is men of centre rather than *excentric* men or average men (bourgeois, exploitative, irreverent, idolatrous, types you brilliantly describe in your essay "The Idolatry of Economy"), what will make us personalities is living by the *logos*—and it is through the liturgy that we become fully aware of the power and the force and the strength given to our lives by our adherence to the Divine Word. The *classical* man (à la von Hildebrand) or the personality knows how to join the worlds—the inner and the outer, the world of spirit and the world of action, the visible and the invisible worlds or, as you might say, the human and the superhuman worlds—because he has a key (the Christian fact or the Incarnational Fact) and then, full of true life and light within himself, he can appreciate deeply the reality, the complexity and the mystery of everything beyond himself: man, nature, civilization, experiences, to use Hopkins's perfect terms, the *instress* of *inscape* and knows by and through all things the beauty and splendor of Our Lord. Thus the writer, the thinker, the artist, will—if he be *classical*—saved from academicism or aestheticism: the plagues of mankind. He will be incapable—as are too many intellectuals, trapped in their horribly egoistic sufficiency—of committing with almost every thought brutal acts of aggression (as Pieper might put it) against existence. He will be incapable—as are too many artists—of generating only the hot and/or cold vapors of their own confused, and even neurotic, subjectivities.

The *classical* mind, the Personality, too, will be able to achieve a genuine *conversation,* having the profound character of *discretio:* it will be his way never to churn up all that is, leaving it shot and scattered and flying (as is the way of many revolutionaries, activists and destructionists), but instead to see all that is in its total meaning, in its wholeness, in its unity, and to direct it or at least, quietly and carefully and protectively, to allow it to unfold towards its completeness, to pass, in a way, from its *necessary* wholeness through the equally necessary dispersions of life back again into its wholeness (and this, Ed, you will understand, is no lapse into Hegelianism). To the *classical* man or the personality, for sure, "everything that happens is something to be adored." Newman, I have often thought, has shown himself to have the *classical* view (in von Hildebrand's sense)—wonderfully in his sermons—and a few years ago an N.D. senior did a great job in showing (without at all forcing the note) how von Hildebrand's canons for classicism applied acutely to Newman's personality and thought. I think, too, that the Christian existentialists (like Kierkegaard, Theodor Haecker, Gabriel Marcel) and the Christian personalists (like Emmanuel Mounier, Maritain, and Berdyaev) as well as the Christian poets (like Hopkins, Claudel and Peguy) and the Christian novelists (like Undset, Bernanos, Ramuz and Williams) have the profoundly *classical* view of existence. In fact, Mounier in a lately published posthumous statement on *personalism* has sharply indicated what it means to live by a *centre* and within a *centre* (here the *logos,* the *word*). Such living makes for a genuine "interiority" and "objectivity." In a passage which I know you will find very striking, he says (and I quote at length):

> Personal existence is . . . always in dispute between a movement of exteriorization and a movement of interiorization, both of which are essential to it, and by either of these it may become encysted, or alternatively, dissipated.
>
> We have already alluded to the misery of the person who has become objectified. It is from this torpor, or even death in objectivity, that the great personalist movements come to awaken us. We are often warned against the danger of becoming shut up in ourselves and it is very real. Of the majority of men, however, and of a great part of our lives, thronged as they are with worldly solicitations,

the truer description is that of Valery [the important modern French poet]: "We are shut up *outside* ourselves." From that kind of imprisonment nothing but contemplation can deliver us.

But within ourselves too, we encounter the same dangers both of dissipation and sclerosis, for they pursue us into our retreat. Excessive rumination dissipates us, too much interiorization leads to oversubtlety, and too much self-solicitude, however spiritual, can engender an egocentricity that grows like a psychic cancer. The cultivation of a certain image of the self in order to preserve and protect it, may then come to fill the entire horizon of life. This may have originated in a spoiled and over-sheltered childhood; as the psychologists say, the "acquisitive" tendencies have overcome the "oblative," so that adaptation to others and to reality have been prejudiced from infancy. The usual outcome is a life that is never sufficiently involved in virile labour and communal discipline: perhaps the greatest evils of our epoch are those of the uprooted and the unoccupied. Ever since the 15th century Western man has been slipping slowly down this slope: every value has been devalued to please the groundlings in a theatre of Narcissus, where even the roles of sanctity and heroism are played by glory and "success," that of spiritual force by "toughness"; where love is debased to eroticism, intelligence to intellectualism, reason to cunning, meditation to introspection, and the passion for truth reduced to the shallowest "sincerities." It is high time, therefore, to remind the subject that he will never re-discover and strengthen himself without the mediation of the objective: *he must come out of his inwardness if he is to keep his soul alive....* there is a true instinct of exteriorization: ... *the person is, indeed, an inside in need of an outside* [italics mine in this instance]; and the very word "exist" indicates by its prefix that "to be" is to go out, to express oneself. It is this primordial motive which, in an active form, moves us to exteriorize our feelings in mimicry or in speech, to inflict the imprint of our action upon visible works and to intervene in the affairs of the world and of other people. All the dimensions of the person are mutually sustaining and constitutive. The pressure of nature upon us and the labours by which we respond to it, are not merely factors making for productivity; they are also forces disruptive of egocentricity, and for that reason they are cultural and spiritual forces, quite as important as power or riches and doubtless more so. We must not, then, undervalue the external life: without it the inner life tends to insanity, as surely as the outer life becomes chaotic without interiorization. [E. Mounier, *Personalism* (1952), pp. 42–44]

And now the point: it is in living in the liturgy, by the *logos* that we conjoin the external life and the inner life (although Mounier does not draw this out), that we become personalities. That is to say, in the liturgy, by the *logos* we live at the centre of ourselves—and of all existence—and we are not alienated from or horrified by existence nor is existence (man, nature, civilization) alienated—or brutalized or exploited or spoiled—by us.

The term *classic* has always, of course, meant when properly understood the *centric* or the *central*—and in the best minds and works of antiquity (e.g., Plato, Aristotle, Virgil) there was a proper interiorization and a meditative search for true forms in the objective world. (Plato does not actually reject the world—only its deformation; he sought, I believe, even as Soloviev, close on our own time, to bridge the gap between the inner and the outer worlds.) I think, too, that in the authentically *classic* mind (which was, for the most part, the Greek mind), there was a sense of *powerlessness,* at least a consciousness that the ascent of being ended finally in what could not be precisely described with firm intellectual clarity; and the Greeks could speak—and not just with patronizing, familiar anthropomorphizing terms—of the gods and of God (although not—since they couldn't—with the Christian awe and self-surrender best expressed in the Christian act of worship). But the "godliness" of the Greeks was inadequate for them to have, as with us in the Christian ages, a consciousness of the unique meaning and mystery and destiny of *each* and *every* living person. It was the Romans who created a *pseudo-classical* world-view—a narrowing of the Greek sense of form into formula. Speaking broadly, it was the Romans (like the Caesars and, on the artistic level, like Horace and Quintilian) who worked away from *centre* towards exteriorization of the most naked kind, towards externalization, towards the *outside* entirely. The instinct— and the action—of the Roman world was inveterately towards the BIG and the PUBLIC and the POWERFUL. And Cochrane is utterly right in speaking of Roman culture—that is, a *pseudo-classicism,* as representing "the apotheosis of power." There were exceptions, of course, notably the magnificent exception of Virgil (about whom Theodor Haecker has written marvelously in *Virgil, Father of the West* and also Herman Broch in an extraordinary novel, a book of love, called *The Death of Virgil*), who possessed deeply the character of *pietas* (or *reverence*), who had a poignant sense of the limits of the world or rather a mystic intimation that the closed world would open up, who had the *anima naturaliter Christiana,* who could, on the power-world, write the phrases of incomparable beauty and wonder and sorrow: "Sunt lacrimae rerum et mentem mortalia tangunt." The words, *anima naturaliter Christiana,* could be, I think, applied to the greatest of the Greeks. But it was not until Christ, the *logos,* that the centre of life—the truly classic fulfillment of all the possibilities (and the realization, too, of all the "impossibilities") of man and of history—became shiningly clear. Equally clear became, as you note, the sadness of the efforts of the ancients to search for philosopher-kings and to set up super-men. Christianity makes forever clear the pathos of any particular man's effort to live unto himself, of any particular society's confidence in living unto itself. At the same time we are aware, as you so well say, of the fact that, in the Christian vision, "there is no destruction of the hope for superhuman existence" and that "the source of this existence is not found in non-existent powers of intellect and will but in the free gift of the spirit."

Appropriately for the rumination of this letter, there is a passage in the Epistle of today's Mass (the 2nd Epistle of St. Paul to the Corinthians, 3:4–9), which perfectly expresses the *classical* attitude in the Christian context (as elaborated by von Hildebrand):

> Brethren, such confidence have we through Christ
> towards God: not that we are sufficient to think any-
> thing of ourselves, as of ourselves: but our sufficiency
> is from God, Who also hath made us fit ministers of
> the New Testament, not in the letter but in the Spirit:
> for the letter killeth, but the Spirit quickeneth.

In addition—and interestingly enough—this is also the feast
of St. Bartholomew, the Apostle, and in the Epistle for this
feast (the 1st Epistle of St. Paul to the Corinthians, 12:27–
31), it is declared that the prime gift of the Holy Spirit is
that of the apostolate:

> Brethren: ye are the body of Christ, and members
> of member. And God indeed hath set some in the
> Church, first Apostles. . . .

Putting these sublime texts together, we are told by St. Paul
that when we have become authentic personalities (*classical*
men), that is when we have "our sufficiency from God" and
are quickened by the Spirit (and so made "zealous for the
better gifts"), then we are endowed to confront with courage
and to give form to the world.

So, Ed, ends my lecture for this occasion. And you can
be the calm judge of whether I have contributed anything at
all to the solid, pointed goodness of your own reflections,
which I honestly admire very much. These pages, anyway,
stand as my extensions and you will, I know, have the patience
to bear with them. As for the total problem of the classical
world-view or views (in the customary sense) I propose to
detail it later. When I get back to school in September, I'm
going to send on to you Mounier's *Personalism,* from which
I made the lavish citation in this letter. The book has just—
that is to say, June—been published in this country and I
have not completed reading it. You may remember that I
mentioned and cited Mounier (as well as Maritain, Berdyaev,
von Hildebrand, et alii) when I was discussing *personalism*
during those late afternoon lectures in the spring. But this
newly available book of his can be, I believe, very valuable
for a lot of my intentions; in fact, it will be given major
emphasis during the first semester of Modern Catholic Writers this coming school year. For impressing the relevance of

personalism as the salvaging philosophy for us all, Mounier's work will be more useful than Maritain's. Mounier touches, in a direct and graphic way, many of the themes around which my courses revolve: ART, CULTURE, VOCATION, EDUCATION, the meanings of History, Freedom, Suffering, Evil, etc. And I think that while you will find the whole book full of comforting—and exciting—insights, you will be especially interested in the section on "Personalism and the Revolution of the Twentieth Century," in which he speaks of "the unique work of the Church, the community of Christians in the Christ, *mingled among all men in the secular work*." It is a small volume but you—and others who read it—will be stimulated to further development and embodiment and personalization of what Mounier sketches. For you, too, it may constitute another *forming* or *holding* or *directive* book. Mounier is no perfectionist, no machine-breaker; he urges us to face our world as it is, to be in truth and deed Christians in Civilization. . . . [12]

After the war Edward Goerner went to the University of Chicago and completed a PhD, then taught at Yale before returning to Notre Dame for a faculty appointment. He is now Professor of Government and International Studies there.

Living Out His Days

In Frank O'Malley's life at Notre Dame there was ample time for visions and revisions, for public speaking, and even for a few hilarious incongruities, such as the teacher becoming political ward heeler. He changed his stand regarding graduate study during the late 1940s and promptly became the coordinator of Notre Dame's participation in the Woodrow Wilson Fellowship program. He was so successful in this that 127 Notre Dame students were named Woodrow Wilson Fellows during the 1945–67 period, a number far out of proportion to the size of the institution. In 1958 he was Notre Dame's representative to a Fulbright conference on higher education at Allerton Park, Illinois. For may years he was also a member of the Danforth Fellowship selection committee for the midwest region which held its meetings and interviews at Northwestern University.[13]

O'Malley always followed the careers of his students with great interest, and one student whose fame and success in later years brought his teacher deep satisfaction was Ed O'Connor, the author of *The Last Hurrah* and *The Edge of Sadness.* As O'Connor's biographer writes:

> One teacher, Frank O'Malley, had a special influence on O'Connor: "the greatest single help for me in college." As a student in O'Malley's freshman course in composition, O'Connor was steered away from a journalism major in favor of English. Later, O'Connor took O'Malley's "Modern Catholic Writers" course, a distinguished series of lectures or meditations about the relation of literature and faith. Long famous at Notre Dame as a course which attracted crowds of drop-in auditors, O'Malley's lectures had a widespread influence on scores of students who have subsequently been active on all levels of writing and editorial work. A feature story in *Time* of February 9, 1962, for example, commented about this course: "Perhaps no one else has better conveyed that sense [of a Christian view of man] to Notre Dame students than witty, incisive English Professor Frank O'Malley, 28 years on the faculty and the University's most inspiring undergraduate teacher. O'Malley plumbs life's most basic emotions, using Charles Peguy to examine the virtue of hope, Claudel to plumb suffering, Kierkegaard to emphasize the shallowness of religion without love. When he reaches students, O'Malley often changes their lives, teaching them to love learning and learn love" (p. 54). The friendship between O'Connor and O'Malley endured. In later years, O'Connor as an alumnus was not one to attend football games or local alumni meetings, but every year for over a decade O'Connor returned to Notre Dame for a week or so to visit O'Malley, to read manuscripts to him, and to lecture in his course. In 1962, the prize-winning book, *The Edge of Sadness,* was dedicated to Frank O'Malley.[14]

When O'Connor died of a massive stroke in 1968 O'Malley went to Boston for his wake and funeral.

O'Malley's own attitude toward football at Notre Dame seemed to be one of somewhat detached amusement and tolerance. Let those who were interested in it have it.

One of his means of keeping contact with his former students for a number of years was an annual Christmas poem printed on a card. The following examples survive:

> Let the Christbrand burst,
> Let the Christbrand blazon.
> Dartle whitely under the hearth-fire,
> Unwind the wind, turn the thunderer,
> And never, never thinning,
> Forfend fear.
> Flare up smartly, fix, flex, bless, inspire,
> Instar the time, sear the sorcerer,
> And never, never sparing,
> Save all year.
> Let the Christbrand burst,
> Let the Christbrand blazon.

THE SAVIOUR

Today adore,
Return the raging earth to Him.
And once more,
He will bless the hard heights of the mountains,
He will give warmth to the cold depths of men.

  The upheaving sea is His
  And the dark sky descending.

  The drained land is His
  And the dry trees trembling.

  The gray faces are His
  And the cruel hands crushing.

  The storming generations are His
  And the wild hearts breaking.

Today adore,
Return the raging earth to Him.
And once more,
He will bless the hard heights of the mountains,
He will give warmth to the cold depths of men.[15]

The King of Heaven

In the windows you may see no light,
At the doors there may be no crowding,
In the voices heard no hint of Him,
No sound of The Name.
But He will come to the house
Through a thousand earth-fed fires,
Crashing a thousand chains.
He will find His way to the city,
And the streets will be bright with His Face,
And the lands loud with His Voice.
Then sleep will not break again or breath tear,
Or the multitudes mourn from room to room,
From tower to tower of flags aflame or falling.
He will come,
And within the eyes of the lonely women
By shaken pillars and shattered walls
Their souls will speak:
"Now does our sorrow seem old
For He is here and the enemy near no longer."[16]

Among his papers there is also an undated longhand draft of a statement apparently used for some campus celebration during the Christmas season. It illustrates, again, his joy in making the religious focus:

The Concept of Christmas

Paging through a weekly publication that makes an enormous impress upon our American time I came yesterday upon an advertisement, gothically illustrated with the magi. The advertisement, sponsored most unobtrusively by the Bemis Brothers Bag Co., contains nothing more than these words: "Thanks for Christmas . . . Because it brings brightness to young eyes and laughter to young hearts . . . it gives pleasure to those who receive, and joy to those fortunate enough to give . . . it brings home closer to those far away . . . it comes as a happy benediction to . . . we trust . . . a well-lived year . . . it retells the Greatest Story Ever Told. Thanks for Christmas." The ad did not elaborate upon the real reason for our saying "Thanks for Christmas"; nor did it indicate the nature of the "Greatest Story Ever Told." The mere fact of its appearance, however, suggests that, no matter how commercialized, the fact of Christmas does make a vast difference to us. Perhaps it is a feast now thoroughly hollowed out for most Americans, its deepest meaning lost in wild street decorations, its absolutely necessary identification with Christ distorted and indeed obliterated in department store window-displays of silly, gyrating Santa Clauses around which the crowds—in a senseless and sentimental—if not entirely—weird perversion of the true act of Christian worship—gather and ogle and adulate.

Be all this as it may, the season and the movement of Christmas do alter the somewhat too-determined course of our lives. Certainly it is a time when we do change, show exceptional charity, extend greetings to strangers—no less than to friends and even enemies, look rather less indifferently into the faces of those whom we are inclined to rush by in the remorseless pursuit of our business, of our individual activity. The mass-movement slackens and some dim awareness of our community—one man, one mind, one spirit, one towards another—renews itself. At Christmas, we are, in a way, restored to one another. This is, surely, an immense, a marvelous "benediction" and "brightness" and a "joy"! And this "benediction" comes because, no matter how desperately or miserably or powerfully involved in the day-laboring of the world, we have as a people retained—and seem to desire to assert—our consciousness of the Incarnational Fact—the Fact of God's descent into history and society—after whom and, in truth—before whom, every man grows and every age flows in His Great Body.

The words of the advertisement I cited at the beginning are an odd and casual and nationally publicized echo—and without intending to be, a reaffirmation—right in the intense midst of the warring complexities and the violent pressures of existence in a distraught mid-twentieth century America—of the utterance that has been described as "the most sublime passage that ever has been or ever will be written, bringing together the eternal act and the temporal act, the Godhead, creation, mankind and showing us their significance." This is the sublime utterance from St. John's Gospel with which every day at Mass you are familiar: "In the beginning was the Word, and the Word was with God; and the Word was God. . . . All things were made through Him. . . . In Him was life, and the life was the light of men. . . . And the Word was made flesh, and dwelt among us. And we saw his glory— glory as of the Only-begotten of the Father—full of grace and of truth."

Since the moment of the Word, the eternal moment that is every moment, every day since the birth of Christ, as the magnificent priest-scholar of our age, Don Luigi Sturzo, has descried, since "the development of His religion and the growth of a Christian civilization, there have been many peoples who, like those before Christ, have had only a glimmer of the divine idea in the world; not to speak of those who, though living in a Christian environment, no longer believe in God. Yet insofar as they sincerely aspire to reform and redemption, they too enter into the orbit of the history of the Incarnation, not only as potentially redeemed but as bearing witness to the necessity for a divine intervention that will realize in mankind the truth that was "made flesh," so that men may see the "glory of the Only-begotten of the Father." This is, undoubtedly, why, out of the most unexpected mouths speaking in the most unexpected places, there come the "Thanks for Christmas" and the acknowledgment of the Word as "the greatest story ever told."

At Notre Dame, of course, it is expected that we, as Christian students and teachers, shall be conscious, in all our works and thoughts, of the Word, Who is the Child of Christmas, that we shall be the daily embodiment of a statement of Karl Adam which reads: "Just as breathing and feeling and thinking are functions of our natural being, so living in Christ is a function of our Christian being." At Notre Dame, too, we are acutely aware of God's mother as the purveyor of His graces, our spiritual mother in whom we breathe and grow— growing always in the only vital sense of growth—of becoming "more Christ and baffling death" (Hopkins). For us, the members of the City of Our Lady, who would express our "Thanks for Christmas," its joy, its benediction, there is intimate and wonderful import in the moving Christmas

hymn to the Church [by Gertrude von Le Fort] in which the
voice of the Church majestically yet tenderly speaks:

> Little child out of Eternity, now will I sing to
>   thy mother! The song shall be fair as dawn-
>   tinted snow.
> Rejoice Mary Virgin, daughter of my earth,
>   sister of my soul, rejoice, O joy of my joy![17]

There were times when Notre Dame's administration honored
Frank O'Malley, perhaps none greater than when they invited him
to give the commencement address for the Summer Commencement on July 31, 1956. He said then:

> I am speaking primarily to the graduates of this summer
> day, assembled for what I can only assume to be your brief
> and inevitably ceremonious last lecture, for which I have
> chosen the following text: "the old question which traversed
> the sky of the soul perpetually, the vast, the general question,
> stood over her, paused over her, darkened over her. What is
> the meaning of life? That was all, a simple question; one
> that tended to close in one with the years."
>
> The woman who wrote those lines lived in the midst of
> the terrible experiences suffered by the British during the first
> phases of the second World War. She felt that all the loveliness
> she had ever known had been spoiled. As the days of war
> accumulated, she grew increasingly tired, tired of struggling
> and failing to maintain the life and the beauty that the bombs
> would obliterate. She found that she who had spoken so much
> and so wonderfully could hardly speak at all any more. This
> woman's way to freedom had been through her power to
> create in art and poetry. But she found that she could no
> longer create. Her life had had its chief meaning in art and
> poetry, and these, in the turmoil, in the chaos, in the turning-
> point of history, she could exercise no more. The doom of
> the world besieged her, pounded at her, crushed her, and
> silenced her. Relentlessly, the moment came when she wrote
> to her husband: "I have a feeling that I shall go mad and
> cannot go on any longer in these terrible times. I hear voices
> and cannot concentrate on my work. I have fought against

it but cannot fight any longer." She went out of her house then and over the downs to the river. She could bear no longer the pressure of the age, the need of lies and phrases. Now she would dissolve herself, her tormented mind and heart in the river of death. She sank then into the irrevocable darkness, the stillness, the deepness.

This was life's end for an artist, the death of one of the most sensitive modern women: Virginia Woolf. What was the meaning of life to be? It was not to be even in what she had thought it to be, in art and poetry, but in dissolution. What is the significance of her life and of her last act?

This: Virginia Woolf was a modern person, a twentieth-century person. It may be said that she was an exceptional person, one of the finest contemporary English novelists, one of the subtlest and tenderest talents and imaginations; and it may be said that from such a superior and rare genius would come exceptional, even extravagant action. In moments of crisis, the average person does not become so utterly wrought, so catastrophically distracted and deranged. A personality, however, like that of Virginia Woolf did not dwell or develop in a vacuum. She came out of a life and a people and lived within a particular culture, within some pattern of human existence. And her environs must have some responsibility for her, must be able to give some accounting of her, some clues to the turbulence of soul that finally defeated and doomed her. She was not so alone as she thought. Many in these generations have experienced her kind of sorrow and suffering; they have not always been able to express it so felicitously, and perhaps because they were not so exhaustively susceptible to changes in the life about them as she was, they would not plunge into the river of death, triumphed over by the civilization that had bred them. The mind and the experience of Virginia Woolf represent, of course, a pitch-point of the experience of the modern world, of many people of the twentieth century, searching for a limited amount of peace and beauty and order and rest, and not finding a vestige of these.

The sensitive, really conscious modern mind often suffers from a weakening distractedness. The essence of its cosmic discontent lies in the incompetence of the mind to reconcile a personal intellectual or aesthetic culture with a huge, complex technological civilization, constructed without consideration or design, and so creative of destruction. The sensitive mind is unable to reconcile its own organic, conscious life with mechanical organization. The problem of the reconciliation of personal culture and modern mass civilization is probably the most central and most difficult facing those who are responsible in any way for the education of modern people. Our multitudinous modern civilization tends to make human life and action less and less free, less and less sure, more and more divided and disconcerted. The mind aspires to be freed in unity, to be truly self-possessed, but instead it seems today to be sometimes losing its very identity. A subjective personal culture trying to reweave into a new design the personality that civilization has unraveled into a thousand threads is not able usually to achieve this synthesis. Yet almost every nation and every decade reveal persons of thought and talent, like Virginia Woolf, affirming the ideal of self-possession in some cult: in aestheticism, in a secular humanism, in the rationale of science, in Marxism or Freudianism, in existentialism, in something that will compensate for the failures, the misfortunes, the stupidities, the distortions.

But art and poetry alone, as the career of Virginia Woolf indicates, cannot be the firm basis of a true spiritual culture, equipping a person to confront the problems of modern civilization, providing him with a mirror into which he can look on occasion and grasp his wholeness, and so enabling him to regather into a unity the self that has been scattered. This true spiritual culture and its compensations our age and our education do not commonly seem to provide. The minds that grope among the developments and within the progress of the age have found it harder and harder to compose their right and true personalities. They look for a faith, they look for spiritual self-possession, and not finding it in the fury and the chaos some of them in the most abandoned and unutterable confusion are tempted to resolve the agony of disorder and self-distrust in self-destruction.

Such an abysmal surrender to oneself and to time is not the way only of women. They really are not weaker than men, but they are sometimes more responsive to pressure.

They are often emotionally and imaginatively more acute than men, less phlegmatic in the moment of danger. They register more completely, more overwhelmingly. I think that one may say of them that they are more *barometric,* readily and quickly marking changes and fluctuations. In their lives and their ways can be found a superior instruction in and a superior revelation of the temper of the times and the meaning of the times.

This is certainly a century of self-destruction, a century of ruin and revolt, a turning-point in civilization. Note, according to a last-week headline, that 1956 will descend into history as the year of nuclear blasts. But this century has also been an age in which, despite war and revolution and conceivably because of these derangements, those who are more responsible and responsive than their fellow-men have been engaged in a gigantic search for the highest values. Serious thinkers and artists of every sort have been engaged in a search for the best values: religious, philosophical, political, and social. And only a few comparatively have found real, imperishable values. They are those men and women who have not despaired when they have been confronted by the confusion of the day. Their careers provide more encouraging indicators than does that of Virginia Woolf. They have been graced so that they could save themselves from the melancholy and the sickness of their triumphant civilization; they have encountered the effective agents and agencies of grace in the world. And one of these, surely, is Raïssa Maritain, herself a sensitive poet and critic who with her great husband Jacques Maritain—the real type of Catholic thinker in and for the modern world—found the meaning of life, the desired peace and order and beauty and self-possession, in a true and adequate faith within the life of the Church. The Maritains are fortunate among those who, searching for an ultimate to strengthen themselves and their world, react against their education and their routine of existence. Raïssa and Jacques Maritain happily found that the ultimate alleviation of the unsettled self was not to be found in self-destruction, although for a moment this did come before them as a prospect, as an escape from the distress of modern culture.

In their hunting for a way out of this distress, the youthful Raïssa and Jacques Maritain encountered in the spiritual underworld of the times prophets and teachers and friends and influences who seem never to have entered the universe of people like Virginia Woolf and who gave the young Maritains powerful directions in their quest for the meaning of life. Thus at the critical time when existence filled them with desperation the Maritains decided not to reject existence but, in Raïssa Maritain's words, "to extend existence credit, in the hope that it would reveal new values to us, values which could give a meaning to life." They entrusted themselves to the Church, where they would find God and man and themselves. They would hear the call of the saints, not the call of "the lost sea voices," of "the strong brown god" of the river. They would experience not the waters of death but the waters of life in Baptism. As Raïssa Maritain records it, there descended upon them an immense peace: "There was only the infinite answer of God. The Church kept her promises." Yes, to the "vast, the general question, what is the meaning of life," there was only the infinite answer of God. For Raïssa Maritain "the reasonings of the philosophers and the scientists could not achieve the splendid realism of the words of the Church." Now she could live in and by substantial poetry, not by the lies and phrases that have afflicted us and that are still capable of driving men into madness.

Virginia Woolf and Raïssa Maritain, sensitive, impressible women each, lived as we are all still living at a changing point in history. They were disturbed by the disasters they witnessed; and facing them was chaos and death or the Church and life, for this is the choice of this century as of every century. But in the heart of Raïssa Maritain there was hope as well as melancholy. She would not dissolve herself with the dissolution of this our world, for she and her husband had resolved the disharmony between their intellectual culture and the life of civilization within the life of the Church. She now had the Christian sense of the significance of human suffering: "When nameless sufferings have purified us, then only can the breath of life which is able to renew the face of the earth blow once again upon our misfortunes and our patience." In the moment of crisis, one must abandon

oneself not to dissolution, but to Providence; one must put
all one's care in God and thus be made free of the world.
Raïssa Maritain knew and asserted that those who arrive at
this blessed state of independence will gaily bear their cross
and faithfully follow the Lord; they will live in His presence,
they will always find Him in the depths of themselves and
will adhere with all their souls to Him Who is above all
thought and Who wished to transform us into Himself by
love. For men in time this is then the meaning of life; in
fact, the very meaning of earthly life is to be found in that
which at first sight seems to empty earthly life of all significance: the eternal and supernatural life towards which the
whole universe and all the centuries march.

The supernatural view, the Christian view of creation and
man and society would be, we know, the reanimating, peace-
bringing, integrating view for all those searching today. Its
universal acceptance would mean the marvelous renewal of
our civilization. But we who do accept the faith with its
theology and philosophy cannot expect this renewal too soon.
We must also make sure that we do not ourselves obstruct
its coming to pass. Since we have the truth, we must not be
afraid to speak it. And speaking the truth, we must not allow
the Catholic creed to degenerate in our mouths into a creed-
ism, becoming then just another ism warring with all the
other isms. We must not fail to realize that the Church is a
complete way of life, the very rhythm of existence, with an
eternal integrity that will permit her to survive not only Communism but whatever evils may rise following the disap-
pearance of the Communists, for it is a fact that the Church
prays over all tombs.

We should also be courageous enough to recognize our
own weaknesses as members of the Church, our own lamentable neglect of our graces, our own mediocre employment
of the Christian life. And we must be sympathetic to those
who are more confused, more desperately confused than ourselves. We must never be complacent or cruel. We must be
sympathetic not only to persons who affirm the values we
deem worthy but we must also be sympathetic to those who,
in part or whole, wrench or ignore our values. We must be
ready to understand always the worth of and even the neces-

sity for the people, as we say, of "dimmer understanding." We shall be looking for the minds of the type of Virginia Woolf who walked into the river of death; we shall recognize their complexity and bewilderment and sensitivity, remembering that by their own admission the Maritains were themselves saved from death by sympathy and understanding, and now they are the agents of grace who save others from despair.

The questions that ring in our minds are those that naturally cannot be answered now. Will the world rediscover and reestablish a genuine culture, uniting the temporal and the eternal? Will the people of this century be able finally to mark out, to trace a spiritual community beneath the flash and the flutter, the goring and the ganging and the smashing of modern men and modern existence? In our crowds, in our streets, what will be found to be final? Today, the world is immersed in a flux of errors, and the Catholic mind cannot by any proud opinions or pious slogans transcend them or overwhelm them. But at least the Catholic mind can be hopeful that every beautiful thing will not be destroyed, can be confident that joy and justice and fidelity and redemption and charity have not departed forever out of the world. The constructiveness of the Catholic in every field of action will lie in great measure in his hopefulness that value and virtue and love can be reasserted in the world, in the suffering universe of men. He will pray—and strengthened by his recollection of the Scriptural words, "And being in an agony and his sweat falling like drops of blood to the ground, He prayed still more earnestly"—he will work, he will create, he will strive, he will endure. Neither darkness nor pain shall vanquish him. He will have courage, the courage to keep his soul composed, his mind free in the face of danger. He will feel himself to be stronger than the death he does not fear. He will know what the wretched ones, trembling with fear, can never understand: mortality leads to immortality.

These realizations ought to be more firmly and powerfully yours because you have come here to this place of Notre Dame, this great and dominant Catholic university of the United States, a place concerned through all the years with integrating a true faith and a true philosophy with the life of culture. In your time here, you must have become better aware of the composition of life, of the nature of true primacy. You must have considered here and found here the answer to "the old question which traverses the sky of the soul perpetually, the vast, the general question, what is the meaning of life?" If you are convinced of your answer, you will not be deluded by the lies and phrases; you will be able to resist the pressure of the age. Possessed as you should be of a true spiritual culture, you will not be too much disconcerted or ravaged by contemporary civilization; you will not feel yourselves prisoners of life, scratching on the walls of your cells; you will not succumb to the sorrows of the savage world. Instead, you will save yourselves and save all those who encounter you in your various works and ways and vocations.

This saving patience of your achievement as religious and laymen, as teachers and scholars, and as citizens of the world altogether may go unheralded and unpublicized. Occasionally you may even think of yourselves as failures because of your lack of discernible fame and demonstrable prosperity. But genuine leadership in society is actually a quiet force, a spiritual force and presence; and the right movement of history and earthly progress is maintained more by the obscure decisions and private actions of ordinary men and women than by those personalities regularly spotlighted in the pageantry of public acclaim. For example: nothing should more stir and comfort the heart of the American Catholic than the sight of the largely uncelebrated though noble and sacrificing womanhood of our nuns. Daily they uphold, with holy serenity and humble energy, the extraordinary edifice of the Church in this country. At least the Lord knows that they shall have their infinite justification and their infinite glory.

Finally, I am honored to speak for all my colleagues in offering to you, the latest bachelors, masters and doctors of Notre Dame, our warm congratulations as well as our prayerful confidence that time will never trap you or the world triumph over you. We your teachers and your friends hope that you will be happy. We hope that you will be happy forever. But we ask you to remember that the happiness of human existence is sometimes sorrow and suffering borne for love.[18]

Clearly, these remarks were intended for an audience largely made up of the nuns who used to attend the Notre Dame summer sessions in such great numbers. The spirit and the tone of the words also borrowed a good bit from a page in his papers that must have been his valedictory to some class: "With confidence, I shall remember. And I hope that you will remember at least my very last words which I utter with all my heart out of my unworthiness and in the face of your presences which I have ever found so beautiful, human and indeed holy. I dare to say: I hope that time will never trap you or the world triumph over you. I hope that you will be happy, I hope that you will be happy forever. But I would ask you to reflect that the happiness of human existence is ofttimes sorrow and suffering borne for love. And loves still brood over our bent world. Love to you, my students, joy to you, my fellow creatures. Peace to you, my friends. Blessings."[19]

In 1972 for the first time the Notre Dame administration invited the student body to nominate one of the recipients of the honorary degrees at its June commencement. To the amazement of a good many people, they nominated Frank O'Malley. The degree of Doctor of Laws, *honoris causa,* was conferred on

a teacher. He came to Notre Dame, as a young man, to learn. And he stayed to teach. Since 1933, he has been a faculty member in Notre Dame's Department of English. Since 1938, he has been Managing Editor and later Associate Editor of Notre Dame's *Review of Politics.*

His world is the word: the word of poetry, and of all imaginative literature; the political word, to set society aright; the word of faith, in the liturgy, in prayer, in inspiration. He has spoken his words to generations of students. His words, and the person who spoke them, changed lives by speaking to minds and to spirits. He speaks his words in his poems, in his articles, in his conversations, and in his classroom. No one who heard him has remained untouched. He lives many lives in many students all over the world, students who call themselves his boys, and who recognize him as father, as teacher.

Notre Dame is a place with a sense of place. It is that because, to use one of his own phrases, "the blood of many men is in its bricks."[20]

O'Malley's reputation for having a way with words also brought him many invitations on the Notre Dame campus to be the spokesman for the administration and faculty on the occasion of retirements or anniversaries, such as the fifteenth anniversary of Father Hesburgh's becoming president of the university, or on the retirement of his old friend, Jim Armstrong, as director of the university's Alumni Office. On the latter occasion he read at the Academic Awards Banquet of June 10, 1967, a paper that he had entitled, "A Letter to Jim Armstrong."

None of us would be here tonight if it were not for the fact that 125 years ago a young French priest went into the Indiana wilderness and founded a school which, extending itself and its influence across the entire land and the world, would ultimately join our lives and our destinies. Naturally the past four decades at Notre Dame have been complicated, changing, struggling, moving, heading for the future. And I can speak for the faculty (and especially alumni faculty here and elsewhere) in saying that Notre Dame alumni have been fortunate in having during these times Jim Armstrong as a central interpreter and communicator of the university's life and happenings. You are a man, Jim, whose heart and mind have always been warmly open to students, faculty, and alumni alike. You have looked out upon this place and its purposes and its confusions with a true humor, that is, a nice and delicate consciousness of human foibles. Yours is a saving and generous humor, the sort that alleviates wounds and permits our life to go on, rather than afflicting and frustrating it. You know, quietly and gently, that our present prepares for a future bright, radiant with expectations, full of sights and events that have never been known, bearing hopes for new realizations, new greatness in teaching, research, and service to humanity—ranging with marvelous liberty through the universe, fulfilling always the object of the Church in establishing universities, which is, as that imperial intellect Newman describes it, "to reunite things which were in the beginning joined together by God and have been put asunder by man." You have, Jim, used your office and its agents and its publications as well as your journeyings handsomely to make us aware of our actualities and our possibilities. For this we are grateful.

Regardless of developments, you discern that the people of Notre Dame retain and will perpetuate what I increasingly—in the often crude and conniving competitiveness of our civilization—consider to be the finest of qualities, the virtue of human decency [a proper regard, a reverence for persons and things]. Each alumnus encountered it memorably during his period at Notre Dame even as it is daily, whatever may be heard to the contrary, to be encountered now among our students. You have ever understood, Jim, that among the famous American universities and colleges it is the capacity for human decency that does distinguish us, that makes Notre Dame—and will ever make her—unique as a community of teachers and students, with the values of that community enduring with us and among us so long as life lasts.

I know that we cannot outwit you, Jim, but tonight at least we can outbless you. So it is not too much to say that you are the very embodiment of this high virtue of human decency, constantly trying to lift its level. We, your faculty friends, have recognized this. As you leave us now—to return we trust as often as possible—we praise you for it, love you for it, and wish you the happiness of a new and unencumbered life with all our hearts. We wish you, your wife and your family *Joy,* remembering that joy is *the echo of God's life in us.*[21]

This tribute brought O'Malley a letter from a Notre Dame Board Member, Thomas P. Carney, Senior Vice President for Research and Development at G. D. Searle & Co. on June 26, 1967, in which he wrote: "I think your tribute to Jim [Armstrong] was one of the most eloquent presentations I have ever heard."[22]

O'Malley's loyalty to his friends and students led him to join them in far places whenever he could. For instance, during the latter part of World War II there happened to be a casual coming together of four of his former students in New York: Erwin Mooney, Jr., Jerry Hogan, and myself at Floyd Bennett Naval Air

Station in Brooklyn and Kenny Beh in Manhattan. We often met on weekends at the estate of Beh's father-in-law, J. T. Kirby in Great Neck. Two of the Kirby sons, C. J. and Arthur, had also been O'Malley students, but they were out of the country at the time. O'Malley would often spend most of his weekend riding trains to New York and back in order to join us for an evening at Kirby's.

None of us knew it at the time, but O'Malley had tried desperately to obtain a commission in some branch of the service. His files contain a letter of acknowledgment from an Assistant District Intelligence Officer dated December 30, 1941, in reply to O'Malley's application for a commission in the Intelligence Branch of the U.S. Naval Reserve. The Navy's test of O'Malley's eyesight showed that he had 7/20 vision in both eyes, far below the requirements. Nevertheless, he next sent inquiries to the Army Specialist Corps in 1942. When that was not successful he wrote to the Marine Corps in Washington, D.C., saying, "I believe I could qualify as *photographic* officer or *air intelligence* officer." Then he made application on June 24, 1942, to the Army Air Force. Finally, when all else had failed he applied on September 7, 1943, to the U.S. Naval Academy in Annapolis for a position as instructor. But the only naval personnel that he was to instruct were the trainees at the University of Notre Dame.

Throughout his teaching career at Notre Dame one of his happiest diversions was into politics. No doubt his family background in Massachusetts had predisposed him toward support of the Democratic Party, and in this as in all else he was intensely loyal. And his loyalty was enhanced by his deep conviction that the nation desperately needed the social welfare programs for which the Democratic Party stood. On this, his life-long sympathies for the less privileged in our society, for the barbers, the soda-jerks, the laundry workers, the Pullman porters, had a bearing. He may also have found a kind of whimsical satisfaction in reenacting in his own life something of the low-level political activity portrayed in James Joyce's "Ivy Day in the Committee Room," or, as Jim Carberry says, of O'Connor's *The Last Hurrah*.[23] At any rate, "he rationalized in an irrational way about the Democratic Party and was proud of being its precinct man for Notre Dame."[24] During the Adlai Stevenson campaign of 1952, "O'Malley wrote an ad supporting the governor, then the target of churlish

McCarthyite sentiment from many Catholics. It ran in the *New York Times* and bore 60 signatures under the headline Notre Dame Faculty for Stevenson. The newly installed President Hesburgh saw the ad as divisive and called a faculty meeting to denounce it. The campus chapter of the American Association of University Professors took up the challenge and battled Hesburgh through the school year."[25]

O'Malley also supported Hubert Humphrey very strongly, and this support extended even into the mundane details of precinct work. He would write detailed reports to the local county chairman, Mr. Ideal Baldoni, listing payments that he had made to his precinct workers.

He was "a great admirer of John F. Kennedy and a dedicated precinct captain for the Democratic Party. As Edward Goerner . . . remembers it, 'We'd be three-deep at the bar talking about Hegel when some ward committeeman would break in to say hello and, just like that, the conversation would switch to Democratic politics.'"[26]

O'Malley's drinking became heavier and heavier during the late 1940s and 1950s. When Frank Duggan was back on campus as a teacher during 1949 he says that "On several occasions I'd run into him at the main gate bus stop at about noon time. His classes were over for the day and mine were too, at least on some days of the week, and we'd sometimes head for town together for lunch. Lunch would be preceded by a beer or two—sometimes three or four or more, so that we'd spend the entire afternoon on bar stools. It was Frank's habit at the time to forego martinis till five o'clock (or perhaps only till four), and it was common for him to forego meals or, when he took them, to eat sparingly and finickily. I once saw him order an oyster stew for supper, eat all the broth, and leave the oysters. . . . [That incident] occurred one night when I drove him down to Kokomo, where he was to give a talk in a Lenten lecture series at a Catholic parish. We left South Bend early enough to get to Kokomo for dinner, but before dinner (or instead of dinner: O'Malley might have had the stew after his talk) we had several drinks. O'Malley drank martinis; I stayed with my beer, most likely, both by preference and because I was driving. By eight o'clock or whenever the talk was to begin he was well oiled, and the parish priest who met us when we came into the hall was clearly apprehensive. The talk came off, however, without mishap, although it must have been apparent to the audience that O'Malley was glowing, and we started back to South Bend (doubtless after some more drinking) in a terrible fog—a literal fog of atmospheric moisture, not alcoholic befuddlement, though there was some of that. The fog was so bad that I kept the car on the yellow dividing line of the road, the only thing I could see the whole distance to South Bend. I had to drive so slowly that we reached South Bend again at dawn. . . . "[27]

Ken Woodward who was part of that generation of students remembers that, "They also sought him out evenings at any of the dozen or so watering holes he frequented, notably the bars in the Hoffman and LaSalle hotels. He liked to refer to these after-hour sessions as his 'evening colloquia.' A certain ritual was involved in approaching him after hours. We students would spot him at the bar, order a drink for ourselves and wait to catch his eye. If he nodded, smiling shyly, we felt encouraged to come closer and make conversation. Sometimes these colloquia would go on for hours, with O'Malley leaning against the polished mahogany while delivering pungent monologues spiked with wit."[28]

But alcohol was becoming a cruel trap for him: "Even with people he knew well, O'Malley was usually shy and self-effacing. He liked to keep a measured distance between himself and others. When faced with someone who insisted on closing that gap he would back off; many of his conversations were held in steady retreat. In fact, he was not a conversationalist except among a handful of old friends and faculty peers. He favored the personal monologue, which collapsed into a mumble when he was drinking, as he often was. On many an evening in South Bend I watched him down eight or nine excruciatingly dry martinis; by the evening's close all that was audible from behind his personal cloud of smoke was an occasional 'My Gawd . . . my Gawd . . .' as he contemplated some affront to his standards for church or state."[29] The cruelty of this, his final illness, lay in the fact that it mimicked the religious intensity that had always marked his finest hours. Worse, it recalled ironically the words of the Apostles after Pentecost when "others mocking, said: These men are full of new wine. But Peter standing up with the eleven, lifted up his voice, and spoke to them: Ye men of Judea, and all you that dwell in Jerusalem, be this known to you, and with your ears receive my words. For these are not drunk, as you suppose, seeing it is but the third hour of the day. . . ."[30]

In 1965 Tom Bergin recognized that alcoholism had brought O'Malley to a life-threatening condition and persuaded him to enter St. Joseph's Hospital for treatment. It turned out to be a stay of six weeks. O'Malley's aged mother even came out from Massachusetts to be with him. His

> delirious rhetoric made quite an impression on the aides who strapped him to his bed. "If there is any among you who has an ounce of Christian charity in his veins, unshackle me from these bonds!" he shouted. Robert Christin sat by his bed for hours while "Frank reeled off plans he had for a student banquet. He recounted the room in the Morris Inn to be rented, the precise seating arrangement, his remarks introducing Father Hesburgh and finally his own speech, which began, 'We are here to recognize the Spirit that brings us together.' It was an amazing performance."
>
> Not long afterwards, O'Malley was back at his old haunts, sipping milk with his Scotch. By the early 70's, he seemed permanently ensconced at the Morris Inn bar, which had a back door he would use to slip away from alumni he preferred not to see. He was also drinking heavily in his room and, for the first time, missing many of his classes. The driver he used to hire to taxi him out of state now was called frequently just to deliver him to the classroom.
>
> At Christmas recess in 1973, O'Malley went home to Massachusetts. He was concerned about his 88-year-old mother, but his sisters were aghast at his own patently failing health. His stomach was bloated; he could hardly eat. Money was a worry. All his life he had been generous toward those in need (once writing a check for nearly a third of his salary to a colleague with high medical bills) and careless about his finances (sometimes keeping $12,000 in his checking account). He was facing mandatory retirement the following June and was melancholy at the prospect of leaving Notre Dame. He examined a condominium on Cape Cod and told his sisters he planned to retire there.[31]

Besides the money that he had so often lent and given to students and colleagues, he had also consistently sent funds for the support

of his parents. His 1942 income tax return included the statement
that for ten years he had been the chief support of his parents.
Since his teaching salary had begun in 1932, he had clearly followed this practice from the beginning, and after his father's death
he had continued sending support funds to his mother for the rest
of his life.

My own last meeting with O'Malley occurred about this time
as I was returning to South Bend one evening on the South Shore
Railroad. When the train reached the station and the passengers
stood up I discovered that O'Malley was aboard. I offered him
a ride back to the campus, which he accepted, and he then excused
himself for a few minutes. When he returned he asked me if I
would have room to take a few of his students, also. I readily
agreed and found that he had about four students all ready with
their luggage right behind him. We stopped at several halls to
distribute them before we arrived at O'Malley's Lyons. There he
thanked me and refused to let me help him with his luggage up
the spiral staircase next to the arch.

This is the same staircase of which Tom Bergin tells:

> During the Easter Vacation of 1974 I was in the Morris
> Inn dining room having breakfast with my family one morn-
> ing when Jerry Rash, the manager of the Inn, came over
> and said to me, "Have you seen your friend, O'Malley?"
> "No," I said, "Where is he?" "There in the corner," he said,
> "and I'm afraid he doesn't have long to live. I've seen several
> terminal cases of alcoholism." I saw him in the far corner
> of the upper deck hunched over his food, his face a terrible
> color of copper. I almost did not recognize him. I went over
> to chat with him and found that he was almost incoherent.
> He had written on a slip of paper the phone number of his
> mother in Massachusetts, and I gathered that he wanted me
> to call and send her flowers for Easter. He was too far gone
> to do it. I saw that he needed to go to the hospital; so I told
> Jerry Rash that, and he said, "I'll take him in the Inn's
> station wagon." After they drove off O'Malley looked up
> and said, "Where are you taking me?" "To the hospital,"
> said Jerry. "Tom Bergin is going to meet us there." But
> O'Malley said, "I'll jump out of this car if you don't stop
> it." So Jerry had to take him back to Lyons Hall. When I

talked to Jerry he said, "He's back in Lyons, but he fell going up the stairs and got a gash on his forehead." I called Father Sheedy and got approval for an ambulance to pick him up, and by then the bleeding had convinced O'Malley that he should go."[32]

The gash may also have turned the metaphor of "blood on the bricks" into a literal fact.

O'Malley lived on for about four weeks in the hospital. His old teacher, Father Leo R. Ward, visited him one day and heard him say only two words: "Father Ward!" Tom Bergin was stopped in the corridor outside his room by a nurse who said, "Your friend is not going to make it."[33] Within a few days after that, on May 7, 1974, he died.

The Holy Cross Fathers offered his family the option of burying him in their Community Cemetery on the Notre Dame campus, and they accepted. The evening before the burial his casket was taken to the lobby of O'Shaughnessy Hall for a prayer service attended by many students and faculty and conducted by priests of the Holy Cross Congregation. The casket remained closed.

The next morning, May 11, 1974, he was buried after a Mass in Sacred Heart Church offered by the university president, Father Hesburgh. The building was filled with faculty, staff, and students, and the eulogy was given by O'Malley's old friend and former dean, Rev. Charles E. Sheedy, C.S.C.:

> Dearly beloved friends of Professor Francis O'Malley!
>
> His beloved sisters! (And we think here of his mother in Massachusetts, alive in her nineties, a lady of power and fortitude, from whom he surely inherited his own tough fiber.)
>
> Beloved colleagues of the faculty!—in the Department of English, and across the colleges of the University. Think of how you have revered his fierce integrity and gained courage from his loyal partisanship.
>
> Beloved priests of Holy Cross! You gave him the only humble home he ever really wanted in his great teaching years. You walked and talked with him, and explored together, in many springtimes, every cherished yard of earth in this calm campus. You prayed with him and worshipped God in count-less liturgies, and Holy Weeks and ordinations—and many

charming marriages of students and solemn funerals of friends—in this great and noble Church of the Sacred Heart, so familiar, so dearly loved.

And how beautiful, how appropriate and fitting, that his mortal body should remain for its long rest (until the King of Glory comes!) in the Community Cemetery, on the campus, among the priests and brothers of Holy Cross. There he will have, as close particular neighbor, his wise and sensitive teacher and preceptor, Father Leo L. Ward, who perhaps above all others gave Francis O'Malley freedom to teach and affirmation of his freedom.

Above all, I would say and he would say, *Beloved Students!* His present and former students, in that widespread and long-extended community of discipleship, which has meant and means so much to you in your affection for Notre Dame. You know that you were everything to him. He taught you to read and write, to love the good and hate the evil. In his own words, which I heard him say more than once, he thought of you as "friends of the work." To me this is a noble phrase. These four words carry both the loving commitment of his affection and his cool view of the objectivity of the common search for truth.

O dear friends, you see that even in exclamatory words of greeting my thoughts are outrunning my ability to express them. I find myself merely reciting a litany of his loves. I would wish to be able to utter some suitable words which might capture clearly his elusive spirit, and make use of these words to inspirit you. But Mr. O'Malley was *your* Mr. O'Malley, as he was mine. His spirit says a different and inspiriting word to each of us.

Yet you will agree that the springtime season of the Resurrection is the most appropriate time for us to mourn his death and celebrate his life. Death and life, two polar opposites: the wall of separation between them is broken down by the Resurrection of Jesus. We think of the sorrow of his disciples, their disconsolateness, their abandonment. Suddenly He lives, and through His spirit their lives are renewed in a fearless and unflagging creativity. Out of a death came a renewal of life, a reconciliation of opposites.

And we may think of a dialectic of opposites in the Beatitudes of the Sermon on the Mount, this morning's reading from the Gospel. We think of the freedom of the truly poor in spirit, of the inward joy of the afflicted sufferer, and of the moral power of the meek and selfless person. All of these stand in opposition to possessiveness, and pleasure seeking, and arrogant pride. The genuine happiness promised by the Gospel is exactly in the opposite direction from the path down which the worldly person seeks for it.

The truth to be found in this dialectic of opposites may perhaps be seen in the life of Francis O'Malley. I think of him as by personal preference a private and withdrawing person, even a solitary person. Yet he carried out a public mission of teaching which through his students has entered helpfully into the cultural stream of our country. The country particularly needs now, and always needs, a more humane and civilized culture, a higher standard of private and public character and conduct, and a nobler public ideal. These are the standards and goals which Mr. O'Malley has regularly taught and personally embodied for his students.

Mr. O'Malley was not at all a faculty activist, nor a political person. Yet when he felt the demand of necessity he spoke out strenuously for the freedom of the faculty. I think what the faculty most admired in him was a quality of steadfast loyalty and fearless integrity. And out of principle, in spite of a personal preference for inconspicuousness, he faithfully fulfilled the duties of precinct commiteeman for his political party for many years.

He was habitually mild and unemphatic in speech and manner of address. Yet when he needed to do so he could speak in outbursts of oratory and prophetic eloquence which would bring tears to your eyes, and sting your nerves and stir up your heart, and move your complacency to a better and more strenuous Christian effort.

Mr. O'Malley was a great Catholic, but I had the feeling that he was not really interested in the controversies of post-Vatican II or the question of Communion in the hand. I never thought of him as liberal or conservative, or of any particular persuasion other than the desire to live as a Christian in the Church. His religion was worshipful and modest,

not clangorous or controversial. He expounded a high ideal
of Christian culture. He introduced his students to the writings of Bernanos and Guardini, Claudel and Peguy, Chesterton and Newman, in a high tradition of Catholic letters
that reaches back through St. John of the Cross and St.
Teresa to St. Thomas Aquinas and the quaint and lovely
English mystics of the twelfth and thirteenth centuries.

But all I have been saying is nothing but bits and pieces
of his life and character. I would want to return to the one
thing necessary for your understanding. This is his love, devotion, devotedness to his students. He did not consider himself
at all. His life belonged to his students. The question agitated
in faculties of teaching *versus* professional progress was
meaningless to him. The University existed for the students:
they were its *raison d'être*. Whatever did not reach the students was a side issue of little interest.

Mr. O'Malley and I were both interested in superior students, in developing programs of study for students of unusual energy and talent. But he did not love them because
they were gifted. The effect was the other way around. His
love and concern conferred giftedness. I have often heard
him describe an undergraduate as "Great" ("a great person")
with exactly the same tone and emphasis that a lawyer might
use in describing Cardozo as a "great judge" or an art critic
might call El Greco great.

So I would think of Francis O'Malley mainly as a "friend
of the work" who spent his life in inspiring and nourishing
a whole network of friends of the work—his students. He
has left us, but he lives on in the fidelity of his students to
the rigorous ideal which he set for them. I know that the
students will remember him in their prayer and work. The
faculty will recall and take new heart from the remembrance
of his courageous steadfastness. To all of us at Notre Dame
he was more a person than a *role,* more a spiritual presence
than a professional. He has been a gift to us, but he was
never wholly of this world. Our opportunity now is to pray,
for him and for ourselves, and to remember, and to go forward with our present and future work, so as to be worthy
of the great teaching he gave us all.[34]

That May eleventh "was one of those soft, grey, and hazy days, with the new spring growth fringing the lake with light green. Lilacs were blooming heavily. We set out from Sacred Heart to walk to the grave, the C.S.C.s in white carrying the golden crucifix before us. It was less a funeral procession than a pilgrimage."[35]

The next issue of *Time* magazine printed his obituary:

> Died. Francis J. O'Malley . . . legendary English professor known as "Mr. Chips" at the University of Notre Dame; after a brief illness; in South Bend, Ind. O'Malley arrived at Notre Dame in 1928 as a freshman from Clinton, Mass., and stayed there for the rest of his life, living in student residence halls. His unconventional, deeply spiritual approach to literature endeared him to generations of students, including Ohio Governor John Gilligan and the late novelist Edwin O'Connor. Students flocked to his courses in such numbers that O'Malley had to screen them for admission. Renowned for producing a prodigious crop of fellowship winners, the quiet bachelor once described his favorite pastime as "writing letters of recommendation."[36]

Newsweek said that he was "the Knute Rockne of Notre Dame's academic faculty, a brilliant English professor who became a legend on the Indiana campus. . . . A shy, dry-witted bachelor who usually carried a furled umbrella, O'Malley entered Notre Dame as a student from Clinton, Mass., in 1928, stayed on as a teacher and never moved out of the dormitories. Lecturing on his favorite theme—the spiritual values illuminated by literature—he drew full attendance even on football Saturdays, when going to his class meant missing most of the pregame festivities and rushing to be in time for the kickoff."[37]

The next issue of the *Review of Politics* contained the following memorial:

FRANK O'MALLEY

> Since its founding in 1939 the name of Frank O'Malley has graced the masthead of this journal. He played an active part in that founding, constantly at the elbow of our founding editor, Waldemar Gurian, encouraging, suggesting, rewriting, planning. Perhaps his most influential voice was felt in the determining of our policy toward a broad humanism rather

than emphasize political techniques. This was characteristic of his own high idealism and his immersion in the thought of Maritain and Newman whom he elucidated so brilliantly in his courses. We deeply regret that death has now removed his name from our masthead and his influence from the Notre Dame community.

Frank O'Malley was certainly the greatest teacher of the humanities in the modern history of Notre Dame. What he did best and wanted to do most was teach. He loved his students and they returned his love with the shining radiance of their youthful idealism. As he grew older he moved more and more toward that center of his life and found less and less energy for the *Review of Politics.* But the present editors, also associated with the *Review* since its founding, are mindful of what Frank O'Malley did in our early days and join with all Notre Dame in mourning him.[38]

It was so late in the school year that the *Scholastic,* the student weekly, held up its tributes to him until the following September when it published:

Words for Frank O'Malley

Frank O'Malley was a teacher.

Unlike many, more concerned with publication and promotion, it was his life with students which earned his reputation. As his friends recall, he was both generous and gracious to his students. One friend said that he spent a great deal of money taking students to dinner, but the crucial thing was the communion that they shared and not the expense. He was a man who loved words and felt their awesomeness in conversation. In helping students with their writing he was a consultant, a fellow traveler. Most often his students would respond to his encouraging concern and begin to work at the edge of their ability. Sometimes their very being would seem to change. Many learned to understand life in newer, more mature ways. All in all, Frank O'Malley lavishly spent himself for his students.

His scholarship was prodigious. He consumed books as others consumed food. Even in his early days in Howard Hall, he would frequently miss meals so that he could continue working. A disappointment, now that he is dead, is that he did not publish more. Much of what he did write can be found in back copies of the *Review of Politics*. His proposal for Christ College is his most representative piece. Embodied in this essay is his philosophy of education, and to a large degree, the man himself. It is unfortunate that Frank O'Malley did not leave a legacy of eloquent volumes. Yet, it was not in the nature of the man to close himself to others to acquire the privacy and quiet necessary for writing. Most of his lectures, however, are preserved in manuscript.

Due to his poetic sensitivity to the anguish of the lonely and suffering, he took it upon himself to exercise a special ministry. Even in the most problematic students—the troubled, the lazy, the dull—he would find goodness deserving of praise. In this he fostered growth where there was often storm and tempest. For example, he always resided on campus. He lived with his students from the beginning of his career as a Prefect in Howard till his final days as a resident of Lyons. Another facet of his tendance of the human things can be discerned in his humanistic political beliefs, and his corresponding work as a Precinct Captain.

In his classes he represented the pulsating life of the Spirit. He nurtured it in others and was often the catalyst for its growth. Incarnational in his embodied Catholicism, he seemed to discern even the most minute workings of the Spirit in others.

His lectures were testimony regarding the good and beautiful things which could be found only through the life of the mind. He lived in tension toward the good and beautiful things, knowing that during one's years, there would at best be moments of ecstasy. His classes were anguished attempts to find words that described the splendors that were continually present to one and the imprint of the Spirit found in all things. He contemplated and created in an interior silence that seemed to make him a lonely figure. The profession that he lived also contributed to this. Such suggestions of loneliness were aggravated by his natural shyness. He lived in an intense awareness of the tragedy of the human condition. But, there were moments of graceful ecstasy. In all of this he was a friend of Diotima, and he shared his best moments with his friends, i.e., students.

It is difficult to find words that adequately describe Frank O'Malley. His life calls for superlatives, but even they lack the razor's edge of intensity. Perhaps the sharp metaphor of the poetic form is more appropriate. One did not meet with Frank O'Malley, one encountered him in an I-Thou relationship. Such encounters were intensely personal. The meaning of his career and the reality of his reputation rest upon such encounters. Perhaps, there is a student of his with the ability and courage to write a dialogue.

Frank O'Malley is a model for imitation. Indeed, for those who knew him well, he seems to represent the limit case. Frank O'Malley, as he shall rightfully live in memory, was a teacher.[39]

Several of his faculty colleagues composed poems in his memory. First, Jim Robinson:

FOR FRANK O'MALLEY

after he died a day or two
in a cool spring as usual here
and deeply green
there a softball sailed
a warm cloud ran
here some with books in hand
after examination time an hour or so
and others hand in hand
and that one magnificent magnolia
in tranquility
in the lake's embrace
that one there

we laugh still
unshared interior laughter
at those enormous cardboard posters
scrawled with names, names
the persons
to take his course that fall
or spring semester
those honored many

the respected ones
everyone
who sought him out
and asked to be somebody there
beyond the cardboard
in his eye
his mind
he knew them all

and how he praised the new ones
in the freshman classes
still
he offers praise
and knows
by the lake's edge
and on the green
where voices float
a warm cloud runs
and quiet time explodes
in a magnolia petal
in the spring
and in the fall
the year begins anew here
and when the freshmen come again
again
he knows them all[40]

Then Ernest Sandeen wrote the poem which is inscribed on a
bronze plaque just inside the front door-post of O'Shaughnessy
Hall's lobby:

WORDS TO FRANK O'MALLEY

What have you done? You lie so still
You strain belief in our mortality.
We can't believe the body of your ghost,
lithe and fleet, has now been exorcised.

Our scholar gipsy, you haunted the conscience
of all our paths and corridors,
you sharpened with light the shadow that was cast
on what we yearned for in dome and spire.

You christened writers of indiscreetly
visionary words, the baptized
and unbaptized alike, while awed
multitudes of the young looked on.

You gospelled four decades of rich and poor men's
sons showing them where the soul is.
And each day you knotted them thongs to whip
the money-changers from the temple door.

When did you first surmise that yours
must be the gift of loneliness?
When did you discover that he
who is loved by all is loved by no one?

Foreknowing, as you did, such cost of spirit
how did you decide? Or did you?
How can a man, a mere man, decide
to make nothing but himself his own.

There were days we scarcely could endure
the fury of that indifferent love
that smiled or glowered in your eyes.

Forgive us if we found it hard
to quite forgive in you your relentless
understanding of yourself.

But we salute you now as then
with love, across no greater distance
than you always kept, immaculate
and warm, between yourself and us.

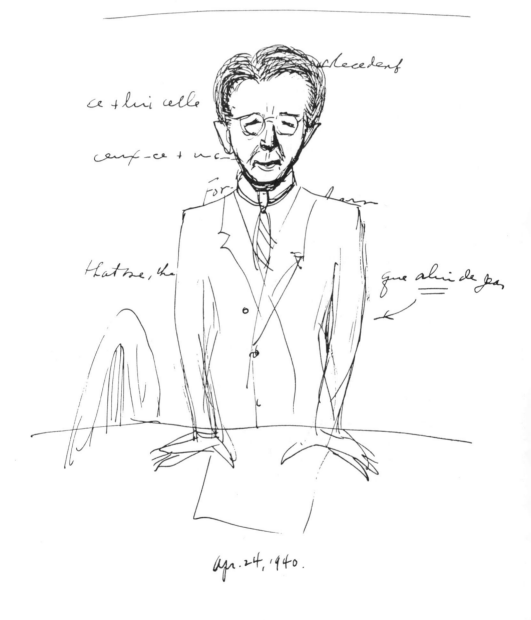

from "Philosophy of Literature" class
notes of John W. Meaney

6
The Impact

The ultimate legacy of a great teacher must lie in his impact on his fellows, students and non-students alike. That O'Malley's impact has not been ephemeral is to be seen in many clear memories, some going back fifty years and more.

———— · ————

I had a great deal of respect for Frank's practical judgment, and never took a step at the University without consulting him first. When I became Chair of Journalism, he worked with me in developing the curriculum, even to naming some of the courses, though he despised the endeavor, thinking journalism despicable. Similarly, I had grave doubts about the Phil of Lit; I was ever suspicious of efforts, so strong in the 1930s, to baptize everything, and Frank must be seen in the light of this movement, his to baptize Joyce and excommunicate Milton, along with those made by Catholic artists and sociologists to baptize their pursuits....
Frank was a prophet. What he cared most about in literature was prophecy, extending his benevolence even to Carlyle, and it is what he cared about in teaching. None of this had an appeal for me. I saw quite clearly that this was what made him a beacon to the students, and saw also that it flourished in the absence of any serious theological thought at N.D. This did not come till after World War II, and even then with not much force, to undergrads [Tom Stritch, '34].[1]

———— · ————

I first got to know Frank while he was my student in several of my courses at N.D. during his junior and senior years as an English major.... Frank, among other courses, took mine in Eliz.-Stuart Poetry (emphasis on the metaphysicals), Eliz.-Stuart Drama (excluding Shakespeare), and Shakespeare. I introduced the work of T. S. Eliot as critic and poet into my course on the meta-

218

physicals, and the aesthetic of Maritain (*Art and Scholasticism*) into my course on the Eliz.-Stuart dramatists. . . . Frank was an enthusiastic student of these writers and thinkers. We had many long conversations about them and the evaluative study of literature. I venture to think that these studies were a major basis for Frank's later development as a great teacher.

Frank was very shy, as an undergraduate and during his early years as a teacher—not anti-social but rather un-social. I don't think that during his entire life he ever had a date with a girl. Many years later he was persuaded by some of his students to attend their Senior Ball. Which he did: he rented white-tie and tails and had a ball! He was the guest of honor in the receiving line. Unfortunately, there's no picture of Frank in tails. He was, in a sense, quite provincial. Though his tastes and knowledge were broad and comprehensive, he never travelled anywhere except to New York and his home town of Clinton, Mass. There's one exception: he did make a trip once to New Mexico with his friend T. Bowyer Campbell, a bachelor history don at N.D., to visit the locale of Willa Cather's novel, *Death Comes for the Archbishop*, at Lamy and Santa Fe. I remember that when I had a small grant to study in Europe for the summer of 1936, Beryl and I tried to persuade him to join us, but to no avail. When he did travel to New York he liked to stay at the Vanderbilt and meet some of his former students under the famous clock, and to go to Tim Costello's Pub on Third Avenue, with its Thurber drawings on the walls, a hang-out of writers and journalists.

There was a mild streak of femininity in Frank's temperament— not enough to raise suspicious eyebrows, but enough to suggest to one of his less sycophantic friends that he seemed to be "descended from a long line of maiden aunts"—a jibe made by someone, either by or about George Bernard Shaw. He was the . . . only son, in a family of girls. It's true to say, and not uncharitable, that he never cut the umbilical cord that tied him to Notre Dame. His loyalty was perdurable and everlasting. . . . I suggested to him in his senior year that he go to Harvard for graduate work—not far from his home in Clinton. It would be the year of T. S. Eliot's tenure as Charles Eliot Norton professor. He was interested, but instead he decided to return to Notre Dame, probably for economic reasons: his mother was a widow and he was on his own. . . .

I had only one regret, in retrospect, in my relationship with Frank during his student days. For a few years I was Faculty Chairman of the Board of Student Publications . . . until I was asked to resign for failure to censor a particular weekly column, written in rather New Yorker style, in the *Scholastic*. Frank was among several applicants at the end of his junior year for the editorship of *Scrip*. Though Frank was a good student writer and had published quite a lot, I appointed someone else. But that did not interfere with our friendship [Rufus W. Rauch].[2]

——— · ———

I knew Frank best during World War II. He was the custodian of our house while I was in the navy. When I told Tom Stritch that Frank was to be the custodian he said, "My God! Why didn't you get someone who had ever lived in a house?"

He used to visit us while we were at the Great Lakes Naval Training Station, and he was distinguished by how lightly he would travel. He would never take a suitcase—just a comb and toothbrush. He didn't even take pajamas. One Sunday morning I went up to call him in time to go to Mass. I had lent him my best pair of pajamas. When I went into his room he was shining his shoes with my pajamas—and if you think he was embarrassed, you're crazy.

One weekend Tom Stritch, Frank, and I drove out to Iowa City to see a football game. We stayed three to a room at a hotel in Davenport. Frank got up first and stayed in the bathroom for about forty minutes.

I don't know how much he knew about football, but he would never miss an after-game party at our house. However, he never liked a party where people sat down. He liked to drift from one group to another with his glass and cigarette.

One of my most vivid memories of O'Malley from the early days was of a time when he and Tom Stritch and I went down to visit Dick Sullivan on Chapin Street. It was a very hot July or August day, and as we started home Tom said, "Why don't we stop in at the Oliver and have a drink?" So when we got to the bar Frank said, "I'll have a Tom and Jerry." He knew so little about drinking at that time that he did not know that that was a winter-time drink.

One thing about O'Malley that I never understood was that for quite a while he was very high on Evelyn Waugh's *Brideshead Revisited,* but later on something turned him off of Waugh. Suddenly it was just a terrible book. And if he didn't like Waugh and you did, you had better just stop talking about Evelyn Waugh.

He was always big for the underdog, for underprivileged people—although I always noticed that he rode the Pullman when he went to Boston. He would often get involved in causes. There was something about the administration's treatment of the librarian Eileen Conley that he did not like; so she became one of his causes. He even wrote a letter to the university president threatening to resign from the faculty unless they did right by her. Adlai Stevenson was another of his causes; he would tolerate no criticism of him.

Frank was the most inept person, physically, that I knew, and he was also very impractical. I once had a date to meet Tom Stritch and Frank at the cardinal's house in Chicago. It was a Saturday evening, and we were going out to have dinner and see the horse races. The date was for 6:00 p.m., and I was there promptly. But then it got to be 6:30, and Frank had not yet shown up. Tom said, "Well, let's go." I said, "We can't go. What about O'Malley?" But at Tom's insistence we did go on. We found out later that O'Malley had changed his plans and gone to Cleveland. Tom knew him pretty well.

One evening at our house as we were sitting having drinks Frank jumped up suddenly and said, "My God! I'm due at Bill Dooley's house in half an hour for dinner!" But that merely amused him. Nothing really shook him up [Ed Murray, '31].[3]

————— · —————

I was a librarian at the university, and I remember that every summer Paul Byrne, the director of libraries, would send someone over to O'Malley's room with a hand truck to collect the library books and bring them back. O'Malley never did it himself.

One day when our daughter was ten years old O'Malley gave her ten dollars to buy herself a copy of *Kristin Lavransdatter* [Mrs. Ed Murray].[4]

————— · —————

He wore shyness like a cloak; although he was gracious and

full of courtesies one didn't enter into his world without invitation.
Should he answer a call to visit which he did only if a favored
few were being invited (and one learned always to mention who
and how many) then he would relax when properly warmed interiorly and talk about some of his favorite characters who were
not of the fold. This he did with deadly finesse in his quiet way
and with a glint in the eye. In time he had learned not to blush
when talking to old married folk who happened to be female.
And he heaped praise on a good shrimp dish in happier times
when he had a taste for real food [Ruth S. Meaney].[5]

————— · —————

There is one idea which the master gave me and even though
I know it to be a commonplace it was, in that undergraduate year,
monumental for me. He explained to us that ideas have consequences in human history, that they in fact are the dynamic which
forms the behavior of ages and that these ideas are to be found
in literature and art. . . . This was an awakening for me. . . .
[O'Malley sometimes used painful barbs on his students.] Think
of the poor fellow whom O'Malley condemned to be drowned in
his own urine. . . . The very best moment I had with O'Malley was
when he came to check me in as prefect. He found me reading
and seemed to find that surprising and interesting. Would you
like to read, he asked, the greatest novel ever written? Yes. Yes.
He went away and came back with *Crime and Punishment*. I
couldn't pronounce Dostoyevski's name but took the book up with
fervor. . . . I have been mulling over the word, "attitudinize," first
heard by me in a conversation with Frank O'Malley. It had tremendous impact, a kind of slap in the face. I was guilty. Wasn't
that what I was trying to do, strike a pose, put on the *right* face
to the world, even though I was uncertain about which face was
right? One tried to pick up the jargon of the sophisticated insiders,
those who knew. A great deal of cant and pretense had to be
learned: "Oh, how delicious, how Kafkaesque!" Something of
the sort. And then O'Malley ripped away the mask with his marvelous word, "attitudinize". . . . I have been thinking, too, about
the violence with which he held ideas and opinions, and expressed
them. He was what Sam Johnson called "a good hater." I think
he offended a lot of nice people. . . . because he did not know how
to disagree politely. He was perfectly willing to pay the price of

being disliked and of risking his reputation, perhaps his job, for the sake of the truth. On the other hand, his enthusiasms and loyalties were also fierce, and often extravagant. He might deplore the business school at N.D. and other horrors of the university and its people, but, at another time, would declare N.D. superb, beyond all other universities of the decade. O'Connor's *Last Hurrah* was the greatest novel of its time.... These are the sorts of virtues and vices which make for a good teacher; they wake people up and make them pay attention [Jerry Hogan, '40].[6]

———— · ————

While fully recognizing [his] skills as a teacher/motivator, [I always remembered a time when] a fellow student walked in a bit late for class and O'Malley verbally leapt upon him with utter malice and vindictiveness, slashing with his scalpel tongue until poor Bob ... was left bleeding and gutted. I was outraged by the injustice of O'Malley's attack and was on the verge of leaping to my feet and demanding that O'Malley apologize to Bob—then and there—for his unwarranted cruelty [J. Austin Sobczak, '40].[7]

———— · ————

The slight, impeccably clad figure twanging the wire strands that used to protect the grass quadrangles as he hurried through the rain to his next class. (Later, when I knew him well enough to ask why, he said simply that he wanted the precise word to describe the sound.)

A different day, a strong March wind. Frank, coatless, striding into the gale, long (for the time) blond hair streaming parallel to the ground.

Frowning at his notes as he cast his pearls before us. (Half of us were honest enough to admit that we didn't quite get it.) Then becoming the transfigured man, abandoning the notes and reciting, say, Hopkins ... Eyes closed....

Not content with a compliment in person for my performance in Robert Speaight's production of *Twelfth Night*, he sent me a note in which he told me he couldn't imagine the role being played better. (His judgment may be questionable, but not his sincerity.)

My first undergraduate conference with him. Both of us taut. His shy smile and jittery eyes. His trenchant analysis of my work. My puny defense. Behind his eyes the intelligence that told him I was floundering....

The two of us sitting on the steps of the porch. The house on Campeau Street where my wife, Mary, my first born, Mike, and I squeezed ourselves into a two-room apartment. I took the moment to tell him that I was leaving the campus and abandoning the idea of a career in professoring. I hadn't the temperament, nor did I have the money to be what was then considered a Catholic parent (eventually we had six) and also fund myself during the chase for the doctorate. He protested. He sputtered. He wished. So did I. I fetched some more beer and we talked late. When he left, he said he understood. I'm sure he merely accepted.

We corresponded for a few years. The exchange became sporadic. Then even the flow of Christmas cards stopped. Most of that record, I have lost. More's the pity!—In case no one has sent you these poems, I do.

TIDINGS
(circa 1938)

Christ in Time!
Christ in the Universe!
Every age flows,
Every man grows
In His Body.

BLOOD OF THE CHILD

From cloudy circle to shining center,
Plods, pounds portentous, primitive thinker,
Wanders reverential, dynastic king,
Earthbred, sunstirred hunters bowing bring
Bone, stone, bull, bird, darklight, devil power
From damp, deep cave, templesteps, startower;
Golden, gripping brain of Plato throbs, burns,
Fullest heart of vigilant Virgil turns,
Peter affirms, Francis, Thomas implore,
All kneeling men fumble, flare, flash, adore,
Know the word made flesh, the great God made mild,
Breath of bright being; clean breath of the Child,
And man's most fickle, violent veins flood
With enriching, ripe, eternal Childhood.

It is obviously an exercise in Hopkins's "sprung rhythm" [William K. Mulvey, '41].[8]

Frank was a great hero of mine and I enjoyed his wit over meals or cokes in the cafeteria. . . . When Father Hesburgh came to San Francisco for a Universal Notre Dame Night get-together I was president of the local club and we arranged a formal dinner and reception for him at the St. Francis Hotel. I had the good fortune to sit beside the guest of honor and took advantage of the occasion to talk about Frank O'Malley. . . . It was twenty-five years or so since I had any real contact with Frank. I had been in the Army and at Georgetown, and had moved to California where I married and was in the process of raising six children. I remember asking Father Hesburgh about Frank O'Malley, whether he was still the "star" of the English faculty, etc. Father Hesburgh's reply stunned me. He said, yes, Frank was still teaching, was still the great favorite of the students, but it puzzled him because he found Frank's speech very difficult to understand. "He doesn't talk very clearly any more," he said, without any comment as to why this was so. . . . Frank O'Malley . . . was the teacher who made me feel I was being let in on the secrets of western civilization, moving me into the company of those who had some understanding of what classical education was all about. At our reunion banquet this year, Fr. Hesburgh made a revealing remark that you may find of unusual interest. He said that when he became president in 1952 Frank O'Malley's salary for the year, including summer school, was $5200. "Now," he said, "We have nine professors whom we pay more than we pay the football coach."

I am enclosing . . . a piece I wrote this summer:

FRANK O'MALLEY
(Memory of a 1941 Class)

The formal nod and bright glass smile,
Unruly hair, defiantly long in a butch era,
One shock standing straight,
Blown there by the wind—
No hat to cover blondish red.
Nervous Good Morning,
Papers unfolded, a manuscript
Born during the night.
Then in smooth tones and cadences
A book or author revealed

With great insight, deep perception.
Proper reverence paid to Joyce,
Dostoyevsky—the back of his hand
To Milton and other pretenders
Who ignore God's real Presence
Whilst playing Christian sage.
He read them all and knew
Their strengths, weaknesses,
Pretensions, hypocrisies, and
Introduced young prematurely jaded
Minds to hidden sources of virtue
In writers whose names were known—till then—
Only to him and God.
His examinations were an opportunity
To show absorption where it was;
Appreciation if it had life;
Rebellion if it did not finally
Feel too juvenile; and a chance
To demonstrate art—at least
In its cradle.
Class was the master's stage,
Not the students' who sat in
Silence and learned and
Accepted or rejected and
Still stayed silent. But a
Mold was forming and a
Butterfly could emerge if
Heaven helped.

[William C. McGowan, '41].[9]

———— · ————

My most immediate recollection is of his manner of dress: it was almost a uniform—the dark suit, the tab collar (and cuff links), and cordovan shoes. Never do I remember a hat—not even in blowing snow—on top of his carefully brushed red head. He was petite, and his eyes often twinkled behind those thick glasses. A slightly feminine quality graced many of his movements and gestures.

Like most English majors, I idolized him in my undergraduate days. He inspired me with his ecstatic approach to learning. And

I must have attempted to imitate him in ways of which I am not aware. I was certainly an ardent member of the O'Malley cult.

Some of my reactions to him have been modified through the years. As I taught—even in graduate school before that—I often wished O'Malley had emphasized scholarly research along with ecstacy. I wish, too, that I had found in him more personal warmth and less inclination to sneer. In contrast, I remember Rufus Rauch as a more personable man. More than most people I have known—and admired—O'Malley created a public figure of himself and then wrapped it around himself for security.

During our University of Chicago days, I had high hopes of his venture to establish a college of the *Right Kind*. I now think he was as unrealistic a dreamer as I was. I have never felt that I knew him well. I knew the public figure in his sartorial uniform, but he was, for me, an exciting, admirable (with some qualifications), aloof man.

O'Malley was an inspiration to me at a time when I needed the inspiration. He caused me to want to do well, and before I had never cared nor had I tried. I sometimes imitated the less admirable traits in his makeup, but that's my fault, not his. He flourished best as an exotic plant in a hothouse atmosphere. I think in 1941 I saw myself flourishing best in that atmosphere. I'm glad it didn't happen that way. I probably would have had O'Malley's weaknesses with very few of his strengths. God rest his soul [Erwin J. Mooney, Jr., '41].[10]

———— · ————

[O'Malley] was not only my teacher but also my friend for many years. He supported me in many ways—encouraged my small talents and showed kindness and an understanding of my positions. I have a feeling that both of us shared an Irish intuitive gift which helped overcome, if you will, differences in our social and personal skeletons.

If I had not been able to discern his *authenticity* I might have been put off by his persistent formal dress (his tab collar shirts, his well-pressed suits, his highly polished shoes—[later, after my days, he did relax his standards to permit use of turtle neck sweaters]. . . .

Our bond could not have been foretold by the accidents of our birthplaces—Clinton, Massachusetts, a small mill town, and

Brooklyn, a brawling section of New York. He often mumbled, and he repeated himself; his conversational language was embellished and idiosyncratic, my own Celtic inclination was to brevity, loudly and belligerently stated (the better to start an argument). So it had to be a shared intuitive sense which, of course, brings with it great dangers.

O'Malley led me to Hopkins and Joyce who remain two of my favorite writers, but I feel that he and I enjoyed a special kinship with Léon Bloy and Peguy and, especially, with Georges Bernanos. It was with these French writers that we enjoyed, I think, our most acute satisfaction and sense of allegiance.

I've thought a great deal about the specific qualities in O'Malley which made him the great teacher he was. I think there is no doubt that he had an unusual talent for exegesis. He was able to extract noumena, distill and describe, explain—and with an *intensity* that eliminated all doubts about the truth and the importance of the pericope. It was the intensity translated by his powerful persuasive voice which distinguished him even from talented teachers such as Gurian and Leo Ward (the philosopher).

This intensity (in his case not a substitute for knowledge) combined with his honest concern for each of his students lifted him to a heroic level for most of his pupils. (He once told me that his mother thought he was a saint.)

There were faults in my good friend. He did exaggerate, he often contradicted himself; he could be sarcastic, opinionated, peevish; he ate too little, he drank too much. And he tended at times to perfectionism even though he railed against it. . . . But then, when he employed that vibrant, throbbing voice, he *was* the perfect teacher. No one who was there could forget the reading of Claudel's words (*The Tidings Brought to Mary*) which induced many self-confident students to weep. (Not long after that he forced surprise and embarrassment when he thundered, "I'll have no truck with tramps!") His eccentricities—closing his eyes, tracing his feminine fingers across his brow, blushing deeply—helped increase his campus popularity, but he was more than a college "character." No academic I've met regarded his obligation to subject matter and to student with so much seriousness, who acted with such fervor and effectiveness, who promoted and practiced justice as persistently, in his way, as Bernanos and Peguy did—justice not only to his favorites but justice for all men.

May his thirst for justice now be slaked and may he rest forever with his own Hero "on his Holy Hill and in His Tabernacles" [George E. Miles,, '41].[11]

———— · ————

Throughout his whole career at Notre Dame, Frank O'Malley paid close attention to national politics and international affairs. This was not simply a scholar's interest related to his editorship of the *Review of Politics*. . . . In the fall of 1939 [he] started conducting informal seminars atop Morrissey Hall on the implications of the war for America. He held those meetings for those of us who shared his interventionist views but more particularly for those who opposed them. This was during the period when a campus poll revealed 80 percent of the students surveyed opposed FDR's interventionist policies. The isolationism of their parents was often reinforced by the anglophobia of some of their own professors at Notre Dame!

In commenting favorably from time to time on FDR's policies, Frank acidly cut through the pious rationalizing of many who urged that America had no interest in or responsibility for Hitler's victims.

Frank O'Malley sensed the brotherhood of man pretty deeply. Poverty excited his concern, and here, I think, literature rather than experience illuminated his sense of our responsibilities. French, Russian, Irish, and English writers taught him that poverty need not be divinely ordained nor unquestioningly accepted [Charles John Kirby, '42].[12]

———— · ————

[O'Malley's] voice was marvelous to hear when he read us stories at Great Neck. I remember thinking he loved words like I loved music—and it was uncanny how much more I understood *because* he was reading. I remember our walks to the pier and just listening—he never talked down to me and flattered me by expecting me to understand every nuance—I stretched!

My recollections of Great Neck at that time are magical. The Notre Dame group was great. . . . *Patsy and the Pilots*, a play by George Miles, with such memorable lines as the giggling Laura-Belle running away from (my brother) Arthur "just fast enough to not discourage pursuit"—and Noel McCarry imitating Zero

Mostell and John Larson at the piano (he taught me so much about improvising) and Bert Kelly and John O'Dea and Bud Concannon and Mooney and [Meaney] and my brothers! Wow—what a group!. . . .

As for Frank, we would sit around him, in semi-darkness, and he would *read*. He read many Conrad Aiken stories to us, and I've never forgotten how I felt the growing horror of losing reality as he read "Silent Snow, Secret Snow" building up to the frightening ending as the boy let go of his last tenuous hold—

And "Mr. Arcularis" came to life, and to death, with Frank's words droning, weaving the spell.

But mostly I remember "The Monkey's Paw" and screwing up my courage to the sticking point and allowing myself to be frightened out of my wits until the frantic moment when he found the monkey's paw and made his last wish, and we breathed again, relieved. He read often.

He gave me a special love for the short story—and I've read these and many others to my children trying to create the atmosphere I remember.

I remember more from him than from my English teachers at school. I remember envying [his] students, imagining what it must have been like to sit in his class. What a privilege!. . . .a kind, warm, too-sensitive man with a love for words that was contagious, fortunately. . . .

But he was sad, too—was it the Irish melancholy? I wish I'd known him better, been older at the time, and understood more his complexity. But even then I was aware how special he was [Patricia Kirby Conover].[13]

———— · ————

Recollections of Frank O'Malley bring to mind the care with which I always approached his assignments in his first year writing course. His demanding standards imposed a discipline which causes me concern even as I write about, rather than for him. Suffice it to say that the subject matter of this letter prompted a pencil draft with corrections and interlineations.

I admire and respect him as do all his English majors. I profited from his courses in the English major sequence, and I was also one of the residents of the fourth floor of Morrissey Hall where we all enjoyed many conversations with him at "night check" [Charles M. Kearney, '42].[14]

———— · ————

He, more than anyone else, was responsible for my decision to switch from a planned undergraduate major in philosophy to a major in English. That may or may not have been the wisest decision for me, for Notre Dame, or for the rest of the world, but I haven't regretted it.

I did a few years of college English teaching myself back in the fifties, and Frank O'Malley was the model I tried to emulate. I hope I had the kind of influence on my students that he had on me and many of my contemporaries. He was a scholarly, unforgettable instructor, with a handwriting to match! I admired him very much [Ed Cummings, '43].[15]

———— · ————

Some tears flowed unashamedly when I read that Frank O'Malley had gone to his God.

Way back in 1939 I was one of those privileged few Notre Damers who, through some providential shuffling of registration cards, managed to find myself in that one section of freshman English Frank O'Malley taught each year. Before that day I had never heard of him; from that day on, I have never really stopped thinking about him.

Most of my adult life has been spent in Christian higher education and Frank O'Malley has been the greatest single influence throughout all these years. When I used to tell my classes that until they read and digested *Kristin Lavransdatter* they would remain partly illiterate and would never understand the meaning of suffering in the Christian ethic, I was only reiterating what this great man said and understood.

When I experienced the minimum of difficulty in composing a master's and doctor's thesis, I knew why I had that strength. Yet in teaching me and countless others how to write and what to read, he also taught us how to live.

Frank O'Malley was the antithesis of our impersonalized, computerized age: he must have found it baffling and horrifying. He impressed upon us in his often shy way that only a person who can love can teach. I doubt if any of us ever forgot that lesson

[Msgr. Anthony M. Brown, '43, President, College of Great Falls, Great Falls, Mont.].[16]

———— · ————

O'Malley strengthened our confidence in our own perceptions and judgments by levelling a withering attack upon much that had been presented to us under the rubric of conventional wisdom.

He did not impose upon us his standards and definitions of what was true and beautiful: rather we were urged to tell him and others what we thought on such matters. It proved to be a hideously painful and quite exhilarating experience. . . .

The oldest and largest human institution in the western world was, of course, the church, and in the life and history of the church O'Malley found the ideal human community, not in its institutional and organizational aspects, which all too often tended to be authoritarian and sterile, but quite literally in the communion of saints, those to whom had been revealed some apprehension of the true dimension of mankind's character and potential. While he developed among his students an appreciation of and admiration for individual artistic genius, he regarded the liturgy of the church to be the greatest single work of art known to man. . . .

During my years at Notre Dame and quite probably during the years that followed there were many among the faculty and the student body who felt that what O'Malley taught (or what they thought that he taught) was so esoteric, so personal, so subjective in the sense that it was based upon personal taste and attitude, that it had no relevance to the real world. He was referred to in some university circles as the Sun God, and there is no question that he made many people uncomfortable. . . . [But] Frank was no dilettante: he was among other things the Democratic precinct executive for the Notre Dame campus, and he managed to outrage and thus awaken great numbers of his colleagues and friends by injecting himself in one way or another into political conflicts at every level. In an earlier age he might have been a warrior bard with his father's sword buckled on and his wild harp slung behind him.

Virtually without exception [his students] bore throughout their lives and careers the imprint of the teaching of Frank O'Malley. I know that that has been my experience since I first came under his influence almost forty years ago. Although I saw him very infrequently in the years after I left Notre Dame and after the war, and although he was one of the world's least prolific letter writers, there are few people I have felt closer to throughout the years, or whose death inflicted upon me such a sense of loss [John J. Gilligan, '43].[17]

———— · ————

Like most of his former students, I cherish O'Malley's influence on my own life. Initially, that influence was overwhelming, as the experience of all great teachers tends to be. In time came the sorting out, the growing up and away that maturity requires. For many O'Malley men, the decade since his death has provided the distance we needed to put the man and his achievement into perspective. . . .

I believe that an era died with O'Malley, an era in the history of the University and in the intellectual life of the American church. We must ask ourselves now how much of what Frank O'Malley stood for so insistently has been lost, and how much should be recovered. . . .

He never travelled outside the United States and seldom inside it. When he did venture forth he preferred to go by train. At holiday time he would book a compartment for the trip back home to Clinton, Massachusetts, to visit his mother and sisters. He never learned to drive, and whenever he lectured within a day's ride of Notre Dame he would secure the services of a favored South Bend taxi driver. "Take me to Grand Rapids," O'Malley would command, and the driver (after picking up a change of clothes for himself) would chauffeur him to his destination. . . .

His final exams were distinctive. Witness this direction from a spring 1952 final: "Try to point out, as well and as personally as you can, the relevance of the realities—indeed the revelations— of *this course* for your own existence and future life and career. (This last question is *not* to be an occasion for *slobbering* of any sort.)". . . .

With the passage of time, some of O'Malley's methods lost their luster for [John C.] Meagher, who has earned three doctorates and now teaches at Saint Michael's in Toronto. "He gave the vague impression that to get any degree beyond a master's was super-ficial," says Meagher. "Those of us who did go on found what he had given us dysfunctional in our next phases of study because

O'Malley had no respect for the technical and scholarly sides of literary investigation, which dominated the graduate schools at that time." While teaching at Notre Dame, says Meagher, "I kept running across students of O'Malley's who had the phrases but didn't know what they meant. It was a parody of education. I found I was concerned with teaching students good techniques in reading literature, not in making grand judgments." Still, like many O'Malley students, Meagher chose the professor to be god-father to one of his sons.

Some faculty colleagues also had reservations about O'Malley's teaching (although most liked him personally). "Sometimes he tended to judge literature by the philosophy it expressed, and his powerful opinions may have overwhelmed some students who were too weak to arrive at judgments of their own," says John Frederick Nims, a distinguished poet. Another poet-professor, Ernest Sandeen, says, "I noticed when I got some of Frank's students that they already knew what they were supposed to think of some authors, like Emerson and Thoreau, though from my point of view they hadn't begun to study them." Both friends and critics, however, acknowledge that O'Malley's approach had compelling strengths. "Frank gave the impression that what he was teaching was a life-or-death issue," says Father Leo R. Ward [Kenneth L. Woodward, '57].[18]

———— · ————

He read poetry with unction and meaning. And somehow, for me Gerard Manley Hopkins made a great deal of sense before the summer was over. Whenever I think of Our Lady, I can almost hear Frank O'Malley reading the poem comparing Mary to the air we breathe.

It seems to me, when I try to recall his teaching technique, that he simply lived the literature he was treating and he allowed the class to experience that "living" with him [Sister Mary Luke Arntz, S.N.D. MA '47].[19]

———— · ————

I also took courses in English at the University of Iowa at the undergraduate level, and one reason I valued Mr. O'Malley was that I had that as a comparison. I had one course at Iowa City in American Drama before 1900—we read about twenty plays, none of any value. There was also a Shakespeare course, almost exclusively devoted to comparison of folio and quarto editions and the problems of establishing an accurate text. After such arid scholarship, it was tremendously exciting to experience O'Malley's flaming devotion to literature as literature. Even at the time (and more so as I grew older), I thought him too selective, too dogmatic, too romantic. But what was true and wonderful was his cutting through to the heart of each literary experience. He did not teach me (or better, I should say I did not learn from him) to read critically but I was inspired to look for the "philosophical" aspect of literature.

I also had his course in Modern Catholic Writers which introduced me to Christopher Dawson, Romano Guardini, and so forth. As it did to many, this introduced me to an intellectual interest in Catholicism and to the new currents moving in the church. I wrote my undergraduate thesis for him on the novels of Graham Greene. (I was pleased yesterday to see Greene had been awarded the Order of Merit by Queen Elizabeth.)

Finally, I was a member of Wranglers, for which he was faculty sponsor. He always attended the meetings—there was always a paper by one of the members, after which each of us commented and O'Malley made the final comment—always appreciative and always drawing together the various remarks. The last meeting of the year was a black tie dinner at a downtown hotel (the LaSalle, I think) where a great deal of beer was consumed by all and O'Malley gave the paper. These papers (I heard three, I believe) were very special, but I am afraid most of us were not in shape to follow very closely. But those banquet meetings were a high point of my college days.

One of the little touches I remember about him was that he always arrived for class carrying seven or eight books—without looking at the class, he would then spend a long time opening each book and finding some passage which he would mark. This seemed to go on forever, and we had a joke that someday he would spend the entire period arranging the books. But finally all would be in order and he would, in what looked like a desperate gesture, grab the knot of his tie, turn his eyes towards the wall, and begin to lecture. Often the entire hour would go by without his smiling or looking directly at the class. But often, too, he would ask questions or ask us to read poems which were being discussed. . . .

Another feature of his teaching was that he would sometimes spend the entire period reading a short story aloud. This, as I remember it, had no connection with the subject at hand except in the way all great literature is connected. I remember three of these stories: Conrad Aiken's "Silent Snow, Secret Snow," Joyce's "The Dead," and a story by D. H. Lawrence—"The Woman Who Rode Away" (?) or was it the one about the boy on a rocking horse? One of the doors that he opened for me was through the admiration of D. H. Lawrence, who was considered pornographic in my household. That of course was one of the wonderful things about him—his openness to modern thought in various fields (or rather, openness to *certain kinds* of modern thought, very closed to others). At a time when Notre Dame was quite parochial in many ways, he was an example to us of the free and enquiring mind (as were M. Fitzsimons, T. Stritch, W. Gurian, and others).

Most of the English majors of my time went off to service before graduating, and several of us returned in the spring of 1946 for one semester. Although he stressed so much the emotional content of literature, he seemed to me always inarticulate about his own feelings. But he certainly made us realize how pleased he was to have us back. On graduation day, he arrived at my room very early (as I was just getting up) to wish me well. In great embarrassment he managed to stammer out that he had looked forward so long to our return that he couldn't believe we were leaving again. Since I was as shy as he was, I muttered a response which was totally inadequate to the occasion, and he went down the hall to bid farewell to my friend Ed Meagher [James E. Newman, '44].[20]

———— · ————

I remember orange hair, red cheeks, the sweep of eyes that knew more than I did, very possibly more than I would ever know, thrilling to what I knew was an exceptional privilege to be in this class as he stood in front of us there, flushed cheeks blowing in and out as he took great breaths belting out those words he read from a written script in an impassioned chant. I didn't want to miss a one. I knew even then, I think, I would have a joy in trying to understand those words, not only then, but all the rest of my life.

He was a wild, funny-looking little fellow, who, in private, off the podium, in any one to one relationship, couldn't seem to find any words at all. In retrospect I think he was even abashed at times, and always embarrassed in one's presence. He was certainly in mine.

How could a mere teacher become such a profound, such an intimate influence in all one's life? I don't know. But that was Frank O'Malley.

I remember how few we English Majors were at the time— about fifteen, I believe. I remember how special we felt to be listening to the man. I remember how life suddenly grew. People that I had seen as, well, people, were now giants. Everything in life, thought, act, heart beat, quickly grew in importance. In retrospect I know of course that I was being made intellectually aware of God's creation—not as an idea but as something real and awesome. Our little group was hungry for this.

The experience was analogous to that of "falling in love." To be flippant (O'Malley would *hate* this)—"ah, sweet mystery of life at last I've found you." Well, life *does* have meaning when you are in love. And seems to lack it when you are not. What is unique about the intellectual experience under O'Malley is that "After O'Malley" I've consistently experienced the intellectual life as "meaningful."

A couple of years ago visiting Bill Pfaff here in Paris—an English major of the 50s—he characterized his experience under O'Malley several times with the repeated summary: "well he just about changed my life that's all!"

There are a lot of things about O'Malley's special interests— they were his, and through them he taught us—that I do not— now at any rate—share. The "cosmic angst" and "prophetic" qualities of modern literature and art, I shy from. I much prefer reading Shakespeare to Lawrence or Joyce, St. John of the Cross to Blake. Or—again to be flippant—Herrick to Hopkins. The beauty of English literature, O'Malley did *not* introduce me to, at least directly. Still, when I'm reading Dante or Aristotle, and have a particularly lucky moment of vision, I'll even at my advancing age hear an echo (not an articulated word) of O'Malley's voice, see him smile, and with particular pleasure think to myself "this is what O'Malley saw."

What I am trying to get at here is that, special interests or not, I think of O'Malley's mind as broad, broader than I can see. And though his was an emotionally charged nature—and surely he had as well painfully conflicting emotions—his mind was highly disciplined, fluid, clear, pure, a music to my memory like a mountain brook [Lyle Joyce, '44].[21]

———— · ————

There were a group of perhaps 25 of us who started on that course in 1940 but were broken up by the war. They included Kelly Cook (lost in combat in Vietnam) who edited the 1943 *Dome* for which I wrote some captions and Mr. Ed Meagher who edited our 1943 *Scrip* and graduated (I believe) as Valedictorian of our class.

We were a fairly intelligent group and quite content with ourselves and our classmates. We felt we were part of the better aspects of American culture. And Frank O'Malley contributed to that feeling. From an ego point of view grade averages from Frank were 90 or above. A grade of 97 or 98 was not unusual. Oddly enough, I think many of us earned those grades because of our dedication irrespective of our latent talent or lack of it.

Some of us had aspirations of being writers rather than teachers although we recognized that the future was bleak from a point of view of earning an income on that basis. But Frank assured us that we should not worry on that score. We were all bright enough and would earn enough to make a living.

Of course, we were all about 18 when we started and Frank was in his early 30s. . . . We started out in his course in Freshman Writing. The school at that time was not noted for its teaching so much as its football. Frank Leahy replaced Elmer Layden in the winter of 1940 as head football coach.

In retrospect, I am not so certain that Frank's course titled "Rhetoric and Composition" (which I note on my report card appears directly below "Commandments and Sacraments") really was about learning to write. Certainly Frank was not concerned about format, content, impact, marketability of the product or, of course, such details as spelling or punctuation. I am not so sure that Mr. O'Malley was a Professor of English so much as a Catholic Philosopher. He inspired rather than taught. When he spoke of the "outside world" he really meant it. Frank was obviously an "inside world" person which became more apparent with aging and his untimely death.

Frank loved young men and he was determined to save their intellectual souls despite the parochial attitude of the Catholic Church of the early 1940s. . . . And he did it through his readings and the intensity of his feelings about those things which he read. To many, he was personally more fascinating than the subject matter about which he spoke. He would have succeeded on the stage were he not exceedingly shy.

His personal appearance and mannerisms would have been considered merely an oddity in another man who had not the unique charisma of Frank O'Malley. One felt just a bit superior while in his presence as is often the case when one is in the company of a person who emanates leadership of one sort or another.

I must say that he inspired me to write—if not well—at least at great length. I typed 10 hours somedays and my typing skills soon ranged to close to 100 words a minute. So Frank taught typing as well as "writing" simultaneously although that was surely not his intent.

I typed enough compositions based on my limited, youthful experiences that I failed both semesters of Freshman Math which was simply a review of high school mathematics. I was too busy typing papers of art for Mr. O'Malley. I did labor. I note on one paper he has written: "My boy. My boy. You do go on and on."

Frank O'Malley exuded warmth and wit. He immersed these characteristics in a pseudo-sophistication that one can mirror in the current columnist and Catholic scholar, William Buckley, although God knows they would be antagonists in their political views.

Frank was too bright to be a member of the Catholic hierarchy which he loved and disdained for its non-intellectual-live-by-faith-alone attitude. I'm sure he fared better under Father Hesburgh.

Frank's wit expressed itself in several ways. He humored us with his symmetry. He often called upon a classmate as "Bob Burns of Bellow Falls (Vt)" rolling the consonants as he spoke. Over a drink at the Hoffman Hotel (postwar) he would humorously chide us with the question: "Did you read your monthly *Catholic Digest* today?" One night he baffled the young male waiter by insisting he was not served the scotch he had ordered. His quiet indignity and assumed horror at the thought put us all in stitches.

Forty years later I can't imagine what was funny about it except for the twinkle in Frank's eye and Frank's "Mother of God. What has been wrot here?"

When I last saw him in 1955 I was with a woman, my wife, so Frank blushed ever more and was in ready retreat. When for lack of anything else to say I observed that we had won the football game that day, he beamed and had a ready retort: "Truly a great triumph for the Catholic Church."

Frank was way above my head in courses that I took in later years when he spoke of the Great Books, of Hutchins, Adler, Maritain, and other literary saints. His reading of "A Diary of a Country Priest" left nary a dry eye in the class. Yet I enjoyed it all for just being in his company. . . .

A couple of years after departing Notre Dame, I was still floundering around wondering what to do with my life. I wrote a classmate, Gerry Hogue, regarding my concern of "living in the community of man, about the mores code and how to adjudge one's life standards." Gerry promptly replied that I should get a job at a department store, perhaps selling men's suits as a start and working up from there. He suggested that Macy's had openings in New York. Gerry replied in part: "and you had no business paying attention to whatever O'Malley might have said. . . . You had all the virtues long before you met O'Malley, you do not have a scholarly mind, and you are too normal to convert sex into mysticism. Consequently all you got from him (like many others) was a sense of inadequacy. Actually you are far more adequate than Mr. O'Malley. You should have taken Journalism under Stritch and rushed from Notre Dame to make a career for yourself in great haste. In short, we are all individuals". . . . I am still perplexed by [O'Malley] as I am sure are many of his past students. But it was good to have known him [Paul F. Carr, '44].[22]

——— · ———

I don't feel puffed up to say that there is a bit more of O'Malley in me than there is in most of his students. I suggest that I drank more with him, talked more with him, debated more with him, and laughed more with him than any of his immediate post-WWII students save possibly Bud Steffen or Kelly Cook. After my graduation from the University in 1948, Steffen and O'Malley motored to South Dakota. . . . We toured the Bad Lands and the Black Hills where O'Malley was truly "a small boy lost in a lonely fen." Though riding a horse was beyond him, he suffered Mount Rushmore with good humor and feared most of all that he would be abandoned in the wilderness with no cigarettes. . . . In the course of the trip we visited Wind Cave National Park and, of course, went deep into the bowels of the earth in the cave itself. I remember making some dumb remark like, "What do you think of it, Frank?" His answer was, "Well, as caves go, this is a pretty fine cave." Years later he had a freshman student from that region who predictably wrote a freshman essay on Wind Cave. The student got the paper back with a typical O'Malley note at the top which said "I know this cave very well and it isn't like this at all."

One of O'Malley's students during my time was Kelly Cook. Kelly could write like an angel and had an especially keen mind and a highly developed and gentle sense of humor. Kelly came back from the Great War with a wife and child—Joanne and Nancy. He completed his work at the University in, I think, 1946 or 47 and was immediately employed by the University as an instructor in freshman English. He and Joanne lived a short distance from the campus on North Eddy Street and this small home became the meeting house for the current English majors—particularly Bud Steffen, Stan Moon, Dick Shaeffer, and me. O'Malley was drinking very heavily during those years and took pretty much of all he ever got to eat from the gentle hand of Joanne Cook.

O'Malley had been waiting for years for some student to come in from the real outlands so that he could engage a young man with a truly rural background to do a senior essay on an obscure writer from eastern Kentucky, Elizabeth Madox Roberts and particularly her book *The Time of Man.* I filled that bill.

I suspect that he had a greater impact on my life than my mother, my father, my wife, and my children all put together. I sense that the real meaning of O'Malley was *direction;* for to a young student with a vast world of thoughts and ideas unfolding before him, the most important thing to grab hold of was *synthesis.* The Philosophy of Literature program, though fairly important in a learning sense, was even more important in a living sense. The childhood verities for which one could be thankful to his parents, the sense of love that comes from marriage and children all actually pale in that vast—somewhat intellectually oriented but more intuitively oriented—art of living—gracefully and harmoniously with the seasons, with other men, with the earth's creatures, and with the hovering spirituality of God and the Church.

We drank a lot at a small cafe at the end of an alley off Michigan Avenue called the Town Club. The signs and the napkins all proclaimed that the bartenders were "expert mixologists." We would tell O'Malley that the University was going to film his lectures in Modern Catholic Writers and the Philosophy of Literature (TV was just becoming common in those days) and then fire him. He would then say that his secret ambition in life was to become an "expert mixologist" and that he could probably do more good at that job than the one he now had.

Another drinking spot was the bar at the Hoffman Hotel. Directly behind the hotel was a Chinese Restaurant. After a long night we would stagger to this place where O'Malley would proclaim loudly to the owner that he wanted "the purest, cleanest, most uncomplicated thing he had to offer." The owner, having heard this same thing a number of times from Frank, would routinely bring him a bowl of steamed rice.

One freshman student was James L. Lamb from North Dakota, an enthusiastic young man who consistently had his hand in the air. One day O'Malley looked at him over his glasses and said as only he could say it—"What ails thee, little lamb?"

Frank always had a fairly cold eye for both the study of law as well as the practice of law. He felt that it was a cold and detached exercise within the community of man—particularly at the corporate or governmental level where the attorney became so detached from those his work ultimately affected that the human result became meaningless. He felt that the dehumanizing process started in the law schools where students first came to realize that what they were going to ultimately do in the community isolated them from the people for whom they would labor—in fact the whole legal learning process was geared toward a certain non-recognition of people in favor of a sort of slavish devotion of the mind toward principle, precedent or what he called the "fact" or the "matter of the fact." The actual practice of law became merely a reinforcement—sinister as could be—of an earlier mindset.

I talked to him at great length along those lines because I had always planned to go on to law school. In his own mind he thought that probably the only honest legal situation he could think of was a case in which two farmers took legitimate positions with respect to the ownership of a cow—the subject matter was human, the lawyer-adversaries as well as the claimants were all in face to face confrontation.

Though he was not simple enough to feel that legal positions or legal situations were not a real source of the contemporary structure, he strongly felt that the execution of those functions should be left to men and women who had a bookkeeper mentality—those with thoughts founded in divination or immortality or, for that part, decency should at all costs avoid the law.

Since it was my intention to return to my own small community in South Dakota where things were pretty much on a human confrontational level he consented to write letters of recommendation for me to the University of Chicago and to the University of Michigan. (Notre Dame was out because its Dean at that time was Clarence Manion—the archtype of the devil in the mind of Frank O'Malley.)

Strangely enough O'Malley had definite partisan political beliefs. He disliked Harry Truman immensely because he bombed two cities off the face of the globe and had a good night's sleep both nights. In 1948 Henry Wallace was his man though he had little stomach for his running mate Glen Taylor, a guitar-playing Idaho Congressman. I don't think he really understood the obvious pitfalls of a Wallace presidency but he viewed him as an honest populist and that to him was a far cry from the likes of Tom Dewey or Harry Truman.

The last time I saw O'Malley was at a time I took my oldest daughter to South Bend to enroll her at St. Mary's College. We drank at the bar at the Morris Inn, talked of time, man, and the world in that wonderful cosmological vocabulary that was peculiar to Frank O'Malley [Owen J. Donley, '48].[23]

———— · ————

I tried to read as much of whomever he mentioned as I could. As a result I have in my library many books I otherwise wouldn't have read, let alone have bought, by writers like Maritain, Dawson, and Berdyaev. My library may be as good an index of what

O'Malley emphasized in his courses as my notes are. Another unacademic effect O'Malley had on a few students—it was a minor joke among the faculty, I think—was that they adopted some of his manners of dress: wore his kind of ties or shirts, for example. . . . [His] influence, I have to say, was not always to the good; the charge that some made against him, that he spoiled some of the better students for graduate study, was correct. He believed that graduate studies in English (and probably in other subjects too) were arid and hollow and that they gave students too little choice in developing their true potential. As a result, some who might otherwise have gone into them probably did not, and a number of students whom I know either failed to complete graduate work or shifted from school to school before doing so. O'Malley's indictment of graduate study was in large measure true: it certainly did not encourage the kind of study that O'Malley was interested in or aim at producing the kind of teacher that he was. It is also true that many students who never encountered O'Malley drop out of graduate school or find it sterile. Still, many of O'Malley's students were predisposed against it. He later changed his attitude, apparently; I've heard in recent years that during the fifties and sixties he was actually encouraging students to do graduate work. Even when I was a student he recognized that some of us ought to go into teaching and that, a doctorate being a virtual prerequisite for college teaching, we would have to do graduate work somewhere. But he was predisposed to recommend unconventional programs, like that of the Committee on Social Thought at the University of Chicago, to which J. H. Johnston went (and which he later left for a more conventional program elsewhere). O'Malley advised me and others to go to the University of Pennsylvania—but as a choice of a lesser evil. Penn had recently opened a program in American Civilization that permitted the study of literature outside the traditional philological approach of English departments with their strong emphasis on Anglo-Saxon. Dick Ames and I started at Penn in 1949, and for several years a steady stream of Notre Dame English graduates followed us— so many that I was once asked by the director of the program at Penn what accounted for it. . . .

O'Malley's effectiveness was largely an expression of his personality and his classroom charisma—also that what he valued in teaching was the conveying of personal judgment rather than the transmission of conventional academic knowledge and skills. It was similarly the habit of personal judgment that he wanted to inculcate in students. For this reason the papers he had students write were never research papers but expressions of their judgment on what they read.

He was more interested in religion than literature; at least his interest centered on the religious implications of literature. For this reason he made much of minor writers in whom he saw important religious or philosophical value and tended to dismiss or deal in a perfunctory way with others—Henry James, for instance—whose writings seemed unrelated to religion [Frank Duggan, '48].[24]

———— · ————

In the first week of March, 1944, newly arrived Navy students (including myself) found themselves in a freshman class in English composition at the University of Notre Dame. The instructor was a thin man with red hair carefully swept past the ears and he was wearing a collar with rather unusual rounded tips and a tie firmly clasped to the collar. He stared back at the class through thick-lensed glasses and with a grimace which passed for a smile.

Someone once said Frank O'Malley didn't suffer fools grace-fully, and, even back then, some of the Navy students seemed to at least sense this disposition. Before launching into the expla-nations of matters to be emphasized in the course, he made clear just what wouldn't be occupying much time—Navy English, which was the real name listed on the schedule. He rather shyly suggested that two days would be sufficient for Navy English and terms such as BUPERS and COM-PAC. The balance of the semester would be devoted to things of somewhat more permanent value.

Also, at the first meeting of the class, Mr. O'Malley asked each student to introduce himself and say something about where he came from or other personal description. There were some 35 persons in the class and all wore identical Navy uniforms.

Two days later the classes met again. As in the first meeting, the various students sat randomly about the room. From time to time, Mr. O'Malley would pose a question, always looking directly at and using the name of the student being addressed. It soon became clear that O'Malley not only remembered everyone's name, home town or whatever, but absolutely recognized every person in the room. All this was apparently done without use of notes and after but a single previous meeting. Also, it is doubtful that anybody was in the same seat the second time around.

About 20 years after leaving Notre Dame, and no doubt after thousands of students came and went their ways from O'Malley's classes, I happened to be on campus at a cocktail party. I noticed O'Malley holding a large martini (apparently not his first of the afternoon) and walked up behind him. He turned around suddenly, glanced at me and without a moment's hesitation, said: "John, how nice to see you." All of which indicated to me a second time that Frank O'Malley, along with various other very individual characteristics, had a sense of recall—certainly one that astonished me.

With the coming of the summer months of 1944, O'Malley would inevitably appear in seersucker suits of the striped variety. He was always impeccably dressed, always in hard heels, always walking fast when seen going about the campus. His glasses had red-shell rims, not exactly what most people were sporting in 1944.

One day he asked the class which magazines were the better ones current at that date. He was always coming up with some leading question quite aside from the normal academics. Though most of the Navy students were of the 18-year-old variety, with a few salts from the fleet thrown in, all by this time had learned to be on-guard when O'Malley casually posed his questions. The most sensitive of human beings, O'Malley could drip acid. Safe answers came back, including *Time*, *Saturday Evening Post*, and *Readers Digest*. I don't remember if anyone had the nerve to mention *Look* or *Collier's*, certainly not *Esquire*.

"*Readers Digest!*" His distaste was shriveling. "*Saturday Evening Post!*" O'Malley spent the balance of the period citing the shallowness of most popular literature. He wondered why students supposedly interested in broadening themselves were so unaware of the existence of periodicals of literary merit. He sought to explain why any effort at creativity was to be preferred to crass repetitive material aimed at capitalizing on broad, and usually low, common taste.

Discussions in O'Malley's class would often run far afield, yet somehow be pertinent. At one session a student with a New England accent named Ken Barry gave some heated opinions about jazz and other forms of music. (Incidentally, everyone in the class with O'Malley had last names beginning with A, B, or C—typical Navy efficiency. I don't know who the X, Y, and Z got for an English instructor.) Anyway, the student was lamenting the fame and fortune of Harry James, trumpeteer and band leader who had supplanted Glenn Miller and the Dorsey Brothers on the popular heap, when the creative musicians of jazz such as Duke Ellington were largely ignored. "The commercial swing guys like James get all the money and glory (and Betty Grable) but you hardly hear about the original jazz artists," he said.

O'Malley looked very pleased. "You've made an interesting observation. We seem to be getting someplace in this class. A person such as Ellington might be remembered later on; but, even if he isn't, he did what he did. That's the point.". . . .

Later during my student days at Notre Dame I had joined a seminar on the Great Books conducted by Frank O'Malley. We usually met in a lounge on the second floor of the Rockne Memorial Building. The books that we read and discussed included some of the expected genre, but with a couple of odd works thrown in. Toward the end of the term, O'Malley asked the group what it thought of the various books he had selected for the seminar. There was considerable weighing in on the side of or against this or that tome of antiquity, the Middle Ages or more modern times. One book, however, drew rather heated views and was seen by several students as a very questionable selection. It was one of O'Malley's odd choices: *Pilgrim of the Absolute* by Léon Bloy.

Complaints centered on the author's (this was autobiographical) strange habits, including one where he went around the streets of Paris begging for the poor while his own family was approaching starvation. "What kind of way of life for a father is this? What if everybody was like this?". . . .

"It's impossible that everyone would be like that," answered O'Malley. "But, I think it's important for us to be disturbed." He said there were values other than those we are in the habit of hearing about. He said we should be willing to listen to them sometimes, and to "let them make us think."

Along about this time (it was a couple of years after the war) we began to hear of efforts to make Notre Dame "a great American university." There were, of course, those who already thought Notre Dame was a decent place of learning. But, this was different. It had to do with the number of PhDs on the various institutional staffs and other symbols of prestige in the world of education. It had to do with money to buy the symbols. Frank O'Malley was always one to boost the university, but this sort of paper conformity presented him with a personal problem. . . . The conformity implied with the seeking of advanced degrees seemed, somehow, alien to him. To be educated, it was not necessary to be certified. Sometimes he seemed to be saying advanced degrees were fine for other people. . . .

It was a time when Harvard and Princeton were still revered, and Notre Dame had its niche. It is hard to believe Harvard or Princeton had anyone like O'Malley. As Carl Jung might have phrased it: Notre Dame had harmony of time, place, and attitude. Later it was more of a university but after O'Malley it was less of a place [John V. Ankenbruck, '49].[25]

———— · ————

Professor Frank O'Malley was one of the legends of this campus. His mind always seemed to be in flight, as though mentally he were on the way to finding an answer that would explain all the mysteries. I would meet him on his travels in the Morris Inn. He would smile, greet me with an enormous compliment, then smile again, as though we were conspirators who shared a secret that not even the great ones could get us to tell. He would shuffle off, leaving me immensely flattered. Out of his presence, I realized that only he knew the secret, and I wasn't in on the conspiracy; nevertheless, he had made himself dear to me. Later, I guessed that the secret was that there is no brass ring; and the sweet smile he wore was the mask to hide his despair. Isn't doubt a part of the whimsy of the Irish? [Father Robert Griffin, '49].[26]

———— · ————

When anyone told O'Malley in his later years that he had become a legend his reply was always, "I'm not a legend; I'm a myth." Ostensibly, this was self-deprecation, but it was not necessarily so: there is a kind of myth that is more than a legend, as in ancient Greece when the myth of the gods was older and more fundamental than the legend of Homer.

———— · ————

[Frank O'Malley] had an enormous influence on me, and indeed still does. A photo of him looks upon me as I write this letter! I think the best thing I can do is to send you a copy of a letter I wrote Kenny Woodward when he was preparing the Notre Dame magazine article on him:

"... His influence on me was entirely in the classroom (and at the Wranglers), plus, of course, nominating me for a job at *Commonweal* the summer I graduated—something that came as a great surprise and which set me on the ink-stained way to which I have now returned.

It has seemed to me that what never was fully understood, at the time at least, was that his influence was not literary or even educational as such, but moral and religious. He gave people a vision of life, a religious vision, one even of sanctity, and a stance—uncompromising, of the highest possible intellectual standards certainly, contemptuous of pedantry and orthodoxy, scornful of material considerations (some of us later found adjustments necessary, especially in this respect). He took bright provincial products of the anti-intellectual and puritanical Catholicism of the time, at an age when doubt dawned, and gave them a new, inspiring, intellectually satisfying Catholicism of Maritain, Bernanos, Bloy, etc., thereby solving a particular problem for them, that of coming to terms with what they were and with their place in the larger American society, but he also inspired them through his own intensity and conviction. He also wrecked some, who never got over the experience and spent the rest of their lives imitating him (I remember him contemptuously dismissing somebody's essay as that of "a little Léon Bloy"). He also left many cold. The true O'Malley man—and it is an astoundingly widespread and influential fraternity; I keep bumping into them here [in Paris], in Tokyo, in all parts of the U.S.—had his life changed in a constructive way, and even when his spell had lifted had reason to be grateful.

But I knew nothing of his own life and would be fascinated to learn. When I knew him, he was capable of travelling—annually to New York and the Biltmore Bar, to Chicago, etc. I gather that later even that became impossible and it was simply Dillon to class to Dillon to the whatever-it-was hotel bar in South Bend, delivered home by obliging busdrivers into the arms of a waiting campus policeman. He would also pick up astounding acquaintances at the bar who probably wondered for the rest of their lives what *that* had all meant. It was the very narrowness of his life that was, I presume, responsible for the intensity of his classroom effect. There seemed to be nothing else in his life. Other splendid people in the English department of the time—Richard Sullivan, Ernest Sandeen, Rufus Rauch—could not have the same effect because they were normal human beings with normal lives, with wives and families and homes and common sense. They were balanced. Frank was obviously unbalanced, and in that lay his power. Was it a personal tragedy or all a great success? That's the interesting question [William Pfaff, '49].[27]

———— · ————

I had come from a Tennessee country public school and had brought only some facility as a newspaper reporter with me to N.D. For me, Frank O'Malley represented the vehicle of transformation, as I suspect he was for many others. I can count at least seven things he did for me:

1. O'Malley was the entree to elegant language, taste, art, and value—to style—in his careful measurement of the truth, goodness, and beauty of everything.
2. In Rhetoric and Composition he introduced me to the critical intelligence through his challenging questions.
3. There I also learned to look at the world around me and to try to capture it in words.
4. His extraordinary ability to convey respect for his students and his high expectations of them motivated me as no one had before to do better work. I would not be embarrassed by his criticism. The Meehan medal, upon his nomination, was an honor because it reflected his approval of my work.
5. In Philosophy of Literature III and IV we discovered where we were in the history of ideas and how the literary sensibility had reflected that history.
6. In Modern Catholic Writers we discovered a Christian *Weltanschauung* through a rich array of writers from Guardini, Maritain, Gilson, and Dawson to Hopkins, Claudel, Bloy, and Graham Greene—a perspective from which we could view and judge the modern world and its cultural development, a truth by which we could live our lives. And it made no difference, later, when I knew better the extent to which he was only

synthesizing the ideas of others; he had put it all together in a way 19 and 20-year-olds could grasp. That vision has served as a foundation on which I have been able to stand, without danger of being swept away by whatever current came along, for almost 40 years. (He also introduced us to the Benedictine monastic tradition; the Holy Rule and monastic associations have stood me in good stead since.)

7. Finally, O'Malley was for me a strong father figure in that I have lived my professional life as an academic and sometimes journalist under his gaze; I would not betray him by compromise of principle or unseemly conduct, by any dishonorable act. His portrait alone hangs on my office wall, but I don't need it to remind me of what he gave me or of his gaze.

[When I heard of his death I spoke a kind of memorial to him in one of my own classes]: "In *Time* and *Newsweek* this week appeared obituary notices for a college professor who published no books, advised no presidents, made no great scientific discoveries.

"You don't know who Frank O'Malley was. He was a teacher, and for 41 years he communicated a vision of the meaning of life, a passion for the truth found in the Word, a thirst for justice, and a respect for personal integrity.

"As *Newsweek* noted, he was taken seriously. On football Saturdays, game time 12:15 or 12:30, his 11:00 class was invariably full, even if it meant missing lunch or the kickoff. His respect for his students' minds and efforts was complete, and one was ashamed to fail that respect. Yet, one knew that Frank O'Malley loved him and believed in him. One left his final senior class meeting with a challenge to go into the world and the memory of his breaking voice, filled with emotion. And I suspect that all who counted themselves O'Malley's students have through all the years felt the burden of O'Malley's trust. I have failed it a thousand times. . . .

"'Mr. O'Malley,' as we addressed him—he wasn't a Ph.D. and I suspect that his students who got doctorates have often, as I have, been embarrassed when our students addressed us as 'Dr.' instead of 'Mr.'—used to quote Paul Claudel's reference to the old Portuguese proverb that 'God writes straight with crooked lines.' When I think of myself as one of O'Malley's students it is sobering, indeed. As mired as one may become in the bourgeois life, one tried to be faithful to his vision, seeing realization of a truly human community of persons liberated by truth and beauty as the justification for one's commitments. But those lines are crooked. One's lack of genius and command of language, one's fear that he would not get through a course syllabus, one's distractions from his students in committee work, one's timidity and embarrassment in intruding upon another's private space, one's bad judgment in taking on too many preparations or courses (O'Malley apparently taught the same five courses for forty years)—all of these and one's pride and selfishness...stunt, divert, block, or abort that love and patient respect that he exemplified and frustrate his kind of success as a teacher....

"O'Malley died last week. The *New York Times* took note of his going. But I would remember his name in honor, and I am only sorry that you could not have sat in one of his classes" [William H. Slavick, '49].[28]

———— · ————

This man said something to us seniors 24 years ago, in May 1950, at the end of our last class with him, which I have never forgotten.

He had closed all of his ever-present, multimarked books, paused, then said: "I hope you will all be happy; I hope you will be happy forever. But always remember, happiness sometimes is sorrow, sorrow borne for love."

I personally have been a recipient of just such a sorrow which can become a happiness if borne for love; many of us have, I'm sure. Perhaps all of us have borne them better, because Frank told us how [Paul Mack Schaefer, '50].[29]

———— · ————

> Sorrow, that saw your face in kindness,
> In silence saw the pity in your eyes,
> Praises now that generative sadness
> From which my exaltation could arise.
>
> Lethargic flesh that yet must be redemptive
> Had only to be touched to be consumed.
> How is it flesh that would not be
>   presumptive
> Now resurrects before it is entombed?

Little dear, bestower of surprises,
Such apathetic patterns you have changed.
I want to live bereft of all inertia.
I want to live loved and estranged.
                    [Walter Clements, '51][30]

———— · ————

*Hugh Hennedy quotes a poem of O'Malley's within his own
poem and then goes on to acknowledge the Hopkins influence in
O'Malley and to express gratefulness for that and so much more,
implying so correctly that his greatness lay more in his teaching
than in his writing.*

YOU, FRANK O'MALLEY, YOU

1

Let the Christbrand burst!
Let the Christbrand blazon!
Dartle whitely under the hearth-fire,
Unwind the wind, turn the thunderer,
And never, never thinning,
Forfend fear.
Flare up smartly, fix, flex, bless, inspire,
Instar the time, sear the sorcerer,
Save all year.
Let the Christbrand burst!
Let the Christbrand blazon!

2

Ah! There's the heart
That read you right, Gerard!
You, Balliol's star and Christ's.

There's the heart,
Pierced by Incarnation
And by Lovescape crucified,
Uttering—even muttering—truth.

3

You, Frank O'Malley, you
Brought me to
The dragon in the door,

To morning's soaring minion
And the woman who was poor.

You, Frank O'Malley, you
Revealed to me
Me, being, as you were,
The first to have me try,
Being the first to pay attention.

You, Frank O'Malley, you
Gave to me
And all the others
Hopkins' great vocational poem
Along with that vocational poem, your life.

You, Frank O'Malley, you
Wrote to me,
No doubt to others,
That you were and would be always
With me in my works and hopes.
You are.

                            [Hugh Hennedy, '51][31]

———— · ————

Students of mine wept openly twice in my years as a teacher—on a raw, cloudy November afternoon in 1963 when a President was assassinated and on a hot, stagnant July afternoon when I read to them an impression of Professor Frank O'Malley written by one of his former students.

Perhaps the latter group recognized the sense of pain as their teacher read slowly and deliberately about a man who was so important in his own life. Perhaps their vicarious experience of sadness was a fitting tribute to a man who had been spoken of frequently by their teacher. Perhaps they knew that their teacher, the pupil, was mourning the loss of the master.

My experience with Frank O'Malley was brief but meaningful. I had tried unsuccessfully to enroll in one of his courses for three and a half years. In my last semester at Notre Dame, my quest finally ended. What I remember most about Frank O'Malley can be narrowed down to one crucial half-hour conversation.

I sat in his office for my final exam. We discussed two things: the Old Testament and the Russian novelist, Fedor Dostoyevski. If there were ever any doubts in my mind about wanting to enter the teaching profession, they were resolved in those critical 30 minutes. The novice had sat with the master. Now he must go out and do.

It was my privilege to share a vision with Frank O'Malley when I attended Notre Dame.

Leo Tolstoy said that "The glory of the good is in their conscience and not in the mouths of men." Frank O'Malley possessed that conscience, and his vision will never be silent in the mouths of men [John C. Collins, '63].[32]

———— · ————

Quite frankly (and I have confessed this to many who were similarly impressed by Frank O'Malley's approach to life), I owe him, under God, my vocation to the contemplative life.

He was God's minister of the Word, and the seeds sown in those days later developed gradually and continue to this day to influence me. In a word, thank God for Frank O'Malley, and may something of his great spirit continue in the halls of Notre Dame [Brother Patrick Hart, '66].[33]

———— · ————

I was one of the first five women to attend Notre Dame, in an experimental course offered by both S.M.C. and N.D. I took O'Malley's course on modern Catholic writers as one of my electives. He was a lovely sad man. His course was one that had a class list of well over two hundred and daily attendance by about fifty. Some days he was incoherent, some days he was eloquent and brilliant, and many days he wasn't there at all. My most vivid memory of him is of the day he had a guest at class . . . Ed O'Connor who read to us from his novel in progress—I believe it was *I Was Dancing*. After class O'Malley asked if I would please come up to the podium (these classes were held in the murky, cool haze of the basement of the engineering auditorium). He introduced me to O'Connor who had known Dad—the remarkable part of this story is that until that moment I had no idea O'Malley was even aware that I was on his class list [Joan Garvey Hermes, '67].[34]

———— · ————

What I remember best is the way he had of creating an atmosphere in his freshman English class in which about fifteen adolescent males were capable of charity. We were encouraged to write very frankly about things which mattered deeply to us, and he made it possible to do so. People who, in other circumstances, might have been biting or easily critical listened with sympathy to very personal writing, and the discussion of books we read in common was conducted in the same spirit. I remember, too, a couple of lectures to his larger classes which drew standing ovations, and deserved them, and I also remember the people who took advantage of the fact that he was a notoriously easy grader and read newspapers quite openly during those lectures. I loathed them for that rudeness—not that I wasn't often rude myself, but because of the lack of respect it showed for a good, complicated, tormented, and holy man. I remember him so drunk one night he could barely talk and could walk only with difficulty; he was angry with me because I hadn't accepted his offer of editing the *Juggler,* something he could have arranged and something I didn't want for a number of reasons. Another time I visited him in the hospital when cirrhosis had begun to kill him and he was terribly embarrassed, as he always was when anyone ever showed him any thanks or gratitude. One of my happiest memories of him was a time in the room of a friend, when he was talking with a few of us about the summer before, during which Notre Dame had opened the campus to a Project Headstart group, black kids aged from late grade through high school who came to campus for a few weeks to see what colleges were like. Some were housed in Lyons, and O'Malley felt that he should have his rooms open during that period—something that must have been very difficult for someone who was so painfully shy. He told us about one little boy who came into his room and looked around at the shelves and said, "Are all these books yours?" "Yes," he said, "and I've read some of them more than once." The kid shook his head. "Man, you must be sick." Frank laughed when he told us this and said, "You know, he's right—I really must be sick!" He told us this in the rooms of a couple of friends who conducted an avant-garde drama group at Notre Dame: he asked them to do a reading of Claudel's *Tidings Brought to Mary* for one of his classes, and they had. He was there to thank them, which was unusual—he almost never went to the rooms of any students.

It bothers me that the writers he cared about have completely vanished from Catholic and other campuses these days, people like Mauriac and Claudel and Guardini and Mounier and Bernanos. I am inclined to think that the greatest of them was Bernanos, for *Diary of a Country Priest,* but none of them can be dismissed, even if there may be greater writers around. A lot of lesser ones are being taught on campus, and you'd think that people with a pretension to caring about religious tradition would be more careful about their own heritage. The French Catholic tradition is especially important.... Anyway, there isn't anyone like him at Notre Dame now, but there wasn't anyone like him before he got there either. He suffered a lot, I think, and apparently his last years were especially difficult. I hope he knew how grateful people were to him. The people I knew—who studied in small classes with him—the ones who are my friends, anyway—all remember him with the most profound respect [John Garvey, '67].[35]

———— · ————

[O'Malley] seemed to hand write each lecture in pen and ink and then deliver them in that quiet voice which brought a stillness to the class and yet the eloquence of his words seemed to speak loudly about the depth of his spiritual feelings [Joseph G. Blake, '68].[36]

———— · ————

Frank O'Malley was one of the most devoted and single-minded men I've ever known. I hardly knew *him;* a *figure,* in a way, an apparition, as he appeared slightly late every Tuesday and Thursday afternoon in our classroom in O'Shaughnessy Hall. The class meeting time was late, too, at a time when there would be few other classes in the building. Suddenly he'd be there—his snow white hair, his immaculate three-piece blue suit, mumbling sonorously under his breath—and we would shut up and listen. He not only created an atmosphere, he was the thing he created; young as we were, stupid as we were, deluded as we were, we knew that. We had the respect for him that we would ideally wish for ourselves. Incredibly, it wasn't sanctimonious and it was sacred. To him, we were something—each one of us. We would all be great artists. We would all make great contributions to humanity. And we worked our asses off, even though everyone automatically received an A in the course anyway. We worked because not to do so would be a violation, a blasphemy. I studied his pet books— *In Parenthesis, The World of Silence*—with a rigor I could never have mustered on my own; and I responded to them as "creatively" as I knew how, always in writing. He'd have us read our work to the rest of the class. Afterwards, speaking of the student, he'd ask "What has he accomplished?" And we had always accomplished a great deal.

At the end of the semester, I had written a play which I presented in class as a self-induced assignment. Afterwards, Mr. O'Malley took me aside and muttered into my shoulder "A great work. Great work," and seemed, I swear, to bless me with his right hand as he spoke. I didn't laugh then as he did that, and I don't laugh thinking of it now. I don't know who Frank O'Malley was. *Mr. O'Malley* was a great teacher; at a crucial time in my life, he did something for me no one else could have done. What else can you ask of anyone? [Michael R. Ryan, '68].[37]

——— · ———

I did not know Frank O'Malley particularly well. I was a student in one of his courses and we chatted on a few occasions outside of class. Yet I felt, and feel, a powerful closeness to the man.

One reason for my feeling is that his understanding of what it is to teach is the most profound I have ever encountered: "Teaching belongs to the active life or, rather, to that activity which is the overflow of thought and contemplation. It is the utterance of truth to people who will grow upon the utterance as mystery and rebel against it as formulation."

Another reason, I think, is that the aspect of the truth he seemed most sensitive to was man's exquisite vulnerability. He appreciated and shared the suffering caused by that vulnerability; he could laugh because he knew the Christian irony that in the cross reside all of man's dignity and worth [Kevin Reilly, '71].[38]

——— · ———

I first came to work for Notre Dame because of Frank O'Malley and the atmosphere he had helped to create there. The booklist for Modern Catholic Authors was given me at a national meeting of the National Federation of Catholic College Students in 1955, that's how close this professor's thinking was to the field of action. At that time, too, Notre Dame was considered the American arm of the revival of Catholic letters, begun by Chesterton and Belloc. And aborted with them, too, some think.

The first thing I did upon arriving in 1960 was to attend his class in Philosophy of Literature.... The place was packed.... What was the technique that made this man so much a legend at his university? ... Assignments included topics that were part of the daily life of the students, campus life.... In treating them as intellectuals he raised up independent thinkers, among them a goodly quantity of Notre Dame football players!

About the content of the student sections many stories are told. Frank was notorious for believing that the learning experience went on between the teacher and the student and all the rest of the institutionalization was dross. He often sent over all A's for his class and when the Registrar would send them back he would say, "Then change them to all F's. Isn't it all the same?" Another time a Dean tells the story that Mr. O'Malley had returned 22 A's for a class.

"But, Sir?" the official questioned.

O'Malley: "What I have written, I have written. Those are my grades, kindly...."

"But, Sir, there are only 20 people in your class."

O'Malley: "Then give the two A's to someone who needs them."

Teaching Baudelaire and Genet went side by side with moderating the literary magazine, the *Juggler.* I remember one time when editor McQuaid locked the office door after an O'Malley protest stopped a story about a mestizo call girl in Nuevo Laredo until "agreement" could be reached. Frank was absolute about his Victorian sexual mores and it often led him into hilarious conflict with the undergraduates. The mestizo story, by the way, never appeared, and we never got to learn how [the author's] brother found those things as a freshman.

Lyons Hall where he lived was an example of the utopian ambiance of Notre Dame's campus. In the years since Father John Cavanaugh laid such a fine foundation for growth and Father Theodore Hesburgh so bravely asserted the true intellectual character of the University a kind of Camelot atmosphere grew up.

Dr. Carberry, an engineering professor and part-time humanist, explains the atmosphere of Notre Dame at that time in this way: "The English Department required a two-year course called Philosophy of Literature at that time, and Engineering had a truly humanistic basic course for its students consisting of a senior . . . cultural seminar in Shakespeare. Yale marvelled at us," says this professor, a graduate of [Yale]. . . . Frank O'Malley used to say, in jest, that he was his own department. . . .

The "O'Malley boy" was something of a national phenomenon. The Dean at Northwestern's Woodrow Wilson Center in the days of that great grant used to refer to Frank as his "stable." . . . In 40 years of teaching, [Frank's] technique varied somewhat. In his later years his voice was so quiet as to be almost indistinguishable at the podium, but he was ruthlessly straightforward, like his teacher, Father Leo R. Ward, who used to say: "We could think it, but Frank could say it."

Frank dwelt on dichotomies, science versus humanism, ethical or theological philosophy versus scientific philosophy. He was at base a synthesist with a synthesist's sense of humor. In his papers we find titles for lectures for the Wranglers, the philosophical debating society of the undergraduates, like "Snakes and demons strangling in a fog." His ignoring of administrative protocol was legendary, some letters from the Academic Dean remaining unopened for 20 years" [Patricia Fenelon, MA, '71].[39]

———— · ————

Although he constantly taught and personally embodied characteristics which inspired and nourished his students, his shyness forced a distance between himself and the other residents of Lyons Hall. One day Frank invited me into his room which the maid later admitted to me was opened for her cleaning services once a month—if she was lucky. I had run into Frank when he was emptying his trash around noon . . . his overcoat lay upon his bed giving me the impression that he had not slept that night, and to the left the walls were shelved with books. . . .

During course registration periods, Frank's class would close immediately. Then the mass procession would begin to his room in Lyons. But the solitary soul behind that door never answered— in four years on that floor I *never* saw him answer his door, not even during the fire at the end of my junior year. So students would leave notes on his door, under his door, in his mailbox, and even in boxes of other students residing on the floor. Students also camped overnight for almost 12 hours outside the English Department, hoping that they could secure that cherished computer card which granted them admittance.

Besides camping and writing letters, students had a third option for gaining admission to an O'Malley course. They could personally ask the professor. That meant that literally hundreds of students followed the master whenever he walked to his classroom during registration week. Their goal? They had to obtain a unique piece of paper—a palm card which read, "Thank you for voting Democratic," on one side, with Frank's signature on the other. . . .

The only public office Frank ever held was precinct committeeman for the campus. His abundance of palm cards was evidence that he cherished privacy over politics. Yet . . . he faithfully fulfilled the duties of committeeman mostly out of convictions for integrity. The Notre Dame precinct was "O'Malley's precinct," with Lyons Hall residents usually working on election day as judges or clerks of the polling place. . . .

One day a week Frank would remain in his room all afternoon until 4:15 when he set out on his journey across the campus to his Modern Catholic Writers class. By the time Frank reached the main sidewalk along the tree-lined quads at least three students had shaken his hand heartily. . . . When Frank passed the flagpole at the middle of the campus, he had talked to at least 15 students who had made it a point to go out of their way to greet him. As he walked by the Business Building, two-thirds the distance he was traveling, Frank walked with 20 or more students who happened to be going that way, too. O'Malley was the pied piper of Notre Dame.

My last class at Notre Dame was Frank's class on Monday, May 7, 1973. Exactly one year later, May 7, 1974, Frank O'Malley passed away. And although I could not foresee his death, Frank could feel its closeness. Somehow, something compelled me to jot down those final words he spoke to us:

> I appreciate the presence, hope, and beauty of your lives. These are the last words you'll hear from me—for the time being anyway. I don't know what's in store for me in the near future or far-off future. And I hope you'll remember

these words. I have a wish and hope for you. I hope that time will never trap you, and that the world will have time for you. I hope that you will be happy forever, and that you recollect the happiness of human existence which is sometimes sorrow and suffering, and sometimes love. My love to you! Peace and thanks!

[Gary J. Caruso, '73].[40]

———— · ————

The people in Lyons Hall who knew Mr. O'Malley better than the rest did so more because of an affliction than any other factor. There were three of us in particular, all members of the class of '73, who suffered from congenital insomnia. So, as bleary-eyed guardians of the dawn, we became well acquainted with the elusive professor who resided in room 327. We were at first a bit apprehensive of the scholarly gentleman; because anyone who kept the hours we did was automatically suspect, even by us. What was it that could keep a man of his stature out until four o'clock nearly every morning? It soon became apparent that his custom was to devote the late evening and early morning hours to spirits found in glass rather than football weekends. But no matter how rigorous the evening or late the hour, the hallway in front of his room was always an open forum for anyone who might be around when he arrived. He is what I think of first when I remember Lyons Hall.

In speaking with Mr. O'Malley it became quite evident that he regarded Lyons Hall as a very special place. He subtly instilled in us a sense of pride in the fact that we lived there. He would at times speak of "Blood on the Walls." To him, the building was no common edifice. It had been blessed by the labors of good people who had lived in it, and as long as the present inhabitants remained true to what he called "The Work," it would continue to be an exponent of that viability and not a Golgotha. I really believe that Mr. O'Malley thought all the people in Lyons Hall were good. Even the lowliest of us, which was at times me, felt that in his eyes we had great potential. He never verbally discouraged a student, and his capacity for coping with their shortcomings was vast [Stephen R. Pallucca, '73].[41]

———— · ————

Although it was...my good fortune to be one of the last

generation of Frank O'Malley's students (I was graduated in 1974), I never actually visited Frank's bedside as he lay dying. In fact, I heard of his hospitalization only a day or two before he died. He had closed himself off in his room for quite a while (the sort of thing he often did. . . . Those of us . . . most of us . . . who rather romanticized his alcoholism did him no favor by excusing or over-looking these absences) and we thought little of it. . . .

I met Frank (I think of him as Frank, although I never addressed him as anything but Mr. O'Malley) at a party in Keenan Hall when I was a freshman. I'd already heard many stories about him from my father, my mother, my oldest brother John ('67), my Uncle Jerry (Hogan . . .), and Henry Rago. I was in perfect shape for the meeting: a self-absorbed adolescent with romantic preten-sions to become a poet. If he had been legendary among people in your class, you can easily understand how, in the fall of 1970, he seemed almost divine. It was a typically dirtball late sixties-early seventies sort of student party with Jimmy Hendrix and Grateful Dead music blaring—I think there was even a hashish pipe circulating—at which this elegantly dressed and soft-spoken gentleman of another generation nevertheless seemed very com-fortable and happy. And accepted. Somebody introduced me to him and he began to speak of my Uncle Jerry and then of my father, and then, saddened and suddenly remembering, of the father of Tim McGarry, a recent Notre Dame graduate and antiwar activist who had only a few weeks before committed public suicide. He tried to describe the father and the son to me but soon dissolved into weeping and perhaps drunken incoherence ("What a good father he was to have! And what a good son he had! Oh, the fathers and the sons!") The few awful moments I watched him slumped in tears against the cinderblock corridor wall will always be a sort of emblem of that terrible time.

[As a teacher] he was brilliant and moving and made you want to read and write and think and talk about books and men and women and angels and God for the rest of your life.

We heard about his death at the beginning of a Jacques Maritain seminar given by the late Professor Joe Evans, another great man and teacher and a dear friend of Frank's. "Let us thank the Ground of Our Being for him," Joe Evans said, and then we all, whether believers or not, joined him in saying the Our Father [Michael O. Garvey, '74].⁴²

I said a brief prayer at his grave recently. [Rev. Theodore M. Hesburgh, '38].[43]

Some have speculated that he might have preferred being buried in his native Massachusetts. But I doubt that. Yes, I feel that he would have chosen that little cemetery on the wooded hill in the Indiana snowbelt. It provides the setting for him to continue his great performance even into the years of his death. Just by lying there on dark, wintry days he brings to mind in visitors who knew him the sound of his insistent voice reciting his favorite words of James Joyce coming almost to the dying fall of a prayer:

Yes, the newspapers were right, snow was general all over Ireland. It was falling on every part of the dark central plain, on the treeless hills, falling softly upon the Bog of Allen and, farther westward, softly falling into the dark mutinous Shannon waves. It was falling, too, upon every part of the lonely churchyard on the hill where Michael Furey lay buried. It lay thickly drifted on the crooked crosses and headstones, on the spears of the little gate, on the barren thorns. His soul swooned slowly as he heard the snow falling faintly through the universe and faintly falling, like the descent of their last end, upon all the living and the dead.[44]

Notes

Chapter 1

1. Joseph Lanigan, quoting a campus story of the late 1940s, in a letter to the author, February 5, 1986.

2. Robert P. Tristram Coffin, *Lost Paradise* (New York: Macmillan, 1934), p. 65.

3. This and other class entries below are from an assignment book that I made in 1936–37 and preserved.

4. James Joyce, *Dubliners* (New York: Modern Library, 1926), pp. 297–298.

5. D. H. Lawrence, *Sea and Sardinia* (New York: Penguin, 1923), pp. 29–30.

6. Harry Sylvester, "The Swede," *Scribner's Magazine* (Oct. 1936): 37.

7. Gerard Manley Hopkins, *A Hopkins Reader,* ed. John Pick (Garden City, N.Y.: Doubleday, 1966), pp. 50–51.

8. From a mimeographed copy belonging to the author.

9. Henry Adam, letter to the author, October 30, 1986.

10. Phillip R. North, class of '39, in a telephone conversation with the author, January 31, 1988.

11. Clinton High School, *1926 Yearbook,* quotation supplied by David A. Hazel, Principal.

12. University of Notre Dame, *Dome,* 1929, p. 155.

13. *The Collected Poems of Charles L. O'Donnell,* ed. Charles L. Carey, C.S.C. (Notre Dame, Ind.: University of Notre Dame Press, 1942), p. 138.

14. William G. McGowan, letter to the author, December 5, 1986.

15. Tom Stritch, "A Lost Breed," *Notre Dame Magazine,* vol. 10, no. 1 (Feb. 1981): 21.

16. University of Notre Dame, *Dome,* 1932, p. 269.

17. Ibid., p. 237.

18. Ibid., p. 342.

19. Francis J. O'Malley, "A Literary Addendum: Willa Cather's Archbishop Latour in Reality—John Baptist Lamy—a Presentation of his Letters, Life, and Associates during the Missionary Years in the Diocese of Sante Fe," unpublished Master's thesis, University of Notre Dame, 1933.

20. Tom Stritch, letter to the author, August 8, 1985.

21. Tom Stritch, "The Notre Dame I Came To," *Notre Dame Magazine,* vol. 9, no. 3 (July 1980): 19.

22. Ibid., p. 18.

23. Ibid., p. 19.

24. Walter Pater, *The Renaissance* (New York: Boni & Liveright, 1919), p. 197.

Chapter 2

1. Eugene R. Fairweather, *The Oxford Movement* (New York: Oxford University Press, 1964), p. 3.

2. Christopher Dawson, "The English Catholics, 1850–1950," *Dublin Review,* 4th quarter (1950): 3.

3. Cardinal John Henry Newman, *On the Scope and Nature of University Education* (New York: E. P. Dutton, 1943), p. 112.

4. Frank O'Malley, "The Thinker in the Church: The Spirit of Newman," *Review of Politics,* vol. 21, no. 1 (Jan. 1959): 16.

5. Tom Stritch, letter to the author, June 17, 1987.

6. Gilbert K. Chesterton, *Orthodoxy* (New York: Dodd, Mead, 1924), pp. 4, 153.

7. Rufus William Rauch, "G. K. C. as a Poet," in *A Chesterton Celebration,* ed. R. W. Rauch (Notre Dame, Ind.: University of Notre Dame Press, 1983), pp. 61–62.

8. Ibid., p. 6.

9. Rufus William Rauch, "Chesterton at Notre Dame," in *A Chesterton Celebration,* p. 5.

10. Ibid., p. 6.

11. Frank O'Malley, "Tribute to Jacques Maritain," *Review of Politics,* vol. 5, no. 2 (April 1943): 243.

12. Tom Stritch, "The Foreign Legion of Father O'Hara," *Notre Dame Magazine,* vol. 10, no. 4 (Oct. 1981): 23.

13. Ibid., p. 24.

14. Rufus Rauch, letter to the author, October 8, 1987.

15. Ibid.

16. Ibid.

17. Ibid.

18. Ibid.

19. Stritch, "Foreign Legion of Father O'Hara."

20. Frank O'Malley, "The Image of Man: Ten Years of *The Review of Politics*," *Review of Politics*, vol. 10, no. 4 (Oct. 1948): 398.

21. Frank O'Malley, *Review of Politics*, vol. 10, no. 4 (Oct. 1948).

22. Frank O'Malley, "Waldemar Gurian at Notre Dame," *Review of Politics*, vol. 17, no. 1 (Jan. 1955): 19.

23. Christopher Hollis, *Along the Road to Frome* (London: Geo. C. Harrap, 1958), p. 160.

24. James Hitchcock, "Postmortem on a Rebirth," *American Scholar* (Spring 1980): 216.

25. Tom Stritch, "The Notre Dame I Came To," *Notre Dame Magazine*, vol. 9. no. 3 (July 1980): 19.

26. Christopher Dawson, *Progress and Religion* (New York: Sheed and Ward, 1938), p. 245.

27. Christopher Dawson, "The Nature and Destiny of Man," in *Enquiries into Religion and Culture* (New York: Sheed and Ward, 1937), p. 311.

28. Robert Roquette, S.J., "France," in *The Catholic Church Today: Western Europe*, ed. M. A. Fitzsimons (Notre Dame, Ind.: University of Notre Dame Press, 1969), p. 222.

29. Andrew M. Greeley, *The Catholic Experience* (New York: Doubleday, 1967), p. 247.

30. Rufus Rauch, letter to the author, October 8, 1987.

31. Philip Gleason, *Keeping the Faith: American Catholicism, Past and Present* (Notre Dame, Ind.: University of Notre Dame Press, 1987).

32. Quoted in Arnold Sparr, "Frank O'Malley: Thinker, Critic, Revivalist," Working Paper Series of the Cushwa Center for the Study of American Catholicism, University of Notre Dame, series 14, no. 2 (Fall 1983). In 1985, Mr. Sparr incorporated that paper into a thesis at the University of Wisconsin, Madison, entitled "The Catholic Literary Revival in America, 1920–1960."

Chapter 3

1. Hugh S. Taylor, "Should They Go to Princeton?" *Commonweal*, vol. 23, no. 16 (Feb. 14, 1936).

2. In the Frank O'Malley Papers, University of Notre Dame Archives.

3. Ibid.

4. Ibid.

5. Document loaned to the author by James J. Meaney.

6. Mimeographed sheet among the papers loaned to the author by J. Austin Sobczak (class of '40).

7. Mimeographed sheets loaned to the author by James J. Meaney.

8. Frank Duggan, letter to the author, January 6, 1988.

9. Between 1940 and 1946 the course apparently changed very little. James E. Newman's notes for the course in 1946, compared with my own in 1940, show that the lectures must have been nearly identical: "[Gissing] wanted at first to apply the Greek idea of tragedy to the wretchedness of a London slum" [1940]; "He seems to have tried to deal with the London slums as a Greek tragedy would do" [1946]. "[Meredith] had a sense of vitality which enabled him to see the teleology of life even when watching the wastefulness of nature" [1940]; "he could feel in himself a teleology in spite of the wastefulness of nature" [1946]. "Meredith thought the brain could have its proper part only if it fused itself with the other elements of man's nature, the animal instincts and other impulses" [1940]; "He was convinced that the brain could have a proper part in activity only if it shared its place with animal instincts" [1946]. "[George Moore] searched for his lost self among the artists and literary circles of Paris" [1940]; "[he] searched for lost self among the literary circles of Paris" [1946]. "[Hardy] was fascinated by the idea of a finite God who designed a perfect world but could not fulfill it" [1940]; "He was interested in the finite God—a God who had designed a perfect world and could not fulfill his plan" [1946]. "Homer says that of all breathing and crawling creatures man is most to be pitied" [1940]; "Of all creatures who creep and crawl upon the earth man is the most abandoned" [1946].

10. Class notes loaned to the author by Joseph G. Blake.

11. Quotations are from notes taken by myself and by my classmate, J. Austin Sobczak, who used shorthand. All lecture quotes given below are from this source unless otherwise noted.

12. Frank O'Malley, "The Faustianism of John Milton," in *The Proceedings for the Year 1950,* American Catholic Philosophical Association, vol. 24, pp. 123–132. The modest, apologetic tone is something not found in his lectures. As Garrett Bolger (class of '48) remarked in a letter to Frank Duggan (August 10, 1978), "He doesn't write the way he talked."

13. Frank O'Malley, "The Wasteland of William Blake," *Review of Politics,* vol. 9, no. 2 (April 1942).

14. Class notes loaned to the author by Frank Duggan.

15. Lecture transcribed and provided by Dr. Garrett Bolger.

Chapter 4

1. Dr. Garrett Bolger, letter to Frank Duggan, August 10, 1978, quoted by permission.

2. From notes loaned to the author by James J. Meaney.

3. Frank O'Malley, "The Culture of the Church," *Review of Politics,* vol. 16, no. 2 (April 1954).

4. Frank O'Malley, "The Thinker in the Church II: The Urgencies of Romano Guardini," *Review of Politics,* vol. 25, no. 4 (Oct. 1963).

5. From a transcript of the shorthand notes taken by J. Austin Sobczak, 1939–40.

6. Frank O'Malley, "Religion and the Modern Mind," *Review of Politics,* vol. 4 (Oct. 1942): 496 ff.

7. Class notes loaned to the author by J. Austin Sobczak.

8. O'Malley, "Religion and the Modern Mind," pp. 498–499.

9. From *Poems of Gerard Manley Hopkins,* ed. with notes by Robert Bridges, 2nd ed. (Oxford: Oxford University Press 1930). O'Malley's personal copy is in the possession of the University of Notre Dame Archives.

10. O'Malley, "Religion and the Modern Mind," pp. 499–507.

11. Class notes taken in 1950, loaned to the author by Michael T. Meaney.

12. Ibid.

13. Information in a letter from Rufus W. Rauch to the author, October 8, 1987.

14. From notes loaned to the author by Michael T. Meaney.

Chapter 5

1. Ed Murray, letter to the author, August 28, 1985.

2. Owen J. Donley, manuscript of notes entitled "Thoughts and Reflections on Frank O'Malley of Notre Dame," given to author, March 5, 1986.

3. Joseph Lanigan, letter to the author, February 5, 1986.

4. Excerpts supplied by John H. Johnston, March 11, 1986.

5. John H. Johnston, letter to the author, March 14, 1986.

6. In the Frank O'Malley Papers, University of Notre Dame Archives.

7. Ibid.

8. Ibid.

9. Kenneth L. Woodward, "The Lessons of the Master," *Notre Dame Magazine,* vol. 13, no. 2 (Spring 1984): p. 19.

10. In the Frank O'Malley Papers, University of Notre Dame Archives.

11. Sparr, "Frank O'Malley: Thinker, Critic, Revivalist," p. 13.

12. In the Frank O'Malley papers, University of Notre Dame Archives.

13. Rufus W. Rauch, letter to the author, October 8, 1987.

14. Hugh Rank, *Edwin O'Connor* (New York: Twayne, 1974), p. 20. Mr. Rank is a Notre Dame English major in the class of '54, who also completed graduate studies there for a MA in '56 and PhD in '69.

15. In the Frank O'Malley Papers, University of Notre Dame Archives.

16. From Notre Dame's *Scrip,* January 1942.

17. In the Frank O'Malley Papers, University of Notre Dame Archives.

18. Ibid.

19. Ibid.

20. Ibid.

21. Copy provided by the courtesy of Dr. Thomas P. Carney.

22. In the Frank O'Malley Papers, University of Notre Dame Archives.

23. Jim Carberry, in a telephone conversation with the author, March 23, 1988.

24. Dean Thomas P. Bergin, interview with the author, October 9, 1985.

25. Woodward, "The Lessons of the Master," pp. 19–20.

26. Ibid.

27. Frank Duggan, letter to the author, January 6, 1988.

28. Ibid.

29. Woodward, "The Lessons of the Master," p. 16.

30. Acts 2:13–15.

31. Woodward, "The Lessons of the Master," p. 21.

32. Dean Thomas P. Bergin, interview with the author, October 9, 1985.

33. Ibid.

34. Enclosed in a letter from Father Charles Sheedy to the author, September 3, 1985.

35. Carole Roos, in editorial notes sent to the author.

36. *Time,* May 20, 1974, p. 94.

37. *Newsweek,* May 20, 1974, p. 78.

38. *Review of Politics,* vol. 36, no. 3 (July 1974): 355.

39. Michael Melody, "Words for Frank O'Malley," Notre Dame *Scholastic,* September 9, 1974, p. 10.

40. Jim Robinson, "for Frank O'Malley," Notre Dame *Scholastic,* September 9, 1974, p. 11.

Chapter 6

1. Tom Stritch, letter to the author, August 8, 1985.

2. Rufus W. Rauch, letter to the author, July 3, 1986. O'Malley's rationalization for not going to Europe may have been hinted at in his

frequent classroom quotation of Ivan Karamazov in *The Brothers Karamazov:*

> I want to travel in Europe, Alyosha, I shall set off from here. And yet I know that I am only going to a grave-yard, but it's a most precious grave-yard, that's what it is! Precious are the dead that lie there, every stone over them speaks of such burning life in the past, of such passionate faith in their work, their truth, their struggle and their science, that I know I shall fall on the ground and kiss those stones and weep over them; though I'm convinced in my heart that it's long been nothing but a grave-yard. And I shall not weep from despair, but simply because I shall be happy in my tears, I shall steep my soul in my emotion. (Modern Library Edition, 1937, p. 239)

3. Ed Murray, interview with the author, October 9, 1985.

4. Mrs. Ed Murray, interview with the author, October 9, 1985.

5. Ruth S. Meaney, memo, January 7, 1988.

6. Jerry Hogan, letters to the author, August 1, August 16, September 6, and October 13, 1986.

7. J. Austin Sobczak, letter to the author, July 14, 1987.

8. William K. Mulvey, letter to the author, October 28, 1986.

9. William G. McGowan, letter to the author, December 5, 1986.

10. Erwin J. Mooney, Jr., letter to the author, August 31, 1986.

11. George E. Miles, letter to the author, January 24, 1988.

12. Charles John Kirby, letter to the author, March 24, 1988.

13. Patricia Kirby Conover, younger sister of C. J. Kirby, letter to the author, February 15, 1988.

14. Charles M. Kearney, letter to the author, November 3, 1986.

15. Ed Cummings, letter to the author, October 20, 1986.

16. Msgr. Anthony M. Brown, in Notre Dame *Scholastic,* September 9, 1974, p. 32.

17. John J. Gilligan (former Governor of Ohio), statement of August 28, 1976, provided by the courtesy of William Slavick. Mr. Gilligan became the first appointee to the Francis J. O'Malley Chair of Law in Notre Dame's Law School.

18. Kenneth L. Woodward, "The Lessons of the Master," *Notre Dame Magazine,* vol. 13, no. 2 (Spring 1984): 15–21.

19. Sister Mary Luke Arntz, S.N.D., letter to the author, June 11, 1987.

20. James E. Newman, letter to the author, February 14, 1986.

21. Lyle Joyce, letter to the author, January 22, 1986.

22. Paul F. Carr, letter to the author, November 3, 1986.

23. Owen J. Donley, letter to the author, February 3, 1986, and manuscript notes entitled "Thoughts and Reflections on Frank O'Malley of Notre Dame," given to the author March 5, 1986.

24. Frank Duggan, letter to the author, July 19, 1985.

25. John V. Ankenbruck, letter to the author, July 19, 1985.

26. Father Robert Griffin, C.S.C., "Letters to a Lonely God," Notre Dame *Observer,* May 15, 1987, p. 10.

27. William Pfaff, letter to the author, February 18, 1986.

28. William H. Slavick, letter to the author, January 26, 1988.

29. Paul Mack Schaefer, in Notre Dame *Scholastic,* September 9, 1974.

30. Walter Clements, letter to the author, March 11, 1988. In a previous telephone conversation on February 13, 1988, Clements recalled an incident when he was O'Malley's student secretary: Former student Ed. O'Connor had brought a manuscript for the master's criticism, and O'Malley was enthusiastic, but he told Clements, "I argued with him for hours trying to get him to change the title. He wants to call it *The Last Hurrah.*"

31. Hugh Hennedy, letter to the author, February 4, 1988.

32. John C. Collins, in Notre Dame *Scholastic,* September 9, 1974, p. 33.

33. Brother Patrick Hart, in Notre Dame *Scholastic,* September 9, 1974, p. 32.

34. Joan Garvey Hermes, quoted with permission from a letter to her uncle, Jerry Hogan, November 19, 1986.

35. John Garvey, quoted with permission from a letter to his uncle, Jerry Hogan, early November, 1986.

36. Joseph G. Blake, letter to the author, July 1, 1986.

37. Michael R. Ryan, a reminiscence of about 1978, quoted in a letter to the author, February 18, 1988.

38. Kevin Reilly, in Notre Dame *Scholastic,* September 9, 1974.

39. Patricia Fenelon, letter to the author, February 15, 1988.

40. Gary Caruso, in Notre Dame *Scholastic,* May 2, 1977, p. 24.

41. Stephen R. Pallucca, letter to the author, April 24, 1988.

42. Michael O. Garvey, letter to the author, July 29, 1986.

43. Father Theodore Hesburgh, C.S.C., letter to the author, December 15, 1986.

44. James Joyce, *Dubliners* (New York: Modern Library, 1926), pp. 287–288.

Index

273